Roadmap to Success

Copyright © 2011

Published in the United States by
Insight Publishing Company
707 West Main Street, Suite 5
Sevierville, TN 37862
800-987-7771
www.insightpublishing.com

Editor: Sandra Pinkoski
Cover Design: Steve Wilson
Interior Design: Dean Lewis

Disclaimer: This book is a compilation of ideas from numerous experts who have each contributed a chapter. As such, the views expressed in each chapter are of those who were interviewed and not necessarily of the interviewer or Insight Publishing.

ISBN-978-1-60013-633-7

10 9 8 7 6 5 4 3 2 1

The interviews found in this book are conducted by David Wright, President of ISN Works and Insight Publishing.

I've done a lot of driving in my life and one thing I have been smart enough to have is a dependable road map. If you don't have a good plan to get from where you are to where you want to go, you will get lost.

I've known many people who have started out in business and thought they had a good plan, but did not achieve the success they wanted. A major problem for many of these people was that they had not sought good advice from people who had achieved success. If you don't learn from the experience of others, you might achieve success but you will probably get there the hard way. You might get lost down many side roads before you find the right one.

ROADMAP to Success is a mini-seminar on how to plan for your success. The successful people in this book have the experience that will help you find what you need to create your road map to success. These perceptive businesspeople were fascinating as they unfolded their own personal road maps and told me about their various success journeys.

I invite you to set aside some quiet time and learn from these exceptional authors. I assure you that your time won't be wasted. It's not often that you can access such a large quantity of quality information that will either get you started or help you get further along on your road to success. This book is an investment in your future—your successful future!

David E. Wright, President
ISN Works
& Insight Publishing

TABLE OF CONTENTS

Chapter One

THE POWER OF YOU

STELLA BALASANIAN

DAVID WRIGHT (WRIGHT)

Today, we're talking with Stella Balasanian, a deservingly well-respected twenty-three-year veteran in the field of Real Estate. Stella has built a stellar reputation for integrity, ability, and honesty. She specializes in single-family homes, condominiums, and apartment buildings in Burbank, Glendale, and throughout the greater Los Angeles area. She is also a certified life and business coach, specializing in coaching Real Estate agents, personal and leadership development, team development, and sales training. She is currently the success coach for Dilbeck Real Estate Real Living in Southern California. She coaches, trains, and consults with leaders and sales professionals. She helps them take immediate control of their lives and businesses and move forward to achieve their goals.

Stella, welcome to *ROADMAP to Success*.

STELLA BALASANIAN (BALASANIAN)

Thank you for inviting me to be a part of the *ROADMAP to Success* anthology series.

WRIGHT

I know you have heard many definitions of success, probably almost as many people as you have asked, but how do *you* define success?

BALASANIAN

That's a great question, David. For each of us, success means something entirely different and it is very important for each person to define this individually. For me, success means happiness, joy, and peace. For me, success is waking up every morning totally excited about my life. Deepak Chopra says, "What people most want is happiness. The ultimate goal of all goals is happiness." (Ref. *The Los Angeles Times,* December 26, 2010.) This is my recipe for happiness: every day I focus on my daily five—faith, love, hope, service, and gratitude. Focusing on these things daily helps me stay positive, focused, and happy.

WRIGHT

So what do you think are the biggest obstacles people face in trying to become successful?

BALASANIAN

I am so blessed; I get to talk to people all day long and I learn so much from everyone I come into contact with every day. I have to say that the obstacles people face in trying to become successful include a few things:

- Lack of clarity on their why, their passion, their purpose
- Fear
- Thought process

Number one, people sometimes have a lack of clarity of their purpose, their passion, and their "why." You see, a lot of people start with their goals first—this is my goal, this is what I'm going to achieve—and at the first sign of adversity, they crumble. I believe there is a step before setting goals that most people miss. That step is getting clarity on your "personal why"—why are you doing the things you are doing? What is your passion? What is your purpose? What drives you? I think that at different stages in our lives we understand different terminology. When I was younger, talking about purpose was way too big for me. But talking about what you like to do and what you are good at made more sense. That then graduated to talking about mission statements and guiding principles. That was something I could wrap my mind around. That then graduated to talking about passion and purpose.

The second thing is fear—fear of failure. I really believe that if you are focused and clear on your why, you can deal with the fear and not be stopped by it. You'll feel the fear, but you won't let it stop you. You'll have a higher purpose. We have all heard "feel the fear and do it anyway."

The third thing is our thought process. Learn to correct your thinking and everything else will fall into place. We must unlearn what we have learned that is no longer serving us. We must learn to change what we are looking for. If we are focused on why something won't work, we will look for and find excuses to justify our thinking. What we find mainly depends on what we are looking for. Part of this process is also learning about how to speak correctly. Words have power.

WRIGHT

So how do you get clarity on your passion?

BALASANIAN

That's a great question and that's part of what I do when I work with coaching clients. I have to tell you, that is the really juicy part of what I do. It's so important to get clarity on your passion. Your why is really what drives you. It becomes your driving force; it's how you go about achieving your goals. Your why is what is running your engine and unless you are clear about that, you will crumble at the first sign of difficulty. If you are up to achieving big things in your life, you are going to have some adversity.

If you are clear on your why, the what and the how you will figure out. If something doesn't work, try something else. Do this until you figure out what works. When you know what drives you, your entire attitude shifts and how you do things shifts. It's an amazing thing to witness. I feel so blessed that I get to experience this with my clients.

Thirty years ago, my parents moved to the states and they were very clear on one thing: they came here because they wanted better opportunities for themselves and their children. They came here hungry to win and hungry to create opportunities for their children. Do you think they didn't have difficulties? Of course they did. They had so many, but they were clear on what they were after and my brother and I grew up watching this.

We grew up watching that adversity and fear are a part of life and they do not stop you from going for the things you want and you don't crumble just because something doesn't go the way you want. My parents—my heroes—taught us leadership. They taught us that when life comes at you, you embrace it knowing that there is something there for you to learn and to grow from. There is no one else on the face of the plant I have more respect for than I do for my parents.

I have watched my brother take all the lessons we learned at home and use it to build his own very successful life. My parents have always encouraged self-expression and as a result, from a very young age, my brother was always very clear on his passion. He loved science and he wanted to serve humanity. It took years of hard work, perseverance, sacrifices, and patience and today he is a very successful surgeon.

Get clear on your passion first; that is what gives you your goals, which then give you your action steps.

WRIGHT

You speak about discovering your passion being so important and how it is the main factor in attaining success. Is passion alone enough?

BALASANIAN

There is a Chinese proverb that says, "Talk does not cook rice." Of course passion alone is not enough. You have to get out there and do your part; so I say hustle or go home. Action is the foundational key to success.

One of my favorite things I have learned from one of my favorite teachers is the concept of "fail forward fast." Until you take action, you won't know what's working and what's not. Change whatever needs to change and just keep moving forward. If you are clear on your passion, you will want to do things—you can't wait to get up in the morning and start your day because you are inspired by your passion and you are inspired by your purpose. We've heard this many, many times before that success comes from the combination of inspiration and perspiration.

It makes me very happy when someone figures out that he or she doesn't have to settle. The truth of the matter is that there is nothing you can not accomplish. We are blessed to live in the land of opportunity. I really believe that the only difference between people who accomplish what they want and those who don't is this: they are making progress instead of making excuses. I know that most people will not start making changes until they are sick and tired of their status quo and until they get to a point where they say, this is where I draw the line, this is no longer acceptable in my life, whether it's a challenge in a marriage or a financial challenge, or maybe you haven't been treating your body very well. Most people will not make a change until they are sick and tired of being sick and tired.

WRIGHT

So why are more people not in tune with their passion if it's something that all people possess?

BALASANIAN

You are absolutely right—we all have it and some people don't know what theirs is. I suggest you start by thinking of yourself as a walking, talking, breathing resume. What does your current resume say about you and does it convey what you want it to say? Some people will find that what it says and what they want it to say are two different things. Most people are so busy with life maintenance that they forget about creating a life that they truly desire.

I think people have forgotten about the art of dreaming. Eleanor Roosevelt said, "The future belongs to those that believe in the beauty of their dreams." Are you living today from your past or are you living today from your future? Are you focused on your future dreams or past failures? As long as people are focused on their goals, they will not be stopped by obstacles. They might be scared but, stopped? No.

Our dreams and our goals are a source of inspiration, don't ignore them. If you are focused on tomorrow's goals instead of yesterday's failures, you will be inspired. You will start taking steps toward your goals and the manifestation of those dreams depend on what you do today. Start today and don't be attached to doing things perfectly. Even if they are baby steps. I love baby steps—they help you build confidence and they will take you toward taking bigger steps one day.

When I work with Real Estate agents about defining their goals for the year, I always encourage them to put things in their future that really inspire them, that make them wake up in the morning feeling that they can't wait to start their day. People are so busy with running around and taking care of everyday life issues that they forget about quiet time—time to reflect, time to dream, time to plan, time to create.

I have a seven-year-old daughter and I see parents running around from soccer practice to dance practice and so on. I think it's our duty as parents to teach our children to dream, to help them build the habit of carving out time and space on regular basis just for quiet time and dreaming time and creating time. My daughter has a dream book and every day she fills it with drawings of things that make her happy.

There are so many distractions today that can keep us from thinking and reflecting. Every day we are bombarded with distractions—the media, the economy, social media, etc. So you really have to be aware and be deliberate about simplifying your life and carving out time and space in your daily life to pray, meditate, think, reflect, dream, and create. Unless you are really aware, you are not going to do it and the day will just get away from you. I think that's part of the reason why people are not clear on their passions—they have not created the habit of taking the time to figure it out. Prayer and meditation promote clarity of the mind, and this takes daily practice.

Once you have clarity around your passion, then it is important to align your actions with your desires. Effort alone is not enough without direction and purpose.

WRIGHT

So how do you align your actions with your desires?

BALASANIAN

I'll give you an example. A few days ago a Real Estate agent came to see me for a coaching consultation. She is an experienced agent who had just changed companies. She said, "I really don't want to put buyers in my car and drive them around and show them homes. I don't want to leave my family at seven o'clock in the evening and go talk to people about selling their home.

I kept listening and observing. After a while, I had to point out to her that it was interesting—she just signed up with a Real Estate company to be a Real Estate agent and yet she is not willing to do the things that Real Estate agents do. So her desires are taking her one way and her actions are taking her the opposite way.

This is an example of not aligning your actions with your desires and setting yourself up for frustration. The truth is that she is not alone—a lot of people do this. I can give you many examples. Most of the time it is subtle and this is why coaching is so powerful. You work with someone who sees and hears things you don't. Here are some practical suggestions for aligning your actions with your desires:

- First you must be teachable and coachable.
- Self-awareness is the key to beginning to shift your energy. Start raising your awareness about your thoughts, your emotions, and your actions. Start noticing how your thoughts affect your emotions and how your emotions affect your actions. Are your thoughts and actions aligned with your desires? This may require that you give up certain thoughts and activities. For example, if you tell me you want to lose weight and you are eating at fast food restaurants five days a week, that is not aligning your actions with your desires.
- Start paying attention to the conversations in your life. You will notice that some people bring joy and positivity and support your goals. You will also notice that it's usually the same people who bring you gossip, complaint, and negative conversation about why you can't achieve your goals. One of my favorite teachers always says you do not have to attend

every conversation you are invited to and I couldn't agree more.

- Hire a coach who can help you get clear about what you desire. This is where your passion comes from.
- Commit with all that you've got to your goals and desires.
- Create an action plan that is aligned with your goals.
- Allow yourself to be assessed on regular basis. The best way, in my opinion, is with a coach.
- Accountability: If planning is 20 percent, then accountability is 80 percent. Time after time I hear from clients, "Because I knew I had a coaching session with you on Monday, I knew you were going to hold me accountable I did more, I accomplished more, I achieved more—" You will dream bigger and accomplish so much more.

A lot of times it just comes down to habits. You are just so used to doing things in a certain way, it's as though you are on autopilot. Breaking that habit sometimes takes a while and it starts with awareness. Align your actions with your desires and watch how fast you accomplish things.

WRIGHT

We haven't talked about balance. Generally, when you think about life balance, you think about females; but men need to balance their lives as well. Is it important to have balance in your life at all?

BALASANIAN

Absolutely. It's important to define your work/life balance in advance and then keep to that ideal as much as possible. For some people, balance seems to be an impossible goal. They believe that there is never enough time to get it all done, which leads to a lot of stress and frustration. I often ask coaching clients to see their weekly calendar or I'll ask them to keep track of how they use their time for a week. Almost always there is a lack of priority management and not a lack of time.

Also, at times when you are up to something really big in your life, in my opinion, it's completely fine and, in fact, necessary to take your life out of balance for a short time to accomplish what you need to do. So yes, balance is important but it's also not something that you achieve once and are done with it. It is something that you work on regularly. If you are focused on priority management versus time management, you have a better chance of getting the important things done and have less frustration and more joy and inner peace. And again, I want to add pay attention to alignment because it is so important.

WRIGHT

You mentioned priority management. How is that different from time management?

BALASANIAN

You can never really manage time but you can manage your priorities. You can't say, "Well, I ended this meeting ten minutes early so I'll put that ten minutes in my briefcase and then I'll pull it out when I need an extra ten minutes." That just doesn't happen. The truth of the matter is that we all have the same amount of time; where we differ is how we use our time. How you see time and how you invest time will have a direct effect on the success you are trying to achieve in every area of your life. For most people, it's not a matter of lack of time, it's a matter of lack of focus and lack of direction.

If you are clear on what you are trying to accomplish and you are committed to what is important to you, you will automatically modify your to-do list. So many things will just fall off your list. We can only focus on one thing at a time anyway, and sometimes multitasking can really scatter your energy, even for some of us who think we are great multitaskers, we accomplish so much more when we are completely focused on one thing at a time. I have learned this the hard way. I have to constantly make an effort to not multitask. So yes, you can never manage time but you can manage your priorities. I always say, "Organize your time around your priorities and you'll become "unmessable" with." I know that's probably not a word but I use it all the time.

Time is the most precious commodity we are born with. For me personally, time is a gift and I can use it any way I want. Learn to invest your time wisely; make empowered choices with your time. If you look at time as a precious gift, you will change the way you use it.

We waste so much time on things that really add nothing to our lives. I often talk about how our mind constantly needs to be fed and unless we are feeding it with good, positive information it's going to pick up the negative, and the negative is everywhere. I suggest you start paying attention to the way you use your time.

Who are you socializing with? What are you reading? What are you watching? How many hours a week do you spend watching television shows that are full of negative information? Sometimes people will say to me that they need to know what is going on in the world. To that I say, "It's one thing to be informed, it's something entirely different to be completely bombarded with constant negative information."

So yes, if you are focused on the things that are most important to you and you start seeing time as a gift, your to-do list will get completely modified and your time will be scheduled around your priorities. A result is that you will experience more satisfaction and less stress and frustration.

WRIGHT

Would you tell our readers a little bit about what drives you to be successful?

BALASANIAN

There are a number of things—simple things:

- I have simplified my life and have become clear on what's important in my life.
- I rely heavily on my faith. I know everything that comes my way is going to serve me one way or another.
- I'm obsessed with wisdom. I pray for clarity and wisdom every day.
- I start every day as a student and I am open and flexible to what I can learn every day.
- I focus on my daily five: faith, love, hope, service, and gratitude.

- I'm very clear on what my purpose is, and I'm obsessed with fulfilling my purpose.
- I love, love, love life and I live it passionately.

I would say one of my strengths is that I don't have to know how to do something to start to do it. When God puts a picture or a desire in my heart, it becomes my duty to live it. "Serendipity" is one of my most favorite words in the English dictionary. I just start and the right people and the right circumstances just show up. All I have to do is make a commitment, take the first step, and then the next step reveals itself to me.

I think probably the last thing is that I fear regret more than I fear failure. So I'm committed to doing what I'm supposed to be doing.

WRIGHT

You talked about people who influenced your life such as your father, your mother, and your teachers. How can people help each other succeed?

BALASANIAN

Our interactions with people can be a huge source of wisdom if we are open to them. We are meant to help and serve each other. If we are aware, if we are awake, if we are paying attention, and we see every interaction we have as opportunity to learn and grow, it's all around us, every day. For example, every time I meet somebody new I look at him or her as my teacher and my student.

The same thing is true about every circumstance we encounter. Every circumstance in our lives is there to teach us something. Always look for teachers in your life. Often, our greatest lessons are hidden in someone we may not like very much. I have had and continue to have some amazing teachers; I have learned so much from them and I continue to learn and always will.

It is so important to have role models in your life and it's important to have people in your life you look up to. I am extremely fortunate that my mom and my dad have been incredible role models in my life and continue to be. They have instilled a sense of work ethic, service, and gratitude in my brother and me that serves us and guides us every day.

Among many things I have learned from my dad is commitment. My dad taught me that a commitment is made with the heart. He taught me devotion to family. I also get my hustle from my dad. To this day I have never heard my father say he's tired. Growing up, this was a big lesson to see my father get up early and go to work every day. He worked hard and not once did he say, "I'm out there working hard to provide for you." He has always provided a wonderful life for us. He would come home and still have energy for us. He was there at every important event and always fully present in the moment. And even to this day, he is always encouraging us to keep dreaming and to keep pursuing our dreams. Of course I appreciate that now because I am a parent now. Growing up, I most certainly did not value those things and up until recently, I took all that for granted. I now know the challenges of being a parent and have found an entirely new level of appreciation for who my parents are. I am so grateful that I came to this understanding while they are alive and I have the opportunity to acknowledge them and appreciate them and thank them.

From my mother I learned service. She is always there for her family and friends and she is there with love in her heart and a smile on her face. Her grace and her beauty are immeasurable. To know her is to love her. I have to say she was probably my first teacher about wisdom and the power of words.

I remember one time when I was probably about twenty years old and I think I had just broken up with a boyfriend; of course I was devastated. The way she approached that situation was so amazing. She said, "Remember when you were in school and you didn't like history very much and you wanted to repeat that course because you didn't like the grade you got? Life is the same way—sometimes you've got to do something more than once to get it right."

After my conversation with my mother, I had a glimpse into the power of words and the importance of wisdom. One minute you feel a certain way, a few words are spoken and your energy is completely shifted and you think differently, therefore you feel differently and you are going to act differently and you are going to have different results.

This has been huge for me. Over the years I have come to have a deeper understanding of this. I have come to a place where I take a great deal of responsibility with my words and I choose to be deliberate with my words. People who come to my seminars and workshops continually say to me "you are so inspiring." For me, that is about the way I choose words. I choose to speak truth. I choose to use my words to empower, to encourage, and to inspire.

Sometimes I hear a client or friend or a colleague say to me, "You said this a few months ago, and it really had an effect on me." Most of the time I don't even remember what I said, but they do because it affected them significantly. I always encourage the use of words wisely because they have so much power; they affect more people than we realize.

How different would our children's lives be if their parents, teachers, and caregivers paid attention to this? If we were always speaking life and possibility and encouragement into young hearts and minds, what difference would that make in the world?

WRIGHT

How did you begin speaking and why is personal power your main topic?

BALASANIAN

I am living my dreams and I want to help as many people as I can to live their dreams also. There is something each of us has to offer that only we can do. I want to inspire you to take ownership of that beautiful gift and responsibility. For me, it's so exciting to help somebody figure out what that is for them; it really comes down to personal power. I hope that through my seminars, workshops, and speaking I'm able to help those who are ready to increase their awareness about their faith, the choices they make, and the power of the words they use.

About faith: I know that if we pay attention and if we are really honest about it, every single one of us has experienced incredible miracles that have happened in our lives already. Start looking for those miracles in your life and in other people's lives. I would even go a step further and say start expecting them. When things are really good, we tend to neglect our faith and our spiritual life, now is a great time to start paying attention to that and bring balance into your spiritual life.

About choices: The power of choice is the most powerful asset we have because the choices we make create the life we have. Sometimes things happen in our lives that we don't have a choice about, but we have a choice about how we deal with those situations. We have more choices than we recognize. For example, you have complete, total control of every single thing that you put in your body. Are you going to choose a donut or are you going to choose a fresh fruit? The choice is yours. You also have a choice in what you feed your mind every single day. Are you addicted to drama and the bad news that plays on the airwaves constantly or are you feeding your mind with positive, healthy things? The choice is yours. Are you going to choose to be around people who nurture your weaknesses or nurture your strengths? The choice is yours.

About words: Words have power. Words hold energy. Pay attention to the conversations in your life. Pay attention to what is coming out of your own mouth.

All these things are not outside of us, they are inside of us, and they make up our personal power. You decide how connected you are to your faith, you decide the choices you make, and you decide what words you use when you are speaking to yourself and to others. So to me, all of that is personal power. Have faith, focus on choices, and speak possibility!

WRIGHT

So what is the message you want people to hear so they can learn from your success?

BALASANIAN

I love what Maya Angelou says: "We delight in the beauty of the butterfly but rarely admit the changes it has gone through to achieve that beauty." I have experienced a lot, I have learned a lot, and I have changed a lot and continue to do so. Ultimately, my message is not about making money, although if you follow your passion you might just do that. It's about being true to yourself and creating your own happiness by living your life passionately and productively. Do what makes you happy, take possession of your personal power, have faith, make wise choices, speak possibility, find your passion, work hard, love your family, and count your blessings. Life is too precious to have a job and a life you don't love.

I would simply say that life is about creating yourself and creating a life you love. If right now is a challenging time for you, then this is a great time to reinvent yourself. Anytime you want to make a change in your life, you must first change your standards. Change what you demand of yourself. Now is an especially good time to look at these things.

A lot of people's emotional resilience levels have been tested recently and continue to be tested. When you are just sitting on the couch, it may not be obvious to you that you are physically unfit. When you have to run around after your kids in the park or you have to run up a flight of stairs, it becomes obvious to you whether you are physically fit or not. The same is true about our emotional fitness level. When we are facing a challenge, that's when we discover our emotional fitness level.

A lot of times people will continue to sit on the couch because they are afraid to find out. So people will stay in unfulfilling relationships, and they will stay in dead-end jobs because they are really afraid to find out that they may not be emotionally fit. This is a great time. Many people now know where their weaknesses are and they have a choice— they can either be the victim of their circumstances or make the necessary changes to create the life they desire. It's an incredible time to figure out what in you should be celebrated, what in you must be strengthened, and what you really want. You can create the life you desire and deserve.

We are living in an era of unmatched opportunities. Wherever you are right now, you can start there and you can build on that. Decide today that you will be bigger than your current circumstances and you will not allow your current challenges define you. You will not change your life until you change what you do daily. To live life on your terms takes courage. I would love for people to walk away with this: We have the power to create the life we desire one baby step at a time. Everything is possible.

WRIGHT

What is your biggest contribution to your personal success?

BALASANIAN

When I hear this question I think about what I would like to be known for. My answer is simply this: I am constantly growing and changing and while I learn new things every day, one thing is constant and will always remain constant—I will always serve. When I sell a house for a client or when I help clients buy their dream house or their first house, it's an honor and a privilege for me—I am serving.

At this point in my life I also serve by inspiring others to dream more, to learn more, and to become more. Albert Pike said, "What we have done for ourselves alone dies with us; what we have done for others and the world remains and is immortal." I also know that I am just starting and the best is yet to come. I am grateful at my deepest levels when I know I have touched someone's life and made a difference, whether I help them with their real estate needs or help them discover their personal power. My purpose is to empower others.

I fear regret more than I fear failure and I think that comes across in everything I do. I also want to say to the reader, "God bless you on your journey. Reclaim your personal power, find your passion, live your passion, and live your life on your terms. I wish you unlimited success. Anything is possible!"

WRIGHT

Well, what a great conversation.

BALASANIAN

I so enjoyed this time with you; it's been a delight.

WRIGHT

It has for me, too. I appreciate all the time you've taken to answer these questions. It's been enlightening for me and I'm sure it will be for our readers.

BALASANIAN

Thank you so much; I appreciate the opportunity.

WRIGHT

Today I have been talking with Stella Balasanian. Stella is a veteran in the field of Real Estate and she is a certified life and business coach specializing in coaching people in personal and leadership development, team development, and sales training.

Stella, thank you so much for being with us today on *ROADMAP to Success*.

BALASANIAN

Thank you so much.

About the Author

Stella Balasanian, a deservingly well-respected, twenty-three-year veteran in the field of Real Estate, has built a stellar reputation for integrity, ability, and honesty. Stella specializes in single-family homes, condominiums, and apartment buildings in Burbank, Glendale, and throughout the greater Los Angeles area. Stella's emphasis on customer service is one of the many reasons for her success. Stella and her team bring their buyers and sellers unmatched attention with extraordinary results. Stella and her team pride themselves on meeting and exceeding all of their clients' expectations.

Stella is also a Certified Life and Business Coach specializing in coaching Real Estate agents, personal and leadership development, team development, and sales training.

She is currently the Success Coach for Dilbeck Real Estate Real Living. She is devoted to working with clients as they uncover their purpose and stretch beyond their self-imposed limits to achieve excellence both personally and professionally. Her authenticity, joy, and energy inspire transformation in others.

For more information on Stella Balasanian, and to order your copy of *ROADMAP to Success*, contact:

Stella Balasanian

The Power of You Coaching
PO Box 1022
Burbank, CA 91507
818-840-8686
info@thepowerofyoucoaching.com
www.ThePowerOfYouCoaching.com
www.Stella4RealEstate.com

Chapter Two

DISCOVER YOUR INNER RESOURCE

DR. DEEPAK CHOPRA

DAVID WRIGHT (WRIGHT)

Today I am talking to Dr. Deepak Chopra, founder of the Chopra Center for Well-Being in Carlsbad, California. More than a decade ago, Dr. Chopra became the foremost pioneer in integrated medicine. His insights have redefined our definition of health to embrace body, mind, and spirit. His books, which include, *Quantum Healing, Perfect Health, Ageless Body Timeless Mind*, and *The Seven Spiritual Laws of Success,* have become international bestsellers and are established classics.

Dr. Chopra, welcome to *ROADMAP to Success.*

DR. DEEPAK CHOPRA (CHOPRA)

Thank you. How are you?

WRIGHT

I am doing just fine. It's great weather here in Tennessee.

CHOPRA

Great.

WRIGHT

Dr. Chopra, you stated in your book, *Grow Younger, Live Longer: 10 Steps to Reverse Aging,* that it is possible to reset your biostats up to fifteen years younger than your chronological age. Is that really possible?

CHOPRA

Yes. There are several examples of this. The literature on aging really began to become interesting in the 1980s when people showed that it was possible to reverse the biological marks of aging. This included things like blood pressure, bone density, body temperature, regulation of the metabolic rate, and other things like cardiovascular conditioning, cholesterol levels, muscle mass and strength of muscles, and even things like hearing, vision, sex hormone levels, and immune function.

One of the things that came out of those studies was that psychological age had a great influence on biological age. So you have three kinds of aging: chronological age is when you were born, biological age is what your biomarker shows, and psychological age is what your biostat says.

WRIGHT

You call our prior conditioning a prison. What do you mean?

CHOPRA

We have certain expectations about the aging process. Women expect to become menopausal in their early forties. People think they should retire at the age of sixty-five and then go Florida and spend the rest of their life in so-called retirement. These expectations actually influence the very biology of aging. What we call normal aging is actually the hypnosis of our social conditioning. If you can bypass that social conditioning, then you're free to reset your own biological clock.

WRIGHT

Everyone told me that I was supposed to retire at sixty-five. I'm somewhat older than that and as a matter of fact, today is my birthday.

CHOPRA

Well, happy birthday. You know, the fact is that you should be having fun all the time and always feel youthful. You should always feel that you are contributing to society. It's not the retirement, but it's the passion with which you're involved in the well-being of your society, your community, or the world at large.

WRIGHT

Great things keep happening to me. I have two daughters; one was born when I was fifty. That has changed my life quite a bit. I feel a lot younger than I am.

CHOPRA

The more you associate with young people, the more you will respond to that biological expression.

WRIGHT

Dr. Chopra, you suggest viewing our bodies from the perspective of quantum physics. That seems somewhat technical. Will you tell us a little bit more about that?

CHOPRA

You see, on one level, your body is made up of flesh and bone. That's the material level but we know today that everything we consider matter is born of energy and information. By starting to think of our bodies as networks of energy information and even intelligence, we begin to shift our perspective. We don't think of our bodies so much as dense matter, but as vibrations of consciousness. Even though it sounds technical, everyone has had an experience with this so-called quantum body. After, for example, you do an intense workout, you feel a sense of energy in your body—a tingling sensation. You're actually experiencing what ancient wisdom traditions call the "vital force." The more you pay attention to this vital force inside your body, the more you will experience it as energy, information, and intelligence, and the more control you will have over its expressions.

WRIGHT

Does DNA have anything to do with that?

CHOPRA

DNA is the source of everything in our body. DNA is like the language that creates the molecules of our bodies. DNA is like a protein-making factory, but DNA doesn't give us the blueprint. When I build a house, I have to go to the factory to find the bricks, but having the bricks is not enough. I need to get an architect, who in his or her consciousness can create that blueprint. And that blueprint exists only in your spirit and consciousness—in your soul.

WRIGHT

I was interested in a statement from your book. You said that perceptions create reality. What perceptions must we change in order to reverse our biological image?

CHOPRA

You have to change three perceptions. First you have to get rid of the perceptions of aging itself. Most people believe that aging means disease and infirmities. You have to change that. You have to regard aging as an opportunity for personal growth and spiritual growth. You also have to regard it as an opportunity to express the wisdom of your experience and an opportunity to help others and lift them from ordinary and mundane experience to the kind of experiences you are capable of because you have much more experience than they do.

The second thing you have to change your perception of is your physical body. You have to start to experience it as information and energy—as a network of information and intelligence.

The third thing you have to change your perception on is the experience of dying. If you are the kind of person who is constantly running out of time, you will continue to run out of time. On the other hand, if you have a lot of time, and if you do everything with gusto and love and passion, then you will lose track of time. When you lose track of time, your body does not metabolize that experience.

WRIGHT

That is interesting. People who teach time management don't really teach the passion.

CHOPRA

No, no. Time management is such a restriction of time. Your biological clock starts to age much more rapidly. I think what you have to really do is live your life with passion so that time doesn't mean anything to you.

WRIGHT

That's a concept I've never heard.

CHOPRA

Well, there you are.

WRIGHT

You spend an entire chapter of your book on deep rest as an important part of the reversal of the aging process. What is "deep rest"?

CHOPRA

One of the most important mechanisms for renewal and survival is sleep. If you deprive an animal of sleep, then it ages very fast and dies prematurely. We live in a culture where most of our population has to resort to sleeping pills and tranquilizers in order to sleep. That doesn't bring natural rejuvenation and renewal. You know that you have had a good night's sleep when you wake up in the morning, feeling renewed, invigorated, and refreshed—like a baby does. So that's one kind of deep rest. That comes from deep sleep and from natural sleep. In the book I talk about how you go about making sure you get that.

The second deep rest comes from the experience of meditation, which is the ability to quiet your mind so you still your internal dialogue. When your internal dialogue is still, then you enter into a stage of deep rest. When your mind is agitated, your body is unable to rest.

WRIGHT

I have always heard of people who had bad eyesight and really didn't realize it until they went to the doctor and were fitted for lenses. I had that same experience some years ago. For several years I had not really enjoyed the deep sleep you're talking about. The doctor diagnosed me with sleep apnea. Now I sleep like a baby, and it makes a tremendous difference.

CHOPRA

Of course it does. You now have energy and the ability to concentrate and do things.

WRIGHT

Dr. Chopra, how much do eating habits have to do with aging? Can we change and reverse our biological age by what we eat?

CHOPRA

Yes, you can. One of the most important things to remember is that certain types of foods actually contain anti-aging compounds. There are many chemicals that are contained in certain foods that have an anti-aging effect. Most of these chemicals are derived from light. There's no way to bottle them—there are no pills you can take that will give you these chemicals. But they're contained in plants that are rich in color and derived from photosynthesis. Anything that is yellow, green, and red or has a lot of color, such as fruits and vegetables, contain a lot of these very powerful anti-aging chemicals.

In addition, you have to be careful not to put food in your body that is dead or has no life energy. So anything that comes in a can or has a label, qualifies for that. You have to expose your body to six tastes: sweet, sour, salt, bitter, pungent, and astringent because those are the codes of intelligence that allow us to access the deep intelligence of nature. Nature and what she gives to us in bounty is actually experienced through the sense of taste. In fact, the light chemicals— the anti-aging substances in food—create the six tastes.

WRIGHT

Some time ago, I was talking to one of the ladies in your office and she sent me an invitation to a symposium that you had in California. I was really interested. The title was *Exploring the Reality of Soul.*

CHOPRA

Well, I conducted the symposium, but we had some of the world's scientists, physicists, and biologists who were doing research in what is called, non-local intelligence—the intelligence of soul or spirit. You could say it is the intelligence that orchestrates the activity of the universe—God, for example. Science and spirituality are now meeting together because by understanding how nature works and how the laws of nature work, we're beginning to get a glimpse of a deeper intelligence that people in spiritual traditions call divine, or God. I think this is a wonderful time to explore spirituality through science.

WRIGHT

She also sent me biographical information of the seven scientists who were with you. I have never read a list of seven more noted people in their industry.

CHOPRA

They are. The director of the Max Planck Institute, in Berlin, Germany, where quantum physics was discovered was there. Dr. Grossam was a professor of physics at the University of Oregon, and he talked about the quantum creativity of death and the survival of conscious after death. It was an extraordinary group of people.

WRIGHT

Dr. Chopra, with our *ROADMAP to Success* book, we're trying to encourage people to be better, live better, and be more fulfilled by listening to the examples of our guest authors. Is there anything or anyone in your life who has made a difference for you and has helped you to become a better person?

CHOPRA

The most important person in my life was my father. Every day he asked himself, "What can I do in thought, word, and deed to nurture every relationship I encounter just for today?" That has lived with me for my entire life.

WRIGHT

What do you think makes up a great mentor? Are there characteristics mentors seem to have in common?

CHOPRA

I think the most important attribute of a great mentor is that he or she teaches by example and not necessarily through words.

WRIGHT

When you consider the choices you've made down through the years, has faith played an important role?

CHOPRA

I think more than faith, curiosity, wonder, a sense of reference, and humility has. Now, if you want to call that faith, then, yes it has.

WRIGHT

In a divine being?

CHOPRA

In a greater intelligence—intelligence that is supreme, infinite, unbounded, and too mysterious for the finite mind to comprehend.

WRIGHT

If you could have a platform and tell our audience something you feel would help them and encourage them, what would you say?

CHOPRA

I would say that there are many techniques that come to us from ancient wisdom and tradition that allow us to tap into our inner resources and allow us to become beings who have intuition, creativity, vision, and a connection to that which is sacred. Finding that within ourselves, we have the means to enhance our well-being. Whether it's physical, emotional, or environmental, we have the means to resolve conflicts and get rid of war. We have the means to be really healthy. We have the means for being economically uplifted. That knowledge is the most important knowledge that exists.

WRIGHT

I have seen you on several primetime television shows down through the years where you have had the time to explain your theories and beliefs. How does someone like me experience this? Do we get it out of books?

CHOPRA

Books are tools that offer you a road map. Sit down every day, close your eyes, put your attention in your heart, and ask yourself two questions: who am I and what do I want? Then maintain a short period of stillness in body and mind as in prayer or meditation, and the door will open.

WRIGHT

So, you think that the intelligence comes from within. Do all of us have that capacity?

CHOPRA

Every child born has that capacity.

WRIGHT

That's fascinating. So, it doesn't take trickery or anything like that?

CHOPRA

No, it says in the Bible in the book of Psalms, "Be still and know that I am God"—Psalm 46:10.

WRIGHT

That's great advice.

I really do appreciate your being with us today. You are fascinating. I wish I could talk with you for the rest of the afternoon. I'm certain I am one of millions who would like to do that!

CHOPRA

Thank you, sir. It was a pleasure to talk with you!

WRIGHT

Today I have been talking with Dr. Deepak Chopra, founder of The Chopra Center. He has become the foremost pioneer in integrated medicine. We have found today that he really knows what he's talking about. After reading his book, *Grow Younger, Live Longer: 10 Steps to Reverse Aging*, I can tell you that I highly recommend it. I certainly hope you'll go out to your favorite book store and buy a copy.

Dr. Chopra, thank you so much for being with us today on *ROADMAP to Success*.

CHOPRA

Thank you for having me, David.

About the Author

Deepak Chopra has written more than fifty books, which have been translated into many languages. He is also featured on many audio and videotape series, including five critically acclaimed programs on public television. He has also written novels and edited collections of spiritual poetry from India and Persia. In 1999, *Time* magazine selected Dr. Chopra as one of the Top 100 Icons and Heroes of the Century, describing him and "the poet-prophet of alternative medicine."

Dr. Deepak Chopra

The Chopra Center
2013 Costa del Mar Rd.
Carlsbad, CA 92009
info@chopra.com
www.chopra.com

Chapter Three

ESSENTIAL
INNOVATION

DR. IRENA YASHIN-SHAW

DAVID WRIGHT (WRIGHT)

Today, I'm talking with Irena Yashin-Shaw, PhD. Dr. Yashin-Shaw is an innovator and an entrepreneur with a unique blend of academic and business experience, which makes her the ideal partner for organizations seeking to improve their productivity and effectiveness through innovation. Using a "top down" and "bottom up" approach, Irena enables organizations to achieve their innovation goals by engaging all levels of staff. She has methods for maximizing opportunities for cross pollination of ideas, harnessing tacit knowledge, enhancing collaboration and networking, and creating the channels through which information and innovation can flow. She specializes in helping organizations acquire strategic approaches to innovation, continuous improvement, and leadership development.

A highly respected international expert in her field, Irena has delivered presentations and workshops on the topics of creative problem-solving for innovation in many countries around the world and has authored and co-authored numerous publications.

Irena's presentations and programs are a unique blend of in-depth, academic knowledge, practical, real-world business experience, and fun theatricality and humor that have made her a favorite on the professional speaking circuit.

Dr. Yashin-Shaw, welcome to *ROADMAP to Success*.

31

Why is innovation the key criteria for business success in the twenty-first century?

IRENA YASHIN-SHAW (YASHIN-SHAW)

We live in a fast-moving world where the pace of change is constantly accelerating. New knowledge is being created at a breathtaking rate. And it is not going to slow down. I came across some statistics recently that were amazing. By the year 2020, technical knowledge will be doubling every seventy-three days. We are on an exponential growth curve when it comes to knowledge creation. This means that by the end of this century, we won't have experienced just one hundred years of progress, it will be more like twenty thousand years of progress. Twenty thousand years ago, Cro-Magnon man was hunting deer in the last Ice Age. We cannot even begin to imagine what our great-grandchildren will be doing in 2099, but they will be as far removed from us technologically as we are from Cro-Magnon man.

The only way to remain relevant in such a world is to innovate. Individuals, businesses, and countries that don't put innovation on the top of the agenda will be left behind quickly because we are already past the information age and very firmly into the innovation age. It is an age where:

- Ideas are the most valuable commodity,
- Strategic partnerships and alliances between very different kinds of organizations or groups are fueling innovation,
- The proliferation of new knowledge is quickly commercialized.

So a business's success in the twenty-first century will very much depend on how quickly that business can respond to market forces to compete in a global economy. The number one rule of long-term survival is adaptability. So building a successful business is about being able to reinvent yourself as the market changes and being responsive to changing times, and that takes innovation.

Some businesses have actually shot themselves in the foot by trying to be better and better at what they do. That sounds like a good thing, right? But that won't work if they're just getting better and better at doing something that the market doesn't want.

Kodak is a classic case in point. They got better and better at making film at a time when the world was changing over to digital cameras. By the time they entered the digital camera business, they were entering a crowded marketplace so even though their products were good, their profits plummeted. Now they have changed their business model aiming to do for photos what Apple did for music—to help people manage their personal image libraries. Going from hard products to digital services was a significant reinvention of their business model, which will hopefully pay off for them in the long-term. It is looking promising. But they were initially slow to innovate and then went down the wrong path before reinventing themselves.

CEOs worldwide recognize the crucial importance of innovation when it comes to twenty-first century business success. IBM released a global study of more than fifteen hundred CEOs from around the globe in 2010 called Capitalizing on Complexity. The study reported that CEOs now believe creativity is an essential leadership competency in order to have successful enterprises. Innovation is not possible without creativity. Business success depends on new ideas, new products and services, and new ways of doing business. In short—innovation.

Businesses that fail to innovate run the risk of losing market share, productivity, profit, and key staff. If that happens, they're in danger of going out of business.

WRIGHT

How do you define business innovation?

YASHIN-SHAW

I find that the term "innovation" is often narrowly defined by businesses as being related primarily to technological advances or inventions. This is a very limiting perspective. Business innovation is much more than installing the latest computer system or CRM software. More broadly defined, business innovation is the application of new ideas to:

- products
- processes
- organizational practices
- business models

Think of innovation as a tool that can help a business to respond proactively to challenges and opportunities presented by an increasingly globalized, knowledge-intensive marketplace.

In a business context, innovation could be a major revision of the business model or core competency, as in the case of Kodak that I mentioned earlier, or it could be as simple as putting up a whiteboard in the lunch room as a way of capturing people's ideas to start the collective problem-solving process on an issue.

Certainly coming up with a great new invention that takes the world by storm and ensures market share for a business is a strategic innovation at its most visible such as the Australian invention of the cochlear implant. What a remarkable invention that is. It has given the gift of hearing to thousands of people around the world. But for most businesses, this type of innovation is not an option. All businesses can aim for tactical and operational innovation on a day-to-day basis. Tactical innovation is where a business produces variations on a theme in relation to its existing product or service offerings, and operational innovation is the continuous improvement to business processes and systems that cumulatively yield increased productivity and profit.

So my definition of business innovation is any new idea translated into action that makes the business more effective, profitable, and sustainable.

WRIGHT

In organizations, what are some of the most common barriers to innovation?

YASHIN-SHAW

Unfortunately, there can be many barriers to innovation in organizations. The nature of those barriers will be different, depending on the kind of organization we are dealing with. For example, in a public sector organization, often the main barrier is its heavily hierarchical structure that squashes new ideas. In a long established Fortune 500 company, it might be the mantra, "That's not how we do things around here," which blocks new ideas and entrenches "group think" (where everyone thinks the same way). In small and medium enterprises, it might be an overloaded CEO who has the responsibility for driving innovation but is so busy that it is a struggle to take time to see the big picture and think strategically.

Here is a list of common barriers to innovation that cause "Innovation Inertia" within a business:

- Entrenched practices
- Group think
- Companies thinking that they are already being innovative
- Focusing only on the day–to-day business and not being strategic enough
- Innovation not a priority for the leaders of the organization
- Staff thinking that innovation is only the job of the CEO, decision-makers, or the research and development team
- Staff not motivated to contribute creative ideas
- Lack of communication or silos within the company that hinder information-sharing and collaboration
- No system for capturing ideas and giving feedback
- Lack of good training for staff
- Believing the myth that you have to be brilliant in order to contribute to innovation
- Believing the myth that innovation only comes in huge leaps forward

WRIGHT

What can organizations do to overcome these barriers to create a company in which innovation can flourish?

YASHIN-SHAW

If we look at that list, we see that the barriers can be divided into three broad categories:

- The way people think or the prevalent mindset of the people in the organization
- The climate or culture of the organization
- The channels of communication through which ideas can flow

Mindset, climate, and channels are the three drivers of innovation within an organization. The best way to overcome barriers is to develop an innovation strategy that incorporates all three aspects. Let me deal with each in turn.

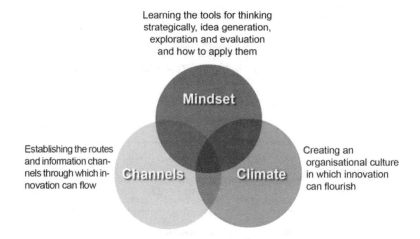

Mindset. One way to encourage staff to think more innovatively and contribute new ideas is for the leaders to ask good questions of themselves as well as their teams. Actively nurture a question-asking culture with questions like:

- What would I see if I examined this situation/idea from a completely different point of view?
- How can we do this differently or better?
- Does this solution look like it will help us meet our strategic plan?

In the absence of questions, we have a dangerous organizational phenomenon called group think. It is a *pattern of agreement where no one questions ideas, policies, or actions.* There is a wonderful quote by Walter Lipman who said, "Where all think alike, no one thinks very much." Obviously, that won't lead to innovation. Kodak was like that. I read an account by the CEO, Antonio Perez, who said that when he first came on board, the hierarchical structure and omnipotence of leadership within the organization was so entrenched that he couldn't get people to disagree with him about anything.

Climate. Creating a climate for innovation is about *consistently* welcoming innovation as a natural part of working life throughout an organization. Building a culture of innovation means cultivating people to think differently, being receptive to new ideas, and being prepared to take the occasional calculated risk. It helps if you have some of these:

- A commitment to innovation by the leaders of the organization. You can't have an innovative organization if the leaders of the organization aren't committed to innovation:
- A system for generating, collecting, progressing, recognizing, and rewarding ideas as well as giving feedback to people who offer ideas, otherwise people will lose motivation.
- High quality professional development or training for staff
- Trust among staff/team members
- Dedicated time for collaborative, creative, problem-solving
- Expectation that all staff be part of the idea generation that will result in innovation
- Tolerance for calculated risk-taking or failures
- Dedicated resources allocated to find, develop, and implement new ideas
- A business strategy that has innovation as an integral component

All of these will contribute to a climate or culture of innovation.

Channels. Having the channels through which ideas and innovation can flow is essential. Without good lines of communication, organizations develop silos of knowledge and experience. This is something that happens often in government organizations and larger companies. But I've seen it happen even in medium sized companies. Here are some suggestions for opening the channels:

- Share the strategic vision for the business with all employees so that everyone is on the same page.
- Collaborate with colleagues across the organization.
- Ask clients for their input.
- Engage with the local community. Many businesses these days are forging valuable relationships with their local communities as well as online-communities. Individuals and groups all around the world can easily collaborate on projects.

Mindset, climate, and channels—these drivers will overcome innovation inertia.

WRIGHT

Suppose leaders in a business wanted to become more innovative in order to improve its competitiveness and sustainability. How would they go about doing that?

YASHIN-SHAW

Different businesses will do this differently. I'll share with you some examples of what some of the businesses I've worked with recently have done.

One medium sized manufacturing organization demonstrated its commitment to innovation by formally articulating it in its business strategy and making it part of the Key Performance Indicators for the executive team. To measure that, the CEO asked for two new product ideas developed and ready for market in twelve months.

Leaders in another engineering firm realized that in order to improve the climate of innovation in the business, they needed to engage and involve their staff much more. The General Manager said, "We have come to realize that if we wanted to improve the innovation climate in our business, then we have to make the employees part of the decision-making process." They started having regular meetings to communicate the company's vision and goals, include them in the decision-making process, and recognize and reward innovative ideas. They provided them with high quality professional development, created an internal business improvement group drawn from all different parts of the workforce, and deliberately included only one manager. Their profit margin has increased by 9 percent without any cost-cutting or price rises.

Leaders in another business simply implemented an active reflection time where they asked all the employees to spend fifteen minutes a day thinking about how they can do better the next day. What a beautifully simple way of encouraging everyone to be part of the business improvement process.

Leaders in one company that had grown very rapidly realized that it was in danger of jeopardizing its achievement due to the fact that the CEO became so busy as a result of the growth the company had experienced that he was doing less of the very thing that had made the company so successful—thinking strategically. He had become too caught up in the operational side of the business. So he delegated operational responsibilities and then went further to appoint key people as innovation drivers in the business. Previously, he had fulfilled that role.

These are examples of organizations that have implemented tactical and operational innovations to improve competitiveness and sustainability. Very often businesses have the resources already within the ranks to innovate effectively; but in order to do so, leaders just need to take a step back and look at the business with a different lens.

WRIGHT

How can organizations tap into the creative potential of their employees?

YASHIN-SHAW

Indeed, there is a huge amount of creative potential that goes to waste in most organizations—brains down the drain! There are enormous reservoirs of cognitive resources languishing in every organization. Most businesses have issues in the "too-hard" basket—those difficult challenges that elude resolution. Chances are that the means to solve those challenges, as well as generate new ideas that can feed the innovation pipeline in the organization, are close at hand but not being used. Usually organizations just need a process for tapping into and channelling the ideas of the employees. Here are a few suggestions:

Set some regular time aside for creative problem-solving and brainstorming. That could be during staff meetings or specific purpose meetings dedicated to particular issues. Have enough structure so that the time is spent meaningfully but not so much that it stifles creativity. Start by defining the issue clearly. The more clearly defined the issue, the better the use of time. Have handy some butchers paper or a whiteboard or some way of capturing the ideas that are generated during the session. Ask people to brainstorm individually first before they go into the group brainstorming. Have a time limit on the process depending on what you want to achieve—twenty minutes to one hour. Select the best ideas to progress. Make sure the team gets some feedback on the ideas they put forward.

Have an effective system to capture ideas. This could be an intranet space where people can contribute and add ideas online. It might be an innovation space or a creative space somewhere easily accessible where people can be comfortable. Usually it tends to be the tea room, which is fine, but it just needs to be fitted out with a few tools by which to capture ideas before they slip away such as a whiteboard.

Suggestion boxes are another possibility, but they have fallen out of favor because they've been incorrectly used in the past. Generally they don't work for a lot of reasons unless they are "campaign-based." A campaign-based suggestion box solicits suggestions about one particular idea only for a limited amount of time, for example, two to four weeks. It is specific, targeted, and contained. Otherwise, most of the time suggestions go into the box and they're just not relevant to what is on the agenda. If you are going to capture ideas, then you must have a process for giving feedback. People don't mind if their idea isn't used; they find it much more frustrating if they put forward a suggestion and then never hear about it again!

Create opportunities for people from different levels and areas of the organization to collaborate. Eliciting different viewpoints and perspectives about a particular issue will almost certainly deliver a richer outcome. So if possible, put project teams together that have a diversity of skills, experience, and insights.

Actively seek input from all parts of the organization. The innovation imperative does not reside solely with the research and development team. It is every employee's responsibility, so ask for input from all sectors of the organization.

Just having a process for proactive knowledge-sharing and collaboration can explode the productivity of an organization as well as help people to feel more engaged and valued. It will harvest ideas that will lead to innovation.

About the Author

Dr. Irena Yashin-Shaw PhD is an innovator and an entrepreneur with a unique blend of academic and business experience, which makes her the ideal partner for organizations seeking to improve their productivity and effectiveness through innovation. Using a "top down" and "bottom up" approach, Irena enables organizations to achieve their innovation goals by engaging all levels of staff. She has methods for maximizing opportunities for cross pollination of ideas, harnessing tacit knowledge, enhancing collaboration and networking, and creating the channels through which information and innovation can flow. A highly respected international expert in her field, Irena has delivered presentations and workshops on the topics of creative problem-solving for innovation in the UK, Russia, China, India, New Zealand, Malaysia, and Australia and has authored and co-authored numerous publications.

Irena's presentations and programs are a unique blend of in-depth, academic knowledge, practical, real-world business experience, and fun theatricality and humor that have made her a favorite on the professional speaking circuit. She currently serves on the National Board of the National Speakers Association of Australia, is a Past President of the Queensland Chapter of NSAA and is the National Professional Development Manager for the organization.

E-mail Irena directly to find out more about her speaking programs.

Dr. Irena Yashin-Shaw

Speaking Edge
PO Box 65 Mansfield LPO.
Brisbane. QLD. 4122. Australia
+61 7 3849 5003
irena@speakingedge.com.au
www.speakingedge.com.au

Chapter Four

COMMUNICATING EFFICIENTLY: A STRUCTURED YET INTUITIVE PROCESS THAT CAN MAKE AN IMMEDIATE DIFFERENCE

PHILIPPE GLAUDE

DAVID WRIGHT (WRIGHT)

Today I'm talking with Philippe Glaude. Philippe's passion for communication and learning started in 1980 while working as an orderly in a hospital learning about human behavior and adapting to different styles and needs. After obtaining a BSc in Biochemistry and an MSc in Microbiology and Immunology, Philippe spend some time in fundamental research. After many years spent in international pharmaceutical companies, selling, managing, training, and heading various departments, Aseret Congruence was created by Philippe in 2001 inspired by the results obtained with effective communication, leadership, and coaching. Since then, Aseret consultants have been involved in the training and development of professionals in North America, Europe, Asia, the Middle East, and Africa with more than thirty corporations, large and small. Aseret owns all copyrights to the U&I, DO™ model and related tools.

Philippe is on the faculty of the International Executive Institute of The Desautels Faculty of Management at McGill University as well as The Institute of Corporate Directors at Rotman School of Management, Toronto University. Philippe is also a member of The International Coach Federation.

Philippe, welcome to *ROADMAP to Success*.

PHILIPPE GLAUDE (GLAUDE)

Thank you very much, David.

WRIGHT

So why is effective communication so important to foster success?

GLAUDE

Communication is basically an exchange of information, isn't it? We share data, feelings, thoughts, what we see, read, and understand about and with people. Efficient communication is the ability to gather precise information, understand its value, clarify its meaning, and use it in a way that brings success in a timely manner.

For example, the Internet is a place where we can gather a tremendous amount of information. The question is: do we know exactly what we're getting? Connecting to the Internet looking for information without asking yourself the right questions beforehand is likely to generate what I like to call a pile of noise. If we don't guide the Web sites to what we need to know, it is unlikely that we will be able to gather the information we truly seek. Communication also means that we make an effort to ask questions in order to decipher the meaning.

WRIGHT

So what are the main communication mistakes?

GLAUDE

In my opinion, the following are the main mistakes we need to recognize and try to avoid:

- Lack of listening
- Lack of adaptability
- Imposing information
- Lack of leadership/courage
- Taking things personally
- Unclear intentions
- Lack of structure

The list of mistakes may seem pretty exhaustive but let me start with what, in my opinion, is the most important communication mistake.

Listening: Lack of listening most often leads to a misunderstanding of information, subsequently leading to making wrong decisions and a general feeling of dissatisfaction.

For example, let's say that you ask Sally, a female co-worker, if she is ready to do something specific and the answer is, "Yes, I'm ready." Are those words, "I'm ready" sufficient to allow you to be confident that she is indeed ready? While it is generally accepted as sufficient, you can't just listen to the words used. Sally may say she is ready when in reality she may not be.

True listening demands that we pay attention to the tone of people's voices as well as their non-verbal expressions. In this case, I may hear the words "I'm ready" but what if the tone of voice is very low, monotone, and even shaky? What if Sally avoids eye contact and her shoulders are slumped. Are there signs that Sally is distancing herself from her words? People's body language may be communicating something different—something that is not congruent with their verbal communication.

Listening also means that you dare ask more questions and say, "Well, you say that you're ready but I have a feeling that you're not." Listening will allow you to truly understand and move in the optimal direction.

Lack of adaptability: Part of listening means that you are also understanding different personalities and different behaviors. We developed a specific model to define and understand behaviors at Aseret, but many others exist and are quite valuable. It's really important to understand people and modulate how we communicate with them.

For example, if I am an expert in a given field and I use all types of acronyms to explain a concept; a layman might be completely lost in the maze of acronyms. In this case, I need to eliminate the acronyms and use complete descriptions.

Another example of adaptability is often associated with energy levels and preferences. If I am trying to communicate with someone who is calm and somewhat introverted in a manner that is highly animated, with extreme changes in tone and oozing with extraversion, I may be perceived as invasive and it may, in turn, generate defensiveness rather than open communication. In this case, it is likely that any information I gather about the person will be limited and possibly even inconsistent with the true nature of the individual. Therefore my understanding will be limited and any conclusion will lack authenticity.

Trying to impose information on others is another mistake. "Group Think" is an example of this. I also call it "the pack approach," in which challenging leadership is viewed negatively, even chastised. Poor decisions are often a result of this.

Lack of Leadership/courage: Lack of leadership or courage is another communication problem. Effective communication cannot work without courage—the courage to say what needs to be said and to ask what needs to be asked.

A striking example of Group Think and lack of leadership is the Challenger space flight in 1986. One engineer was convinced that the O ring was going to leak and create problems. Sadly, it was later demonstrated that the individual, in spite of trying to get his point across, was not "allowed" to fight the system and counteract the pack approach of making decisions. We need courage to ensure that information is shared and understood in order to make the best decisions.

Taking things personally: Another mistake is to take things personally. As a result, valuable information may not be shared because instead, people become defensive. Goleman defined this as Emotional Intelligence.

Unclear intentions: Unclear intentions also cause miscommunication. The simple fact of understanding and being able to express one's intent can guide the entire communication process in a logical manner and make it overall congruent.

Lack of structure: Finally, lack of structure in how we communicate also leads to poor gathering of information and often misled decisions.

WRIGHT

So what are potential consequences of ineffective communication?

GLAUDE

While many consequences may be rather limited, other outcomes can be dramatic. Wars are often the result of miscommunication or poor understanding of information. World War I and II are examples. Other consequences are family conflicts and divorce. One of my close friends is a divorce attorney and he often says that one key problem is that people don't talk, they don't communicate, and they don't try to understand each other. In teams, people may not communicate effectively and the consequences range from conflict to mistrust to loss of revenue and reduced productivity.

Going back to Challenger in 1986, miscommunication can quickly lead to bad decisions, which in turn may generate catastrophic events. The lack of listening and courage to challenge the status quo is the sad reality in too many corporations. There are many examples of leaders in corporations who decided that they didn't need to change anything. As a result, they didn't listen to the available information and eventually it really hurt the company. In the 1980s, IBM had a chance to become the leader in operating systems but as a hardware company, its leadership decided to outsource software development to Microsoft. That simple decision as you know had titanesque consequences. Early in the new millennium, AOL and Time Warner merged for the wrong reasons. Communication was limited to the two CEOs. We know the result of that merger.

Other consequences of poor communication is reduced motivation and disengagement of teams and individuals, therefore generating decreased productivity, misuse of people's potential, limited ability to adapt, increase in negative feelings in the company, and disengagement. An alarming number of studies are showing that the workforce is endemically disengaged from their job. This consequence is terrible because, at the end of the day, not being engaged—not caring—produces poor performance as well as a lack of productivity and innovation. If you don't care about what is going on around you, how effective are you in trying to make it better?

WRIGHT

So what do people need to do to communicate effectively or efficiently?

GLAUDE

We need to slow down, take the time to communicate effectively, have a clear intent, and listen. But what am I saying? Slowing down in today's world seems rather impossible or at best, incongruent with reality. It seems that way at times, yet there are many examples of situations where slowing down, is in fact, the solution to expediency.

Let's find an answer—at least one—to the following question: why do I need to communicate with efficiency? As mentioned earlier, the advantages of efficient communication will come in terms of productivity, profitability, job satisfaction, better harmony in teams, couples and families, and an overall desire to improve. Increased profitability will save time. Increased job satisfaction will save time. Better harmony will reduce conflicts and, save time. We need to listen more effectively and especially more actively. We need to better understand others' situations and realities, and everything that affects their life and ours. We need to adapt our behaviors or our communication style to others'. We need to have a dialogue to be able to identify needs and perceptions of others so that we can start to understand better, welcome ideas, avoid judgment, and finally, have enough humility to communicate effectively.

WRIGHT

So are there key skills and attitudes for effective communications?

GLAUDE

The skills and attitudes we need to develop are linked to what I mentioned so far.

Building a road map to your success must also include a structured approach. Structure provides a framework that leads to increased and more predictable results, it saves time, leads to better planning, and an increased ability to become a role model for productive communication.

I mentioned adaptability as a key factor in effective communication. Let me share an example where effective planning helped someone become more adaptable and efficient. In the majority of our training and development programs, we encourage clients to engage in structured follow-ups. Simply put, we gather a number of participants on a weekly or bi-monthly teleconference (or webinar) and ask them to share how they have applied the methodologies in their actual work environment.

One day, a salesperson (let's call him Peter), told us the story of a client he had had a very difficult time to see. In fact, Peter told us that he may have spent a total of five minutes with the customer in the last five years. By all standards, it is practically impossible to communicate with and influence someone with that amount of face time. During the training program, Peter had decided to make a last effort with this important customer. You need to know that this customer was a physician who literally influenced the prescribing habits of hundreds of physicians in a large United States city.

Peter's behavior style shows he tends to be a Socializer. On the other hand, the physician was more of a Director. In our model, those two styles are complete opposites and have a very hard time connecting. Peter decided that he needed to change his communication approach with the customer. On his next visit, Peter was more businesslike, less chatty, and much more organized. He was prepared to discuss specific treatment data. The physician noticed the change very quickly and for the first time in five years, invited Peter into his office where they discussed products and treatment options for twenty-five minutes.

Because of Peter's ability to adapt, he was able to connect in a manner that made sense for the physician. In addition, Peter was invited to visit monthly in order to provide support to the physician and his staff. Not adapting and not taking the time to reflect and plan resulted in Peter spending only five minutes in five years with the customer. In one day, careful planning and taking time to adapt his behavior to better connect with this physician allowed Peter to spend twenty-five minutes of quality time and provide value. Peter not only adapted, but he also structured his communication, asked meaningful questions, and listened.

Any communication structure should aim to first understand people, situations, and information. Second, the structure needs to allow people to clearly identify needs and situations, and confirm initial understanding. The structure then takes us to a discussion—a dialogue—with people in order to develop solutions and ideas. Finally, any structured communication should include a review of what was discussed, clarify understanding, and the participants must collectively agree on the best next steps and optimal timelines.

WRIGHT

In the context of today's business models using the Internet, isn't communication overrated? Do we still need to communicate effectively?

GLAUDE

I think we do. The Internet is incredibly valuable and I use it every day. Businesspeople around the world use the Internet to find information and transmit solutions. But unless we send the right question to the Web site we are visiting, we may only gather a lot of gibberish. The Internet tends to produce a lot of noise and a large amount of unverified information. Apart from a number of chat rooms or the few blogs that are truly valuable, the chance to collect noise rather than usable information is rather high. Efficient communication allows us to better filter the collected data. Technology has yet to prove that it can replace having somebody standing in front of us telling us about what they feel, telling us about what they think, and being able to filter not just the words, but what they mean through emotion and non-verbal expressions.

For example, if you're worried about chest pains and you look up "chest pains" on the Internet you're going to find dozens of sites that describe what chest pain may represent. In spite of the high quality of information you can find, it may be very unsettling for many people. Whatever one finds on line about health, further confirmation or a proper diagnosis involves communicating directly with a physician who will have the ability to ask questions, listen, and take into account hundreds of little details before helping you come to a clear conclusion about your specific situation.

WRIGHT

So how effective are we in asking questions that engage people and create a dialogue?

GLAUDE

This is a very important question. I've seen greatness, the abyss, and everything in between. Some individuals have the ability to seamlessly inspire others to share information. Typically, these people genuinely want to understand. As a result, it guides their listening ability and ensures that their questions always aim at a profound understanding of others. In doing so, these people inspire trust, which, in turn, fosters more sharing. Skilled communicators ask questions that engage people and encourage them to express what is really going on. Oprah Winfrey and Anderson Cooper are fine examples of the type of persons I just described. I would argue that each reader can find at least one individual around him or her that exemplifies these traits and try to find inspiration in that person's abilities.

Much too often, questions are leading, limited, and geared toward what the "interrogator" wants to hear. The intent is often to get a point across and not to understand others.

The other day, I purchased a cake pan and a cookie sheet at Williams Sonoma. As I am walking toward the exit, a salesperson tending a stand in the middle of the mall stopped me and asked if I had purchased the goods for "my lady."

"I purchased those goods for myself," I said.

He proceeded to ask me if "my lady" cooks, to which I said yes. He then started on the terrible things that cooking can do to women's hands. The questions were aimed at one thing and one thing only—get me to agree that cooking can be harsh to hands and therefore, I needed to purchase the fantastic cream on display. The intent was clear—get me to purchase the cream, not to understand my needs. The questions were therefore aimed at leading me to buy something. It was not communication, it was a pitch. The questions were just a vehicle to take me for a ride. While it may be seen as a good strategy to sell cream in a mall, the same line of questioning is also used in situations that are supposed to generate a discussion, not a sales pitch. This example is one illustration of what I see every day.

Extensive reading and years of experience have shown me that we are rather ineffective in using efficient questions to generate a dialogue that will foster trust and understanding of needs. It may be a sign of the times. Everything is done rapidly and results are expected almost immediately. The pressure to perform in a highly competitive environment seems to influence our inability to take the time to understand.

We often compensate low quality with high volume because it seems more effective, simple, and practical. But is it? Is it faster, more productive, and easier? I would beg to differ. That young man's behavior at the mall did not lead to a sale. In fact, it inspired me to avoid people standing next to their stand in the mall and I am not the only one.

We need to develop our skills in asking questions that uncover needs and feelings. For this, our intent needs to be oriented toward understanding others. This intent helps us relax and pay attention. As we pay attention, we listen and ask more productive questions. The immediate result is that we gather the correct information, which, in turn, helps us make the best decision at that moment.

If I quickly engage a potential customer and realize early that he or she does not need my services or are not ready yet, I can effectively decide what my next steps will be. I can continue to communicate and develop our relationship, whatever the business result, or I can move on. In both cases, I have understood needs, respected the person, fostered trust, and optimized time.

WRIGHT

So what are the questions people need to ask to better communicate?

GLAUDE

Efficient questions first stem from a clear intent. As discussed earlier, and in the context of productive communication, an example of a clear intent is to truly want to understand people's needs. This in turn begins the process of trust, which fosters a desire to share information. Efficient questions engage people and let them express what they think and feel. Examples include: "What do you think about that situation?" "What is your opinion on this?" "How do you feel about the attributes that new hires need to have?" Such questions engage people in a dialogue.

I believe there is a specific sequence—a structure—that can make us optimally effective with questions. Questions first help identify what is true at the moment. Building success involves that we ask ourselves: what are we doing today that has caused us to be successful or not successful? These are actual situation questions. Then we need to ask questions that identify what we want success to look like in the future. In the context of building a road map to success, asking questions on outcomes is of the utmost importance.

Some examples of preferred situation questions are: "Describe to me what would be the ideal situation" or "Please describe how you would like to see this instead of what it is today." In addition to looking at today and the future, good questions address the relative importance of moving from the current situation to the preferred situation: "How critical is it for us to change," "How vital or how important is it for us to innovate or to modify our direction?" Questions need to help us feel the urgency of a certain situation and help us understand what is going on.

Once urgency has been discussed, we need to ask people how they feel about it: "So how will you feel about doing this?" "How will you feel about changing the way we do things right now?" "How important is it for things to evolve?"

When the level of urgency or importance is established, questions have to address the "How." For example: "So how can we do this?" "How do you think we can accomplish what we said was necessary to be done?" These questions will enable people to evaluate specific actions in order to build success.

Finally, we need to identify the what-ifs: "What if we don't do it?" "What if we can't accomplish what we just decided is so important?" "What if we don't find a solution?" "What will happen if this plan fails?" These are questions that enable us to "feel" the urgency or, on the contrary, may help us realize that we don't need to do much.

Children teach us a lot. Watch how inquisitive children uncover information simply because they are not afraid to ask questions. They are most often candid and well-intentioned. Adults have "unlearned" to ask questions. There is one question in particular that adults seem reluctant to ask. We don't ask why enough as adults, especially not in business. Asking why helps our understanding. It helps in challenging the status quo. As a result, it may help us consider more options in creating success.

We need to talk about hope, talk about how determined we are to create success, and be open to solutions, ideas, and opinions.

WRIGHT

I was trained throughout my life to ask questions. The greatest thing anyone ever taught me was the difference between open-ended and closed questions. The closed question is one that is a question to which you can answer either yes or no; generally you learn nothing from it.

Everything you have said has been open-ended—how do you feel, what do you think, what if. It probably takes more than fifty words to explain it. So you're actually learning rather than just someone agreeing with you.

GLAUDE

Isn't that what communication is all about? It's about learning, it's about gathering information, understanding, verifying what it means, taking the information, and being able to do something with it that will bring success. Questions can't just aim to lead us in one predetermined direction; that's what we need to challenge.

WRIGHT

So what is the role of listening in today's business communications?

GLAUDE

As mentioned earlier, I would argue that listening may be the most important skill we can ever develop. To support this, I would like to refer to Carl Rogers. He was a very astute and dedicated American psychologist and a pioneer in developing the value of effective listening. As a therapist, he demonstrated that we need to listen but listen with intent, not just listen because we're supposed to. We're to listen because we care—listen because we want to understand.

Of the many people who followed Freud and influenced Carl Rogers, Otto Rank was maybe the first to talk about or popularize the fact that therapists—or anybody who is trying to provide help to promote health—need to be patient centric. In short, he meant that therapists had to move away from being the center of knowledge and let patients take leadership in making optimal decisions. For this, therapists needed to listen, not just tell.

Translated into the business environment, it means that business needs to be customer centric in order to develop better solutions.

The concept is more than seventy years old and it tells us to listen. Are we just finally getting it? Maybe we are finally realizing that what has often been identified as "touchy-feely" concepts are actually sound business behaviors. Listening is all about paying attention to what people need, want, and desire. When we understand this, we can build things that are necessary and provide services and products that are going to serve a purpose. We need to be able to listen to the people who define the market. If we don't, we're in trouble. The same applies to our lives and dreams.

Google has grown tremendously by listening to what people needed. The Internet was originally built on a system that was more hierarchical. As the demands on the system grew, it was getting more and more difficult to look through the network of data and its layers to find information. It was getting too laborious. Google listened to the fact that people needed something simple. As a result of their listening and intent to build success, they created a new system. Who would argue with Google's success today? Who can argue that listening does not pay?

WRIGHT

So in your opinion, what is the current level of listening skills in business?

GLAUDE

I think it varies tremendously. In general, listening ability in business is rather poor. But we have examples to demonstrate the value of effective listening.

I just shared the example of Google, a company whose leaders were able innovate and have the courage to be better listeners. Throughout history, innovations came from people who had the courage to challenge the status quo. These people paid attention, they listened, they adapted, and they thrived.

Here is an example of my rather harsh perspective on the business world's ability to listen. I've worked in different industries and sometimes, when there is a long tradition of doing business in a certain way it may inspire a fear of innovativeness. When we're scared to do things differently, we don't listen, we don't want to listen, or we don't want to listen to what we could be doing differently. To the "what if," questions, the answer is almost always: "We could lose what we have." This often stems from the fact that changing anything may affect the bottom line. We know that business today is all about the bottom line—profit—and it's all about the stock market giving value to what we do. There are numerous examples of leaders who don't listen very well until the market realities force them to listen. But then, it may be too late.

WRIGHT

So is there a model for effective communication?

GLAUDE

There are many models, in fact: Carl Rogers, Otto Rank, and many of their contemporaries as well as more recent individuals such as Peter Vale. These people have laid the foundations for various concepts and models. What we believe at Aseret is that any communication model needs to be simple. In this case, we call it U&I, DO.

U&I, DO stands for Understand, Identify, Discuss, and Organize. First, Understand the situation and understand the people—try to put yourself in their shoes and understand why you're going to interact with them. Define your intent and objectives.

Then Identify more specifically what their needs are, their perceptions, and their feelings. This requires you to start asking questions, listen, dig deeper, and further develop your initial Understanding. It is important to remember that, in addition to understanding the needs of others, you have the responsibility to express your own needs and make them understood.

The third step is to Discuss ideas, meanings, concepts, and feelings and address the various needs and what solutions or actions will help fulfill those needs. Discuss is the step where solutions are created based on the expressed needs.

Once you've done that—you've discussed and you've found solutions—then you need to Organize the steps to make it happen. This final step is crucial and it is too often skipped. There needs to be a mutually agreed upon plan with timelines for action steps to take the ideas and solutions and give them life.

U&I, DO is a cycle. Every new idea and every new item you discuss needs to go through the same process. You need to re-understand, re-identify, and re-discuss new solutions and organize next steps again.

When we came up with U&I, DO we believed it was simple. We were obviously biased and hoped others would feel the same until one day a client said, "That's interesting because what I understand about this model is that until you and I really work together, we cannot do anything." It is simple. Until you and I speak together—until you and I communicate and understand what we're trying to do—we cannot really do anything, which is a beautiful way to present it, especially when it comes from people who were just introduced to the concept.

So that's the method; that's one of the structures we can offer to develop optimal communication.

WRIGHT

So how much can we plan our communications with others?

GLAUDE

Many of our clients say, "Well, we can't always plan because there is always a new situation. Somebody may barge into my office and ask for an immediate solution to a problem I have not had time to contemplate. How can I prepare for that situation?"

Human beings generally tend to avoid preparation. This is especially true in the current business world where thinking on your feet and making instant decisions is seen as being strong and decisive. We all need to plan and prepare better.

Going back to the situation presented in the first paragraph, one of the first things we say to people is that if you're not ready to communicate effectively, delay the discussion. Take the time to say, "Let me see you in five minutes—" (or ten minutes or in an hour). This will allow you to at least ask yourself how you can plan the discussion effectively. We suggest planning a U&I, DO interaction. Identify what you understand of the person and his or her situation as best as you can. Plan questions to clarify the situation and needs. Before the actual meeting, you may call the person back and inquire, "What exactly do you need? What kind of answer are you expecting and why? What are you looking for?" Ask questions and engage in a discussion before you start discussing solutions.

When you have the discussion, you are better able to create a dialogue and organize the steps. It is possible to plan each step in advance. The conversation may not always happen exactly the way you planned, but it gives you a chance to prepare your approach. It is Winston Churchill who said, "He who fails to plan is planning to fail." Ask yourself, "What am I going to listen to?" "What are the potential emotions am I going to have?" "How will I control my emotions?" "Do I have the courage to listen and do I pay attention to what other people are going to say?" We often know that a conversation is not going to be easy. The question we need to ask is: "Do I still have the courage to engage in a productive discussion and move past my emotions to get to the heart of the issue?"

Going back full circle to one thing I mentioned earlier is the need for humility. You can plan to have humility, you can plan to say that you don't know everything, and you can plan to pay attention and listen.

Here is a secret: the more we plan and use a structure, the more it becomes a part of us and the easier it gets, and the more effective we become. It is just like riding a bicycle—we use the method without ever really thinking about it.

WRIGHT

It occurs to me that we've been talking about communication and almost exclusively in business, but it seems to me that everything you have said also applies to relationships and in our personal lives as well.

GLAUDE

Yes, you are absolutely right—it is the same thing in relationships.

I remember one sixty-two-year-old gentleman was in one of our training programs on selling skills. During the final break, he came to me and said, "I've gone through dozens of these programs and I've seen it all. I'm going to retire in two years, so what we are doing here is not going to change much for me professionally. But there is one thing I need to tell you. As I pay attention to communication skills, I realize that even though you talk about selling skills, it really is communication skills. I'm going to need to apply that with my wife when I retire because I'm going to be with her twenty-four hours a day. I'm going to need to be much better at communicating with her than I have for the last thirty-five years."

It's not just about business, it is about people, it is about our life, and it's about our relationships.

WRIGHT

This has been a great conversation, Philippe. I've really enjoyed it. I've also learned a lot. I've taken copious notes here and I think our readers are really going to get a lot out of this chapter.

GLAUDE

I hope so and that's the intent. If we can start communicating just a little better every day, we can all make an immediate difference around us and plan a better, more successful tomorrow.

WRIGHT

Today I have been talking with Philippe Glaude. Philippe is the Founder and President of Aseret Congruence LLC, which is a company created in 2001, inspired by the results obtained with effective communication leadership and coaching. Aseret Congruence consultants have been involved in training and developing professionals in North America, Europe, Asia, the Middle East, and Africa, with more than thirty corporations, both large and small.

Philippe, thank you so much for being with us today on *ROADMAP to Success*.

GLAUDE

It's been my pleasure. Thank you very much, David.

About the Author

Philippe Glaude, a graduate of Collège de Montréal, earned a BSc in Biochemistry and a MSc in Microbiology-Immunology at Université Laval.

After working as a research and teaching assistant, first at Hôpital du Saint-Sacrement, working on skin and tissue cultures, then at the Dental School of Université Laval focusing on the immunological disorders of the oral mucosa, Philippe joined the Pharmaceutical Industry in 1990.

Sales, marketing, and clinical research were his primary roles the next four years before joining the management team of Leo laboratories, a subsidiary of the Leo Foundation in Denmark. From 1997 to 2002, Philippe Glaude was employed with Fournier Pharma Inc. as the Director of Training and Professional Development and later, Director of Sales for Eastern Canada. During his tenure at Fournier, Philippe was a member of the Board of Directors.

Aseret Congruence LLC was founded in 2001 in the U.S. The company's primary areas of focus are human resources development and effective communications. Aseret's customers range from non-profit organizations to Fortune 500 corporations. Management, coaching (training of coaches and executive coaching), negotiation, communication skills, decision-making processes, competency models, strategic development, and team dynamics are areas of expertise in which Philippe is a consultant for organizations such as pharmaceuticals, healthcare, banking, law firms, aeronautics, manufacturing, and mass market products. Aseret Congruence LLC developed the U&I, DO™ model and the associated tools in 2002.

Philippe is also on the faculty of the International Executive Institute of the Desautels Faculty of Management at McGill University as well as The Institute of Corporate Directors at Rothman School of Management, Toronto University.

Philippe is a member of the International Coach Federation.

Philippe Glaude

Aseret Congruence LLC
419 Sprite Road
Louisville, KY 40207
502-895-7293
pglaude@aseretcongruence.com
www.aseretcongruence.com

Chapter Five

PLANNING TO SUCCEED— THE "RIGHT TURN" ON YOUR ROAD MAP TO SUCCESS!

AMY LETKE

DAVID WRIGHT (WRIGHT)

Today I'm talking with Amy Letke is a successful human capital and leadership consultant who speaks to us from real-world, real-learned experiences as a business owner, entrepreneur, and founder of Integrity HR Inc., a human capital consulting and outsourcing firm. Her real-world experiences are backed up with both the operational know-how of running successful entities as well as having completed the academic discipline of a master's degree in Business Administration. Ms. Letke is working toward a doctorate in organizational development.

Ms. Letke, welcome to *ROADMAP to Success*.

Let's begin our discussion with your experiences in building a road map to success.

LETKE

It's interesting to think about how one builds a road map to success. Depending on what the desired outcome is, it can be easier to accomplish than you might imagine. Many of the successful business professionals I've worked with over the years have quite different road maps, but they do share very common elements to success—they're willing to take chances to be successful, learn from mistakes, and they know that it's not likely that something will magically happen for success to be waiting on the doorstep. The road map is an intentional process that involves creating personal winning habits and behaviors through *Success Planning* and *Success Measurement*. Let's jump in and start first with Success Planning.

Success Planning involves the following steps:

1. Visualizing dreams and goals,
2. Determining what's ideal,
3. Verbalizing those goals,
4. Creating the driving force with goal-setting for determining when the dream will be yours

Success Measurement involves taking those dreams and goals, and creating specific measurements to ensure success in achieving those things that are most critical.

It's no secret why leaders of businesses create strategic plans and mission, vision and values statements—those who do see nearly 30 percent or greater bottom line success when employees understand and embrace the mission, vision, and values in an organization. Whether you're creating a successful career map or a successful acquisition of an organization, the process is the same. To achieve even greater success, we have to have vision, a mission, and values to help guide our journey and reach the desired destination.

How many times in the past have we seen people who wished for something to happen, perhaps to win a new car, find the new perfect job, or exciting new profession, but they didn't take any action? The results were not staggering—nothing was accomplished. Without the vision, a plan for that vision, actions, and measuring for outcomes, the performance is the same—no results.

"There are three types of people in this world: those who make things happen, those who watch things happen, and those who wonder what happened. We all have a choice. You can decide which type of person you want to be. "

—Mary Kay Ash

In creating our successful career map, we can associate it with a vision of taking a beautiful French Riviera vacation, with multiple stops to enjoy Europe at its finest. For example, we have to first create what that itinerary looks like, decide where we are going to stay, and where we're visiting on our journey. Next, we prepare by getting our suitcases packed, heading to the airport to board the plane, and arriving at our destination—seaside. Even a task as simple as planning a trip will not be successfully executed if the plan doesn't tie into the vision for the trip. Without having the vision of where we want to go, we cannot appropriately plan to execute the trip successfully.

If we take a look at processes frequently used in business, we can garner elements to correlate to our personal plans for success through the *Success Planning Process*. Below are the steps in the Success Planning Process.

1. **Mission**

A mission is your expression of what you or your organization does. Your mission tells a customer, employee, shareholder, vendor, or interested job candidate exactly what you are in business to do. It's also representative of dreams and goals from a very high level.

2. **Vision**

A vision is a picture of your desired future expressed in a way that resonates with all members of the organization. The vision is shared with employees, customers, shareholders, vendors, and candidates for employment and creates shared meaning about what your organization wants to become.

3. **Core values**

Core values are traits or qualities that are considered not just worthwhile, they represent an individual's or organization's highest priorities, deeply held beliefs, and core, fundamental driving forces.

When I think about that in terms of life experiences with executives I have worked with for many years, success is somewhat like the journey I just described. It comes by having a clear plan and a clear road map by which to gauge their businesses themselves and even their leaders. Achieving superior results is not only the result of these executives being prepared for that trip, and implementing their plan throughout their organization, but also having a defined personal plan. It's not just about the business, but also about creating a personal road map for success.

WRIGHT

Do you think it's intentional or accidental?

LETKE

Sometimes success can be accidental—perhaps we have a little luck on our side and we find a great parking spot in the first row at the airport before we leave on our journey, or we have amassed enough frequent flier points to upgrade to first class. However, most of the accidental success is just that—unplanned, unintentional, yet it brings a nice ray of sunshine into our world, doesn't it? However, if we're really looking to achieve greater goals, such as improving the business's bottom line, purchasing the larger home by the lake, or saving enough money for the kids' college, relying on luck isn't going to be the way to make that happen.

There's an old proverb that states, "If you fail to plan, you're planning to fail." How many times do we get our plans out of our thoughts and commit them to writing? How many times do we think deeply enough to develop a vision for where we want to take our businesses, our departments, and even develop our personal goals? Probably more times than not. If we do not have something in writing to measure ourselves or others, we're probably not going to hold ourselves accountable to those goals. Proof in point: *only 8 percent of people follow through on New Year's Eve resolutions!* It's no wonder that fitness clubs love to gear up at year end—they know that "good intentions" will boost their customers, at least short-term in January! There are millions of people who are thinking, "Wow, it's time to get in shape," but how many of those people are going to stay accountable to reaching their goals? Maybe 8 percent, which isn't a whole lot of them.

So when we think about developing a plan, we can certainly better predict our successes when we actually create our written *Success Plan.*

"Success depends upon previous preparation, and without such preparation there is sure to be failure."

—Confucius

WRIGHT

So who do you think needs a road map to build success?

LETKE

Anyone who wants to achieve consistent, measurable success should have a personal and professional *Success Plan* itinerary. The reason we want to have that is because we've got to create what our vision is—what that dream is that we want to achieve, whether it's personal in terms of success or perhaps more professionally driven. Isn't it critical to define the dream or what the vision looks like? We need to develop that because it is going to help guide us on our journey to help us be more successful.

WRIGHT

So how should a business or individual create a road map for success?

LETKE

In order to create our own road map for success, we need to determine where we truly want to be. From that vision or dream we then create a means for communicating and measuring that vision. Leaders understand that creating the dream is one thing, and documenting that dream is another. It is just as critical to then be able to engage other people so they understand what that vision or dream means to them and what their role is in achieving the success.

Creating the vision *(Success Plan)*, engaging other people, following a very systematic process *(Success Measurement)* to develop what that road map looks like, and most importantly actually getting it in writing is really critical in helping us achieve that overall success.

WRIGHT

Would you give our readers some key steps in planning for a successful road map?

LETKE

First of all, when you think about creating your own Success Plan, you need to start by thinking about what it is that you want to *be,* what you want to *do,* and what you want to *have;* with respect to the interactions between your thoughts, feelings, and actions. Take a look at the example below of an iceberg - only a portion of how we see ourselves are visibly revealed to others - those items are above the water's surface. However, below the water's surface is where the vast amount of "ice" exists, what cannot be seen easily by others, but is imperative to helping us achieve all that we choose. Consider the following:

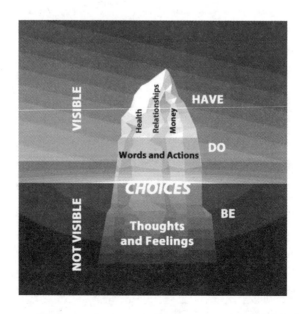

Your thoughts and feelings in this area, like that of the iceberg, are not readily visible to others; however, they are very real. Each item in this image serves a different purpose and there is a definite order of progression that must occur. As an example, you must *be* something before you have the ability or desire to *do* something. Then, once you have done what is necessary, you will *have* what you want. The foundation of this "iceberg" principle starts at the base of the iceberg, what's vast, not seen and all critical.

Your thoughts and feelings will take turns being in control. The combination of these two will determine the *choice* that you make. Your choices show up in the physical sense by the Words you speak and the Actions you take. These are the first visible signs of what you want. Finally, when you have said and done everything necessary, you will have what you want. You will be able to perceive with your senses that you have achieved your goal.

This iceberg principle is why you should have goals for *be, do*, and *have*. Do you *have* what you want within your business, your professional life, your team, and personally? If not, then you need to determine what you need to *do* to acquire what you want. Finally consider, who do you need to *be* to do what it takes to have what you want?

Brad Sugars states, "You need to have vision and you need to think big," when it comes to thinking about being successful. We first have to visualize what success looks like and visually create a picture so we know the answer to "how am I going to know when I get there?" So we've got to think about first and foremost the power of harnessing what our vision looks like and how we prepare and actually write that vision down and deploy that vision. A sample of our MAPS *Success Planner*™ *(Management & Planning For Success Planner)* can be downloaded at www.amyletke.com.

If we're a business owner or leader, we've really got to determine how we're going to paint that picture and be willing to share the vision with our teams. Not only is painting the picture crucial, but we must demonstrate that we have full belief in the abilities to succeed, because if we don't fully engage our minds and have the belief that we truly are going to "make it happen" then we have a high potential for failure. So first and foremost we've got to have that power and that vision, be able to harness it, and be able to share that with other people.

I think secondly we also have to really think about how we're making every day count. We know that, as a professional or individual business owner, there are so many things we can spend our time on. It's easy for us to get distracted in what may be someone else's urgent, but not so important kinds of things. Making each day count, making sure that we are working through the plan and working through that vision in our preparation to achieve the goal is really important.

There's a story from last year about some workers who were working on a trash collection route. Every day they were picking up trash and cleaning up after Hurricane Katrina.

One of the workers on the route was asked, "What kind of work are you doing today?"

"I'm just cleaning up somebody else's trash," he responded.

A second person on the crew was asked the same question, "What kind of work are you doing today?"

"Well," he responded, "I'm making $8 an hour and I'm going to go home and that's all I'm going to do today."

The third worker on the crew was asked, "And what kind of work are you doing today?"

"Today I'm helping rebuild a community as a result of a very devastating hurricane," he said.

What's the difference in these three stories? The first two workers had not made any personal connection to the work they were doing. But that third person had completely connected with the vision— whether it was a company vision or a personal vision—and clearly understood that his role was doing something to contribute overall and making that day count. So when we think about how as business leaders we have the ability to engage our staff and other people, not only do we have to make each day count for ourselves to achieve our own success, but we have to be able to engage other people to help them understand how what they do leads ultimately to the overall success of all.

WRIGHT

So what are those additional elements that help us in creating the road map?

LETKE

I think some additional elements that are really key include making sure that we have specific goals and accountabilities. Not only do we have an overall vision of how we see our success and define what success is going to look like, but then we actually have to develop written 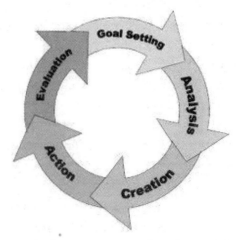 goals and accountabilities to help us execute the plan. Goal-setting should be an ongoing process to help us create, analyze, take action, and evaluate the results.

The first step, as outlined in the MAPS *Success Planner* walks us through this process:

Step 1. Capturing Your Goals

Brainstorm as many potential goals that are most important to you by category:

- Business
- Family
- Personal development
- Social
- Health related
- Money
- Spiritual
- Other

Goals should be personal to us; be positive and be in the present. For it to be personal, include yourself in the statement; for it to be positive, use words of affirmation. To remain in the present, think of having already achieved the goal.

For example, a goal would be, "I deliver successful sales presentations and my close ratio is 85 percent." It meets the criteria of being personal, positive, and present. The more actionable and emotionally tied these goals are to the individual, the more they tie back into our mental energy to help us put forth extra effort and commit to achieving them. Write as many goals down during the brainstorming process as you can.

Step 2. Filter and identify the most important goals from brainstorming

- Capture three to five goals where energy will be expended to create a "Future Reality"
- Identify what the goal is
- Why do I want this goal?
- What are the consequences of not achieving the goal?
- Who else stands to gain from the goal?

This step helps to establish the "future reality" of achieving goals, and connects our emotions to it, as well as other people around us who stand to gain from the achievement of these goals.

Step 3. Complete the MAPS *Success Measurement*™ Worksheet to tie in the details to analyze goals

- Identify three to five goals from Step 2
- Add details from the goal-setting to bring the goal to "life"
- Set due dates
- Establish the reason for each goal—the best ones are goals where the positive impact reaches others
- Identify why achievement is important and consequences of failure

Step 4. Make sure the goals are SMART

Each goal written in Step 3 should be SMART: Specific, Measurable, Attainable, Relevant, and Time-Bound.

1. **Set Specific Goals**—Your goal must be clear and well-defined. Vague or overly general goals are not helpful because they don't provide sufficient or specific direction. Remember, you need goals to show you the way. Make it as easy as you can to get where you want to go by defining precisely where you want to end up.

2. **Set Measurable Goals**—Include precise amounts, dates, etc. in your goals so you can measure your degree of success. If your goal is simply defined as "To reduce expenses," how will you know when you have been successful? In one month's time, if you have a 1 percent reduction, will that mean success? Will success be achieved when you have a 10 percent reduction in two years' time? Without a way to measure your success, you miss out on the celebration that comes with knowing you have actually achieved something.

3. **Set Attainable Goals**—Make sure that it's possible to achieve the goals you set. If you set a goal that you have no hope of achieving, you will only demoralize yourself and erode your confidence.

However, resist the urge to set goals that are too easy. Accomplishing a goal that you didn't have to work hard for can be anticlimactic at best, and can also make you fear setting future goals that carry a risk of non-achievement. By setting realistic yet challenging goals, you achieve the balance you need. These are the kinds of goals that require you to "raise the bar" and they bring the greatest personal satisfaction.

4. **Set Relevant Goals**—Goals should be relevant to the direction you want your life and career to take. By keeping goals aligned with this, you'll develop the focus you need to get ahead and do what you really want. Set widely scattered and inconsistent goals, and you'll whittle your time—and your life—away.

5. **Set Time-Bound Goals**—Goals must have a deadline. Again, this means that you know when you can celebrate success. When you are working on a deadline, your sense of urgency increases and achievement will come that much quicker.

Having SMART goals ensures we have a means for measuring success and evaluating goals for the future. Download a sample of a MAPS *Success Measurement*™ Worksheet (*Management & Planning For Success Measurement* Worksheet) to help you create your goals at www.amyletke.com.

Something else to consider: when we create goals that are very meaningful personally, then we're more likely to spend our time on them. For example, when I think about a challenging goal, such as doubling revenues in a twelve-month period, if I tie it to the benefits such as shared rewards with my staff, my clients, and my family, and tie "how they each benefit," there is even greater opportunity that by creating that deeper emotional connection to the goal, it will be achieved.

WRIGHT

You have worked with organizations and individuals to help them improve and plan for success, so what are the key components of your assessment process that could help the others achieve the road map?

LETKE

In addition to creating vision, mission, values, and goal-setting, the next component is to have a solid understanding of "where we are today" so we can set plans for the future. This can best be done by taking a good look ourselves and organizations through a personal, professional, and organizational SWOT analysis to evaluate our internal Strengths, Weaknesses, Opportunities, and Threats.

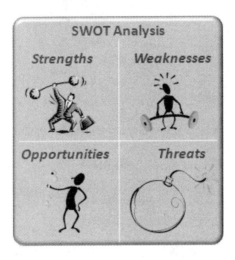

This process helps us gain an understanding of our internal strengths and weaknesses as well as external opportunities or threats. This process is used frequently during strategic planning within organizations and provides critical insight into the overall strategic plan itself.

When looking at this chart from a leadership perspective, sometimes it's difficult to be objective about these four quadrants. That's when we use the 360-degree feedback assessment tool. It is designed specifically for leadership development.

How can a 360-degree evaluation make a difference for me personally or at work? Consider this example:

Most animals that live in the wild live in a very competitive environment. Let's take the wolf, for example. If the wolf is successful in its world, it must constantly be looking for opportunities and threats. Wolves must gather information from all directions and elements to get a complete read on the environment and what they must to do to survive.

In business terms, this translates to gathering input on our performance from all points to ensure we are doing the job we want to do, at the level of performance to *make a difference*. The 360-degree feedback is becoming a very common tool in human resource management for performance improvement. Simply put, it is a mechanism for evaluating someone's performance based on feedback from everyone with whom the individual comes in contact— supervisors, coworkers, business partners, subordinates, sometimes even customers or the general public. It is a method of collecting input from many sources in the employee's environment. This can be a powerful tool in providing feedback to employees regarding how they're doing in their work.

This method of collecting evaluative input is an excellent source of motivation for employees because it provides a truly honest and forthright assessment of how employees and their performance are viewed by a variety of people who have a stake in the performance.

In the more traditional method of performance appraisal, supervisors meet with employees one-on-one to discuss performance. By contrast, the 360-degree method uses confidential input from many people who can truly respond to how an employee performs on the job. The manager and employee meet to discuss the feedback received. This type of feedback helps employees see through a different set of eyes, where they can "see themselves as others see them" and allows them to seriously examine their present behavior. It can reveal areas in which employees are performing particularly well and those areas in which there is room for improvement. It may even reveal "blind spots"— those areas others see as opportunities for improvement, but are completely unseen by the employee. It also provides information for which neither the employee nor their supervisor may be aware of, and gathers specific input to allow employees to adjust their performance accordingly.

The most challenging aspect of the 360-degree evaluation is the concern about confidentiality. When implementing this type of evaluation, it's best to ensure that what is shared will remain strictly confidential. Likewise, explain to each employee that he or she will be evaluated by many people, including those who know the employee's work the best. Employees typically will find this methodology to be more "fair" from their vantage point. When they consider this process, as opposed to being evaluated by an individual supervisor or manager who has limited knowledge of what they do, they see the value in this type of evaluation. They will conclude that the 360-degree feedback is more accurate and equitable than other traditional approaches and puts all employees on a level playing field. This review process is equally helpful for the supervisor. It can provide a more accurate assessment of an employee's performance and help eliminate accusations of favoritism. The 360-degree process provides greater objectivity and because the feedback is submitted anonymously, it provides a supervisor with the most unbiased and accurate information from which to draw performance conclusions. Using a third party to administer the 360-degree process can also aid in building trust with the process and ensuring anonymity.

Most people are not able to see clearly how their performance is either enhancing the work situation for others or detracting from it.

This evaluation method can help reveal these areas and allow employees to improve how they do their jobs, thereby creating greater harmony and better productivity in the workplace. The 360-degree evaluation will help employees identify their strengths so they can build on them. At the same time, it addresses their skill gaps. It is a process that leads to continuous learning, team-building, growing self-confidence, and improved productivity.

Sounds like a winning system, right? It can be, but your organization must be ready to accept the change from the traditional method of employee evaluation. Your formal and informal leaders must buy in to this idea and see the value of its adoption. Some questions to ask yourself include the following:

- Is your organization committed to continuous learning and employee development?
- Are you willing to make the changes necessary organizationally to do this?
- What is the level of trust in your organization? Will your culture support honest and direct feedback?
- Is senior management willing to lead the way and participate in a 360-degree evaluation?

If you cannot answer "yes" to these and similar questions, then your organization may not be ready for 360-degree evaluations. While this can be a powerful and positive tool when tied to strategic goals and individual development, you might consider doing more research on the subject before implementation.

Whether you're building a successful organization or a personal success plan, even higher levels of performance can be achieved by having a good road map to success with solid mission, vision, values, goal-setting, and leadership assessment, as well as creating talent charts and assessing the greatest strengths we have within our organizations to help achieve incredible results.

I think we really have to look at how we assess ourselves, the people around us, and the organization to help us really achieve success.

WRIGHT

Why is having a road map important to us as leaders or individuals?

LETKE

Road maps, such as goal-setting and performance management, help provide excellence in developing personal and professional vision and direction. They provide the "where we're going" and the metrics to determine how we'll get there. When we're without the "tools" to help us be effective personally or professionally, it's as though we're outside on a pitch black night without a flashlight, having no idea where we're going to go and walking through the darkness. This can be a very frightening experience, which could be remedied simply with a flashlight to provide the guidance and direction. Road maps help us guide ourselves along the journey to success, and they also help us to lead and mentor other people. We need to take what we're learning in our personal and professional life, along with what our vision is, and share that talent with other people.

Having others hear and understand more about the vision helps an employee or coworker understand where the road is leading, and their stake in the plan. Having a road map as a leader can be incredibly influential to those around us so they know clearly what our vision is and what our expectations are, and then they can see how these fit into the "bigger picture" and plan overall.

WRIGHT

It's been my experiences that many of us want to have guarantees when we go into business if we're entrepreneurs or into a new job. Is our success predictable when using a road map?

LETKE

Success psychologists indicate that 95 to 97 percent of the people in the world do *not* have written goals and fail, while 3 to 5 percent have written goals and *succeed*. Success can be very predictable when we use a road map. When we have a plan, we also are able to measure our success and we can hold ourselves accountable. We're much more likely to achieve success when we truly desire it, we are willing to make the sacrifices associated with that desire, and when we actually have that road map so we know we are on track or we are not. It's a good way to gauge when we may get off course and how we are going to get back on track to achieve this ultimate goal. Zig Ziglar once said that, "A goal casually set and lightly taken will be freely abandoned at the first obstacle."

So when we have a road map to success and we have written criteria that state very clearly where we're going from a visionary perspective, how we're going to get there utilizing our goal-setting, and how we're going to engage and involve others, we clearly have more than just a very great chance of achieving success. We will achieve success when we truly are engaged and committed to the process, when we engage other people, and measure that success every step of the way.

WRIGHT

What do you think are the biggest obstacles to achieving success?

LETKE

"Your *attitude,* will *determine your altitude*" is a great message for how you see yourself as a professional and to see yourself driving toward success and whether you're going to attain that success or not. So when I think about the obstacles to achieving success, they are as follows:

1. Not having a clear plan.
Many people get lost after they decide to pursue a certain goal. Most goals are merely a progression from where you are to where you want to be. You need a clear plan from A to Z so there's no guesswork. *Solution:* Use the MAPS *Success Planner and* MAPS *Success Measurement process* and goal-setting principles outlined in this material and found at www.amyletke.com.

2. A shortage of time, money, or other resources.
We often are enthusiastic about achieving a certain goal, but fail to do our homework before embarking on the course. *Solution:* Before you set out on your goal, identify the amount of time you will need to put into it, the costs you will incur, and

the resources you will need to obtain and use them. For the particular goal of launching a home-based or start-up business, these could include software, equipment, books, staff resources, online marketing needs, shopping carts, and time to learn the specifics of managing your new endeavor.

3. Unfocused mindset and/or poor attitude.

If you don't have the mindset and attitude of a winner, you have less chance of succeeding. *Solution:* Find successful people and create a circle of them around you. Study them. Talk to them. Listen to their language. Learn from them. Adopt the mindset of success by thinking and speaking positively. Adopt the attitude of success by seeing obstacles and setbacks as learning opportunities.

We all make choices each day. We can choose to be positive or we can choose to be negative. When we make the conscious choice to be positive and to find the "silver lining" sometimes in that grey cloud we have the energy and awareness to achieve the greater success. Being positive, engaging, and encouraging with those around you helps to achieve significantly higher levels of performance.

4. Lack of support or guidance.

You may hit some roadblocks on your journey to success and get stuck, not knowing what to do next. On any journey, support and guidance are essential. On a road trip, it's your map or navigation system. *Solution:* find a mentor, coach, teacher, friend, or partner, who will hold your hand, guide you, and support you until you reach your goal. Then you can celebrate the success together!

WRIGHT

How would you summarize these methods for preparing a road map to success?

LETKE

When creating a road map for success, whether it is personal, professional, or organizational, we need to create our:

1. Vision, Mission, and Values
2. Create Meaningful Goals using a *Success Planner* and *Success Measurement* Process
3. Conduct a SWOT analysis for the business, and a 360-degree inventory of ourselves and leadership

These are just the initial steps to establishing solid practices to achieve success. It takes dedication, commitment, and action to reach your goals, but it doesn't have to be overwhelming. By living day-to-day with your goal in mind you can achieve success. Next, be certain to assess the team and determine how connected the team members are with the vision. Do they see the direction where you're taking the organization or a process or a project, and can they become part of that vision?

Next we need to establish our goals and priorities to be able to become effective in measuring our progress along the way and then we also need to develop a means in which we can stay engaged and excited in this process.

As I think about what we discussed today, I am reminded by a poem I learned many years ago that reminds us always to "forge ahead" to achieve goals and accomplish much success:

Don't Quit

When things go wrong as they sometimes will,
When the road you're trudging seems all uphill,
When funds are low and the debts are high,
And you want to smile, but you have to sigh,
When care is pressing you down a bit
Rest if you must, but don't you quit!

Life is strange with its twists and turns,
As every one of us sometimes learns,
And many a failure turns about

When he might have won had he stuck it out.
Don't give up though the pace seems slow
You may succeed with another blow.

Often the goal is nearer than
It seems to a faint and faltering man.
Often the struggler has given up,
When he might have captured the victor's cup;
And he learned too late when the night came down,
How close he was to the golden crown.

Success is failure turned inside out,
The silver tint of the clouds of doubt.
And you never can tell how close you are,
It may be near when it seems afar.
So stick to the fight when you're hardest hit;
It's when things seem worst that you must not quit!

—Edgar Albert Guest

Do more than just read about developing a road map for success. Take action to define yours by using the tools in this book. Do it for yourself and encourage those around you to do the same. Have the desire and put forth the effort to achieve incredible results!

WRIGHT

Well said, Amy. I really appreciate all this time you've taken with me today, Amy, to answer these questions. Goal-setting and effective planning is always an important topic and I think you have some unique views on how we can accomplish these effectively. I'm going to think on these and I'm sure our readers will enjoy this part of the book.

LETKE

Well, David, thank you, and I'm again honored to be a part of this book and look forward to sharing many more concepts with many of your readers.

WRIGHT

Today I have been talking to Amy Letke. Amy is a successful human capital and leadership consultant who speaks to us from real world, real learned experiences. She has been a business owner, an entrepreneur, and she has founded two companies, Integrity HR and HR Review LLC, a publishing firm for human capital and educational materials.

Amy, thank you so much for being with us today on *ROADMAP to Success*.

LETKE

David, thank you so much, and here's to much success in bringing goals to life and achieving dreams!

About the Author

Amy Newbanks Letke has more than twenty years' successful business experience as is a successful human capital and leadership consultant who speaks to us from real-world, real-learned experiences. She has been a Fortune 500 executive, human capital strategist and consultant, business owner, and an entrepreneur. She has founded two companies, Integrity HR and HR Review LLC, a publishing firm for human capital and educational materials. Ms. Letke is a certified senior professional in human resources as well as a global professional. She is a successful business consultant and empowering international speaker on topics including developing superior leaders, success in goal-setting, successful job performance skills, recruitment and retention of top talent, and coaching for top performance.

Amy Newbanks Letke, GPHR

Integrity HR, Inc./amyletke.com
2013 Frankfort Avenue
Louisville, KY 40206
877-753-0970
www.amyletke.com
www.integrityhr.com
info@amyletke.com

Chapter Six

BE HAPPY, ACHIEVE MORE!

ROZHY TALISMAN

DAVID WRIGHT (WRIGHT)

Today I am talking with Rozhy Talisman. Rozhy says that the power of a smile is sufficient to ignite a lifetime of happiness. She understands the power of happiness and how it relates to everyday life. As a published author and successful business professional, she has gained valuable knowledge on how to apply happiness to reach her goals. From childhood she enjoyed making people smile and as an adult, she recognized that happiness is something we can all achieve. Reaching fulfillment and happiness in one's life is her definition of success and she applies it with love and sincerity in all her seminars and publications.

Let's take a brief look into her background and inspirational process. As a child, she embraced music and writing as fuel for her soul. Friends and family frequently commented about her enthusiastic personality and passion for life. She was gifted with a charismatic, happy personality. By having this ability and awareness from such a young age, it led her into a deep and mature understanding on the subject of happiness and the importance of cultivating it. She educated her mind and spirit to help others become the creators of their world and happiness.

Today Rozhy is sharing with us strategic points to create your happiness; happiness is the road map to success, says Rozhy. She will guide you to discover your gifts and create your own world. Let Rozhy transport you and me to the land where dreams come true. Unveil your inner artist and cultivate and express your skills to ultimately create the world you have always wanted. Smile and sing along with Rozhy; it will be an experience of a lifetime.

Rozhy, welcome to *ROADMAP to Success*.

ROZHY TALISMAN

Thank you very much David, thank you for having me, it's an honor, and a pleasure to be here with you.

WRIGHT

So how did you come to write books about happiness?

TALISMAN

David, writing has always fascinated me. Your question has just taken me back to a couple of transforming experiences I had that led me to writing books about happiness. The first one happened when I was in fifth grade in my grammar and spelling class. My teacher's name was Theresa, who said to me, "Rozhy, you are always full of joy. Will you please tell the whole class your secret to always being happy?" Her question took me by surprise and after a bit of thought I proceeded to answer her question.

"Simply put," I told her, "it brings me joy to see my classmates laughing and smiling." I then asked her, "Am I in trouble or something, Miss Theresa?"

"Of course not," she said, "I would just like to know your formula for always being happy because your positive and happy way of thinking will be the key in helping you open the doors to your future."

Being so young, I didn't have the slightest clue of the impact that her words were going to have on me in my later life. I absorbed her words that still vibrate and ring in my heart today.

In a later occasion, I recall I was taking a class in free writing at Mesa College in San Diego California. Our teacher asked us to write a descriptive paper of a significant story that has taken place in our lives. I wrote about a dream I had where I traveled throughout the universe. I was just another astral body blending in with the stars and planets. I experienced a beautiful sensation of floating and rotating like dancing to the rhythm of a cosmic melody in a marvelous ethereal and heavenly setting. My professor gave me an A+ on my paper and wrote me a note.

"Rozhy," he wrote, "you have an amazing way of expressing your visions, realities, and concepts. Do not let this gift of yours go to waste."

My teacher's words were very inspiring they helped me discover the talents I did not know I had. The beginning of my quest for happiness had just begun.

We are all given gifts; there are no exceptions to this understanding, David. It is wonderful to realize that we all have hidden treasures in need of being unlocked. It is marvelous when we finally awaken our artists within and are able to utilize them as tools to be happy and successful, thus overcoming pain, suffering, humiliation, and issues with low self-esteem.

I believe there are no accidents—everything happens for a reason and everyone we meet along the way has a sign or a precious lesson for us. We shouldn't ignore these signs, I learned to always pay attention to the people around me and communicate with whoever is next to me. I truly listen to everyone who talks to me and those I cross paths with.

We are all connected through our Divine Maker. We have been given the choice of free will and are able to choose happiness over sadness and success over failure. I have chosen to make people happy through my stories, music, and live presentations. I love seeing smiles on everyone's face. This is what inspires me and got me started on writing books about happiness, David.

WRIGHT

So why do you think happiness leads to success?

TALISMAN

That is a great question, David. A very successful and wonderful man influenced my life and thinking process enormously. His life story, which I am about to share with you, implanted and reinforced every day of my life the thought that happiness leads to success. His name was Leo.

He became the man of his family when he was ten years old because his dad left them. He had to work to support his mother and sister. They lived in a small town and after school he would go door to door in an affluent neighborhood asking the residents if they needed any help. It started out with waiting for hours at people's doors just to have them come outside to tell him that they didn't need any help.

Finally one day, someone answered and was in need of some help. His name was Mr. Ruben and he was a very prominent and well-respected man who owned several mills.

He saw Leo and asked him, "What are you doing here, young man?"

"I'm waiting to meet you," answered Leo. "I know you are a very busy person and you might need someone like me who can help you out when you get tired."

Mr. Ruben said, "Hmm, as a matter of fact, yes, young boy, I get exhausted sometimes. I could use your help, come on in."

Leo was a very happy boy. He whistled and sang while he worked; his happy spirit was contagious. Mr. Ruben enjoyed having him around and soon, believe it or not, Leo became Mr. Ruben's private assistant, getting paid good money—very good money for an eleven year old boy. Leo was proud and made a promise to himself that for as long as he was alive his mom and sister would never need food or shelter.

He loved studying and was very intelligent. He was full of dreams and goals and liked to talk to Mr. Ruben about them. Mr. Ruben decided to help him pay for his studies and of course, with a lot of sacrifice and hard work, Leo graduated after a few years as an accountant at the age of seventeen, and became Mr. Ruben's business accountant. At the age of twenty, he became the shareholder and general manager of one of Mr. Ruben's lumber companies.

After a few years, Leo decided to start his own company and Mr. Ruben gave him his blessings. Leo became the sole owner of a lumber company when he turned twenty-nine years old and at the same time he got married and started a new life. Throughout his life, he owned several lumber companies and got involved with other related businesses thus becoming a much respected successful business man. He always kept in touch with Mr. Ruben and looked after him until he passed.

In his personal life he was a spark and the heart of the family. He was loved by everyone he touched. His wife and eight children felt very fortunate for having Leo as a husband and father. He was joyful, funny, loving, and passionate. He played the guitar and sang beautiful harmony. People used to call him the little jingle bell. He enjoyed helping family and friends in need and got pleasure contributing to others' happiness and well-being.

This man taught me the true meaning of life. I learned from him that there are no limits to what you can do and that I can make my dreams come true with perseverance, passion, and determination. This man is my beloved dad, Leo, who is now in another dimension and continues to watch over me. He showed me that happiness is true success and it goes beyond mind and matter.

This is the main reason, David, why I firmly believe that happiness is the foundation of true success.

WRIGHT

Rozhy, when we refer to success we all seem to have different perceptions. How do you define success?

TALISMAN

Most commonly, success is referred to or pictured as achieving or accumulating material things like money, titles, possessions, or things of that nature. My definition of success is a little different—inner happiness leads to wholesome success. They both are interconnected and go hand-in-hand. Success, according to my belief, is based on the discovery of one's purpose on Earth and the enjoyment of fulfilling this purpose with passion, determination, faith, and love. Loving what you do makes the journey fun and exciting.

There are a few essential points that contribute to one's well-being and happiness that I recommend for examination and practice to achieve wholesome success. They are:

- Be thankful and appreciative of who you are and what you represent and possess.
- Live a harmonious family life by prioritizing and cherishing the time we spend with our loved ones.

- Love and be passionate in what you do.
- Eat wholesome foods, engage in physical activities, and embrace mind, body, and spirit wellness.
- Learn to meditate and be peaceful.
- Enjoy the outdoors and appreciate nature and its bountiful wonders.

The words and love of my grandmother, "Mama Mia," kept me grounded and aware of the importance of appreciating my life. She always said to me, "Hija [daughter], you should always be thankful for what you have. Realize that there are others who do suffer and are at a disadvantage, so be happy and appreciative." She was right; I have been very fortunate and am thankful for all life has given me. I thank all my gurus, especially Mama Mia for showing me these values.

In my mid twenties, I realized what my passion and life purpose was. It is no secret anymore. I discovered a magic formula and love sharing it with others to guide them in the creation of their happiness in both their personal and business worlds. In my upcoming book *The Art of Creating Your Happiness* I will introduce it to all my readers. I encourage people to pay attention to those who have been placed in their life and tell them truths that sometimes they might not like or are not ready to hear. These are all teachers in disguise and they are in your life for a reason; listen to them and thank them. Practice as often as possible going inward to discover your true self and hidden virtues. These teachers will guide you in finding out your life's purpose. Happiness and success will follow.

I have worked very hard, studied, and prepared myself to learn how to create my happiness and see my dreams turn into reality. I have also worked hard to put a roof over my head that paid for my vacations and other financial needs, but when I finally decided to follow my call and accomplish my main mission on this Earth I can truly say, David, that nothing compares to this feeling of pursuing one's dream and accomplishing one's purpose. This is what I call the true meaning of success and it always attracts financial rewards as well.

I am very fortunate to have in my life four daughters and one son whom I love and respect profoundly. Among the lessons I have learned from their pure love is the true value of life and family. For the last twenty-six years, I have lived with a wonderful man who is my best friend. He has always been my support and has taught me the meaning of patience, endurance, and unconditional love. I have nine angelical grandchildren who remind me every day of leading the way to the stars and becoming their role model in the search for happiness. Their purity and innocence inspired me to compose the song titled "Thank You," which hopefully will be played all over the world soon.

Let's imagine creating a world where everybody pursues their dreams without being afraid. Where everyone helps each other find happiness and follow his or her passion with blind faith. We can do it! Start by discovering your purpose, write your plan, prepare yourself, speak and live it, walk toward your targeted direction, and like magic you will soon start seeing every piece of the puzzle fall into place and you will experience wholesome success.

WRIGHT

So do you think being unhappy prevents people from achieving success?

TALISMAN

Taking into consideration the type of success I defined in the past chapter, yes, I definitely think that success based on only material or intellectual achievements it is not true success. In my belief, the creation of our happiness is the foundation for wholesome success. Happiness breeds lasting success based on inner joy.

Being unhappy means focusing on the negative and seeing the defects or wrongs of others instead of the qualities. To not appreciate what you were given, negatively judging yourself and others are also symptoms of unhappiness. Feelings of void and dissatisfaction, searching for more money, material possessions, extra marital relationships, and the abusive consumption of alcohol and drugs are also notorious character traits of unhappy people.

I've had the good fortune of having met and of working with wonderful people who have put their trust in my mentoring and training. They have given me permission to speak about them without mentioning names. I'm pleased to share some of the results from these dialogs, hoping that someone can benefit from them.

After analyzing and making some evaluations, I divided the results of these dialogs into two groups, A and B. It is also a self-test. If you want to have some fun, find out to what group you belong. Where the most points come from that you score determines the group you have more affinity with.

Group A—The Happy-Successful Group

- Their personal life is their priority.
- They love what they do.
- They are enthusiastic and positive thinkers.
- They show integrity and honesty.
- They lead by example, not by intimidation.
- They do not criticize their competitors.
- They do not compare themselves with anyone else.
- They compete with themselves, not with others.
- Their family is always included in the pursuit of their dreams and passions.
- They believe with blind faith.
- They do not have doubt or fear of following their passion.
- Family plays a very important role in their life.
- They share their knowledge, accomplishments, and money with others.
- They do not diminish or put anybody down.
- They smile often.
- They are thankful and appreciative.

Group B—The Successful Group

- They do not speak about their personal life.
- They are very passionate about their work and material possessions.
- They highlight their credentials and intellectual accomplishments, not the personal.
- They make negative connotations of others.

- They lead by intimidation.
- They are passionate and enthusiastic when they talk about the money they are making.
- They are concerned about competition.
- They are skeptical about sharing with others.
- Family does not seem to play an important role in their life.
- They refer to clients as units and numbers.
- Their entire theme is about work, trades, acquisitions, and fitness.
- They seem to be indifferent to the problems of others.
- They are too serious. They rarely smile.
- They are lonesome.

Do you have your results? What group do you belong to? Group A displays a more wholesome concept of success. Their family life is integrated but independent from their work life. They seem to be well-grounded and concerned about their inner happiness.

Group B, on the other hand, has also reached financial success but doesn't display a joyous family life. This may be a good time to make an evaluation of what you would like your success to be based upon and make the proper changes and decisions in your life. You can create wholesome happiness to reach a more fulfilling and joyous life. It is in your hands.

I can proudly say that I have helped a few group B's become Group A's; it is a great satisfaction to contribute to people's happiness and self life fulfillment. Either way, I wish you the best and if you would like to contact me, please find my information at the end of this chapter

There are some basic steps you can take to begin action. I recommend starting by being more conscious of your thoughts and habits. We are energy converters and have the power to convert from the negative to the positive and vice versa, so be very careful. In my book, *The Art of Creating your Happiness*, I share seven magic principles I use as my rule of thumb to help myself and others create our desired world. These principles are the tools needed to create happiness. Either way, regardless of your results on the quiz, I wish you the best in your pursuit for success.

WRIGHT

So in your opinion, what role does happiness play in our current society?

TALISMAN

Sadly, wholesome, long-lasting, inner happiness plays a very small role in our society. Programs and concepts of happiness should be integrated into our society.

The modern world seems to be misled and or misinformed on what true success is. Glamour, money, and power seem to be the essential focal points in the media and entertainment industries. This trend even includes some motivational speakers and writers who seem to link success solely to material possessions.

This distorted concept of success, without linking it to happiness as inner virtues, is what causes among a lot of young people a desire to make lots of money quickly. And because they don't have the proper guidance or maturity at this age, they get into confusing depressing mental conditions that sometimes cause them to make wrong decisions such as stealing and selling drugs.

I believe it is time for schools to start teaching more about inner skills when children are very young. There should be more programs in schools like the Montessori system, which is a method that focuses on the child's happiness and development, not on the teacher's. There should be colleges and universities teaching the development of wholesome happiness, a virtue that helps us deal with problems and obstacles later on in life. Violence and depression will also decrease dramatically.

According to the American Medical Association (AMA), 80 percent of all illnesses in our country are related to stress. Stress increases the probability of cardiovascular diseases and occupies the forefront of other deadly illnesses. Several thousand years ago in India, laughing therapy was used to improve health and relieve stress. I am sure we could all use a little bit of this therapy in our days.

In corporate America, there is also an urgent need to kindle sparks of happiness into the marketplace to reduce illnesses caused by stress, to help people be happier at their jobs, and perform their duties better. We should not have to outsource jobs anywhere else if we teach our citizens the value of performing their jobs happily. We need to retake our role as a parent nation by being a model to be duplicated by other nations—one based on the power of smiling and other virtues that promote the concept of achieving being happily successful.

We should give full support to our spiritual and political leaders, artists, performers, musicians, and poets who transmit uplifting, positive messages. Our vulnerable youth deserve positive mentors as role models. Our children ought to have a better future and a world based on a solid foundation where long-lasting happiness and internal peace are the main components.

In the meantime, as the creation of happiness takes place in our society, let's voice our wish to create more peace and joy on this Earth. We all have the potential of creating happiness, change our habits, and choose our actions. Let's start by performing activities and work we love while in some way we serve humanity by smiling and doing something for others; doing so elevates one's spirit. Let's get closer to nature and get involved in mind, body, and spirit practices. We will soon witness a wave of inner happiness that will start manifesting. We need to start with ourselves. Do you think this is a good idea, David?

WRIGHT

I think so, yes.

Will you tell us how you learned that in business being happy increases productivity?

TALISMAN

To better explain, I would like to share some stories with you that incorporate the interconnection between happiness and productivity. I will actually start from the time I discovered the formula to create my happiness.

Everything started when I was about fifteen years of age. I would dream about becoming educated, working and getting married in the United States. Thirty years ago in Mexico, my country of origin, society thought that women should not go to college and have careers. They should just learn domestic chores in preparation for marriage. I never agreed with this mentality, so I decided that getting married was the only choice I had to free myself, to be treated as an adult and get a higher education, which would help prepare me for my future.

When I first arrived in the United States, I didn't know what supernatural miracle had happened for the dream of my early adolescence to become reality. All I knew was that all the pieces of the puzzle fell into place. Shortly afterward, I realized that the mysterious process had been the discovery of a formula to create happiness and materialize my dreams. This formula is composed of a simple method to creating one's happiness combined with the application of seven basic principles that provide the necessary tools to accomplish this.

An important point was revealed to me—the importance of being open to the unlimited land of opportunities and possibilities, meaning that if one door closes, others will open. Be always alert. When someone knocks, you must open the door and welcome the opportunity.

To incorporate my happiness formula in the corporate world, I first analyzed all the business experiences and challenges I faced. Then I learned from the experiences and challenges of others who wanted to share their stories. The results demonstrated repeatedly that happy people are long-term higher achievers, just like in the story I am about to tell you.

The story of Phillip: Phillip was employed by a large technology company for approximately ten years and their management's leadership style was one of intimidation. He seemed to be under a lot of stress. He was beginning a family and had little time to spend with them. He loved his work but the business atmosphere was not conducive to happiness and harmony.

When Phillip had a new job offer with a smaller company, he called and asked my opinion. I suggested that he meet the owner and top management to find out what kind of expectations they had of him and to see if they were a match with his own expectations. He took the job and has been working for the company for a little more than five years; the company has been showing consistent growth and profit. He is now a shareholder. He has the freedom to choose to work from home; his company encourages him to spend time with his family. He enjoys many vacations and personal days off. The company even pays for his martial arts classes. He wrote a book that was supported by the president of the company. He enjoys his personal life and loves his work; he is a happy person and one of the company's top producers.

I believe companies and employees should share similar values, goals, and objectives. Respect, care, and loyalty must be the foundation of their relationships. Employers should hire employees who love the work they do. Employees of all ranks and positions should be introduced to principles of happiness and promote continual motivation.

Happy employees stay longer at their jobs and their performance is far superior to the unhappy ones. A positive working atmosphere is not only healthy and stimulating, but also profoundly inspiring.

WRIGHT

So what are the biggest obstacles trainers and apprentices face in order to transmit the concept that happiness leads to success?

TALISMAN

I believe that one of the biggest obstacles trainers and apprentices face is themselves. Many managers are satisfied with their techniques and believe their apprentices are the problem when in reality most of the times it's the way they lead. They need to embrace change and become educated in the subject of happiness.

I would like to share with you a story about a small business engaged in wireless services and products. The story is about Blanca and Ron. Blanca was interviewed by Ron who applied for an assistant manager position. Ron was the hiring manager.

The interview started with all of us introducing ourselves to one another. Ron began by telling Blanca what he does. He explained everything about the company. Ron spoke too much and had no idea about how to relate. His conversation had no relevance. I had to interrupt because it was part of my job and asked Blanca, "Why are you in sales?"

"Because I love selling without selling," Blanca replied. I asked her what she meant.

"I see sales as an opportunity to offer a service or a product that the client needs and I can do a great job meeting their expectations."

Great answer! This is one of the answers I needed to hear from someone who loves what she does. Usually if trained, guided, and motivated properly, people will perform great.

Ron continued asking her questions about salary, commissions, and other similar subjects.

I interrupted again to ask a second question, "Blanca, what part of sales do you like the most?"

She answered, "When the client signs the contract, gives the check, and begins glowing with happiness."

The two answers Blanca gave were enough for me to know she was going to be a great employee if coached properly. The interviewer needs to select and be aware of what questions and answers are important in order to find out if the interviewee is a match

Blanca was hired by Ron. Later, I discovered Ron and Blanca had personal conflicts that interfered with their performance. I guided Blanca to focus on her qualities and potential. I helped her visualize her goals, write a plan, and take action. I educated her on the importance of team work. I shared with her the principles of happiness. She needed reassurance in that she was doing a good job. Quickly Blanca gained self-confidence. Two years later, she became the sales manager and contributed to the expansion of the Latino market. She now trains her sales executives to generate leads mainly from referrals because of the excellent customer service she practices.

Ron, the manager on the other hand, could not concentrate on his job due to the long hours he was working. He was moody and his leadership skills were deteriorating. I helped him develop a plan for time management so that he could have more time available to engage in happy activities. He was open to change and understood the importance of his well-being to perform at his best. Managers are role models to their apprentices. He now has other managers under his wing and is doing a great job hiring, motivating, and keeping them happy and productive.

Ron and Blanca are two of many professionals who were not aware of the role happiness and positive leadership play. Currently they have achieved personal and business growth by embracing happiness as the foundation of success.

As a result, this business has opened up other locations nationwide with this model as their common denominator: happy employees properly trained and motivated result in long-term top producers.

WRIGHT

So what mistakes does management incur when the result is unhappy and unmotivated employees?

TALISMAN

One of the most common mistakes I have seen is poor management leadership. There are different types of management. The one I am going to elaborate on is management by intimidation. This most commonly results in unhappy and unmotivated employees. I have found out that a team leader who practices intimidation very often does not have a stable and joyful personal life. Intimidating managers and leaders believe that when their subordinates do not meet their expectations or fail to be productive, their way of motivating them is insulting, threatening, or punishing them. These methods are known for having the reverse results—poor production and a negative atmosphere.

I'm going to share a personal experience. In 2007, when the Real Estate industry collapsed, I decided it was time to learn about the corporate world and put my Real Estate profession on the back burner. Most of my life I had been an entrepreneur, this time I was hired as a high executive salaried employee. Here is my story.

Natty, the VP of Marketing of this company, recruited me heavily; she did a very good job selling me her business. I was employed by a midsize company as the VP of National Sales to develop their Latino division. I was very excited with this new venture. Leon, the owner and President of the company, was a young man who had just moved from New York after selling his company for hundreds of millions of dollars; he needed someone with my expertise. The day he hired me he said, "You are exactly what I was looking for."

It was five minutes to 9 AM as I walked through the glass door of my new job's office building. I approached the receptionist and said, "Hi. I'm the new employee, may I see Natty please?"

She said, "Nope, she's not at this office today. Hold on."

I waited until she was off the phone, "How about Selena?" I asked. Selena was Natty's assistant.

"Let me see if she is available, hold on," the receptionist replied.

I felt rather awkward and I thought to myself, "If this is the way the receptionist whom I consider the first and most important impression of a business answers the phone telling people "hold on," and does not know how to welcome clients and new employees, I am curious about what kind of atmosphere prevails in the office. Selena came out after a while and took me to my office and left me there. I began to realize what a great opportunity this experience was going to be for me to learn the dynamics and internal affairs of the corporate world.

Every experience I was faced with helped me understand both aspects of business—the managers and the employees. I also realized that companies lack the happiness touch and strategies are much needed to create a harmonious team-oriented atmosphere. They were also missing pre-hiring techniques, training, and continuing motivation.

The first day of work is basic for the new employees' first impression and foundation of trust and loyalty toward their company, needless to mention the importance the way how the telephone should be answered and the courteous phrases these employees need to utilize at all times. A company must view their employees as the core of their business; they are as important as customers. Employees are a great means of advertising and referrals. Companies should cater to their employees constantly. Happy employees bring happy, loyal clients on board. Indifference and conflict among employees, regardless of their rank, shows poor management.

Oh my goodness, David, you should have seen the anger, envy, lack of motivation, and depression these employees manifested. Conflict reigned in this environment. They were unhappy and unmotivated. Many employees and leaders of companies suffer from unhappiness and lack of inner motivation; their job becomes simply their means of surviving.

A few months were more than enough for my research at this place. My discoveries reinforced what I already knew but had never experienced personally. We as employers and/or higher management are not more important than the average employee. When we feel we are better than others, it means our mind is out of control. That is called ego. Ego is the monster that creates separation and differences. Every employee is a beautiful, unique, and special human being. Happiness is an art and success is a state of mind and spirit that we all can unveil, cultivate, and master.

If readers relate to this story, remember that there is a solution to create a more joyful life, either as an employee or an employer. I can help, and, David, I can assure you that there is a way to revert an unhappy or de-motivated spirit to a happy and enthusiastic human being.

WRIGHT

So do you have a plan or program to help businesses, top management, and sales professionals achieve more?

TALISMAN

Yes, David, thanks for asking, I believe sales is the heart of a business and that all businesses sell in some manner, so I developed a program called "Be Happy, Achieve More." Be Happy, Achieve More reaches professionals of all ranks, titles, and positions as well as companies regardless of their size.

The first part of this program introduces the primordial steps to happiness and it is complemented with techniques and strategies that are easy to apply regarding attitude, kindness, ability to follow directions, how to listen and focus, motivation, time management, social skills, etc. The second part, I call "the art of selling." In it I include customized plans to strategize the generation of leads, customer service, client retention, closing the sale, and an emphasis in building a relationship for a lifetime. The dramatic increase of revenue and profits is the main objective.

My programs are designed to build happy professionals and motivate everyone to be the "best and most wanted." The following principles will help anyone who wishes get started now to becoming the "Best and Most Wanted:"

Attitude

Knowledge

Perseverance

Authenticity

Thoughtfulness

Awareness

Patience

The dismal economy we are currently experiencing should be viewed as an opportunity to capitalize, change, and renew. It is time to return to the old fashioned ways of doing business that were based on personalized attention. We must revert to a more personable and customized attention. The best way to compete in the marketplace is not offering a good price and an indifferent attitude, but to welcoming our clients with a smile and an authentic happy attitude. This is the only way to excel during a difficult economy. All leaders must take responsibility and retrain their fellow workers to make an effort in treating every person the way he or she would like to be treated. Remember that clients and customers are the ones who dictate and choose those with whom to do business.

After twenty-seven years of experience in sales and business development, I am proud to present to you this program, which can become the most powerful tool for any company and will boost sales and production to unimaginable heights. Be Happy, Achieve More also contains excerpts that guide everyone who participates into inner discovery, reflection, healthy thinking, and a positive attitude.

WRIGHT

So have you had any role models in your pursuit for happiness and success?

TALISMAN

Yes, David, I'm very fortunate to have had great role models. My dad, Leo, is one of them. I told part of his story previously in this chapter. Another one is my grandmother who was perhaps one of the main figures in my life. With her exemplary life she spoke more than words could ever say. She was loving and passionate, and when she disciplined her beloved ones she was serious and strict.

As a child I wondered why she never had any boyfriends around, she was a beautiful lady. I imagined her falling in love with Pedro Vargas, a famous Mexican singer who sang romantic songs beautifully. One day we went to watch one of his movies where Pedro falls in love with a girl in the movie, I wished deep in my heart for this girl to be my grandma, but, no, it never happened

I was about twelve when finally one day I asked Mama Mia why she hadn't gotten married again. She was very serious when she answered, "Oh no, little daughter, I want to be a good example for you and the rest of my family. Your grandfather is still alive somewhere." That day I realized the kind of woman she was because she had given up her life for what she believed.

After my dad married my mom, Mama Mia started her own business; she did not want to be a financial burden on my dad. Back in the 1960s it was not common for women to work. She started a sewing factory in the back of her house and managed up to fifteen people. They made sacs for grain and seeds to feed animals. For a lady who had not even gone past second grade, she did outstanding. I'm so proud of her. Wherever she is, I send her all of my love.

David, I could go on and on about my role models and what they signify in my life, but I am just going to mention some of their names and phrases I remember them for:

- *Papa Polo (my dad, Leo):* When you fall, stand again, never give up.
- *Charlotte Blob:* The discovery of our purpose and fulfilling it is the most important assignment we must complete.
- *Linda Goodman:* The way the magnetic circle of money works is based on the more you give the more you receive.
- *Dr. Wayne Dyer:* The more you talk about what you don't want, the more you have it in your life.
- *Jack Canfield:* To succeed, you must have a well structured plan.

- *Deepak Chopra:* To make an important decision, think about the people you love and how it will affect them.
- *San Jeunim:* Education builds spirit.
- *Buddha:* Envy, anger, and attachment are the worst enemies of mankind.
- *Jesus:* If you had faith of the size of a mustard seed you could move mountains.
- *Mahatma Gandhi:* Relinquish power to get power.

David, some of these great men and women have passed already and some are still in this world, however, they all have had something in common—the desire and passion to share their wisdom with mankind. They have taught me love and compassion on one hand and willpower and determination on the other. I send them my love and appreciation.

I invite everyone who would like to honor their gurus and mentors to remember and thank them for their contribution. Make a list of them and the important things they did or words of wisdom they spoke. We must remember that we are all interconnected, breathe the same air, and are all part of Nature and the Divine. We have the potential to also be role models; it's up to us how we want to be remembered.

WRIGHT

Will you tell us more about you Rozhy—your music and your poetry?

TALISMAN

Yes, David, of course I would love to. I was born in Guadalajara Mexico. From my childhood and to this day, I have been surrounded by family members who love music. My mom played the piano; she sings and dances even today at her eighty-four years of age. My dad played the guitar, sang, and created beautiful harmonies. My dad's sister is a professional singer and music composer. At her eighty-five, she still sings and writes poetry. She is a published author and renowned song composer.

One day when I was about six or seven years old, my grandmother heard me singing and said, "Hija [daughter], please listen to your key, you are totally out of tone. Oh my gosh, her words were like a dart in my heart, but it was a dart that did not kill but incited improvement and courage. I said to myself, "I am going to learn to sing."

My mom taught me how to be graceful and follow the notes. "Let the music take you, go with it, listen to the pauses and the changes," she said. At the same time, I started asking my aunt to teach me how to sing in tune. She told me I needed to learn how to breathe through my lungs and sustain the air in my diaphragm. She also gave me tips to follow the key properly.

After a couple of years of practicing very often, I decided I was ready to sing a song in front of my grandma again. After she heard me, I saw her face shining with happiness. And said to me, "Well, not bad, not bad at least you can sing in the right key and tone. Keep on practicing." I realized for the first time that I could sing and dance rhythmically. This was also the beginning of my passion for music and another steppingstone to being aware that there are no obstacles we cannot overcome. I was very humbled and happy for my accomplishment.

From that time on, people liked my voice and I began to be invited to family and friends' parties to sing. I also sang, read poetry, and danced at the school events. I loved it; it was another way of making people happy.

In the early seventies, I recorded my first record with La Familia del Valle, a group formed by one of my brothers (Azhul) and two sisters (Tessy and Nene). They are the creators of the version in Spanish of *Una Paloma Blanca*, our biggest hit. The translation is, *The White Dove*, which was written by George Baker. I was already married with my first three beautiful princesses so I decided to be a stay-home mom and was not able to participate in performances.

In the late nineties, after all my five children were older, I recorded my first album/CD subtitled *Y Ahi estare (And I Will Be There)* with songs in English and Spanish that contain compositions of two of my brother's and one of my own. In 2008 I recorded, in English and Spanish, my first motivational CD, *The Art of Creating Your Happiness*, an audio CD where I reveal my Magic Formula and its seven principles. Its music is original. For the first time, I also interpreted parts of my song, titled "Thank You." It is a very inspirational and uplifting melody that hopefully will be played and sung all over the world.

In 2009, as co-author, I wrote, *Leading the Way to Success,* with Jack Canfield and other renowned authors. And Volume II of *ROADMAP to Success,* which will be published in 2011 as co-author with Dr. Deepak Chopra and other respected authors. I am working on having my chapters of both books available in Spanish for summer of 2011.

This year of 2011 will see the birth to my audio/CD "Be Happy, Be Successful." I will have it available for summer.

Presently I am working on my book, *The Art of Creating your Happiness Volume I,* dedicated to women who have been cheated, betrayed, and deceived. This book and my CD album will be available in English and Spanish at the book and music stores early 2012. My music director and producer, Leo Morales, is working on composing and selecting our musical themes.

For information on my music, books, and novelties, feel free to contact me by phone or visit my Web page and blog.

WRIGHT

So to conclude our segment here with you Rozhy, what farewell message would you like to share with our readers?

TALISMAN

Of course, David, first of all I would like to send a very special invitation to all of you to join me at my happiness workshops and/or presentations. I also encourage you to read my books and listen to my music. I would be honored to add a little bit of wholesome happiness to your lives and put a smile on all of your faces.

I want to thank you, David, for inviting me to be a part of this gathering of well-known authors, especially Dr. Deepak Chopra who has held a special place in helping me grow spiritually. This is the second time I've had the privilege of working with you; I am very grateful. I also want to thank our readers and ask everybody to remember to practice having a happy attitude and positive thinking, along with uplifting activities. Action will give you the motivation to make the necessary life changes and decisions you need to lead a wholesome road to success. Happiness is the foundation of success. Enjoy the journey, be happy, and achieve more.

Thank you, David, for the opportunity of letting me share my message of happiness.

WRIGHT

Well, thank you for being in our book and thank you for taking all this time to answer all these questions. I've really learned a lot here today and I'm sure that our readers are going to as well.

TALISMAN

Thank you, David.

About the Author

Rozhy is originally from Guadalajara, Mexico, and has lived in the United States for more than twenty-five years. Among other courses and certifications, Rozhy obtained a degree in Business and in Real Estate. These professional achievements helped contribute to her success in business, however, the true elements that have propelled her to reach such great heights have been her outstanding abilities as an entrepreneur, her personal experiences, and, overall, the happiness she carries within. Rozhy gracefully says, "I hold a "master's degree" in Happiness from the University of my Life."

Based on scientific research, happy employees stay longer at their jobs and their performance is far superior to those who are unhappy. A positive working atmosphere is not only healthy but motivational and inspiring. Rozhy has spent years proving this theory repeatedly. Her business ventures and trainees have all had the chance to flourish because of the upbeat atmosphere she creates to promote happiness and positive results.

She has developed several programs for businesses and corporations that seek to increase their employees' productivity and loyalty. She specializes in uplifting the spirits of key employees to helping them be happy leaders and manage by example to take their companies to the top. She will guide them with a subliminal strategic plan to understanding the importance of a positive attitude to excelling in their responsibilities, thus joining other companies that will lead through these difficult times and grow stronger for the years to come.

Some of the titles of her programs are:

- "Be Happy, Achieve More"
- "The Power of Your Attitude"
- "Happiness is Contagious"
- "How to be Happy in Difficult Times"
- "How to Create Your Happiness After Your Heart was Broken"

Rozhy says, "It is an art to create your happiness and cultivate success. If I could do it, you can do it, too."

Rozhy is available to everyone who wishes to achieve happiness and success and partake in any of her programs either individually or as a group.

Rozhy Talisman
The Happiness Motivator
877-533-8093
Rozhy.t@gmail.com
rozhy@rozhy.com
www.rozhy.com

Chapter Seven

MANAGING CHANGE: THRIVING IN TODAY'S HEALTH CARE MARKETPLACE

PAMELA SHAHEEN

DAVID WRIGHT (WRIGHT)

Today I am talking with Pamela Shaheen, Founder and President of the Delta Collaborative, a consulting and coaching firm specializing in change management. The organization works with healthcare clients who are wrestling with multiple changes—declining reimbursement, healthcare reform, changing professional roles, and empowered patients to name just a few.

Pamela is a highly regarded healthcare consultant, executive coach, and senior administrator with more than forty years' experience in healthcare. In working with clients, she has directed complex organizational and community change efforts.

Based on her years of experience, Dr. Shaheen has created a five-stage model—a "road map for success"—to assist her clients in effectively leading their organizations in today's turbulent healthcare environment.

Pamela has a bachelor's degree from Michigan State University and a master's and doctorate from The University of Michigan. She is a noted speaker and author in the healthcare field.

Pamela, welcome to *ROADMAP to Success*.

PAMELA SHAHEEN (SHAHEEN)

Thank you, David. I'm delighted we're having this conversation. I'm looking forward to sharing my perspective on how organizations can become and remain successful.

WRIGHT

We all want to be successful in leading the organizations we're responsible for, so how do you define "organizational success"?

SHAHEEN

I'm glad you asked this very important question. To be successful today, healthcare organizations must be able to effectively manage change. As I'm sure you are well aware, being able to manage organizational change effectively is often elusive. In fact, many change initiatives never get past the initial implementation phase, much less making it to their first birthday!

For example, many hospitals are now engaged in making changes to improve their performance and the quality of care they provide. One approach has been to empower any member of the surgical team to call a halt to the operation so the team can reassess how the procedure has been handled and to point out deficiencies. This approach is patterned on the airlines empowering their pilots to cancel a flight if they believe something is wrong.

In contrast, the healthcare process is very difficult to implement because it changes the dynamics of power, especially between the nurses (who love it) and the physicians (who hate it). Sadly, because this change approach often doesn't incorporate strategies to discuss and deal with this authority shift, a lot of change efforts revert back to the status quo in about three months" time—resulting in a significant waste of money and an increase in the frustration of team members. How sad.

Based on my years of experience in working in this field, I believe the following are key characteristics of healthcare organizations that are navigating successfully.

The first is having effective leaders. Organizations won't move forward unless leaders have a vision of where they want to go, a passion for getting there, and an ability to bring everybody else along. Bottom line: if there are no visionary leaders, there are no committed followers.

Second, the organization must be nimble—able to adapt and reinvent itself as its environment changes. This capacity is becoming more important as the pace of change accelerates in all fields—especially healthcare.

The third characteristic is maintaining profitability. This particular adage holds true whether or not the organization is for-profit or not-for-profit. Often when consulting with leaders of nonprofit companies, I have to remind CEOs that they need to write on their wall the following statement: "There is no mission if there is no margin."

Characteristic four reflects organizational resiliency—the ability to bounce back in the face of defeat. Leaders need to be focused and optimistic. Employees have to maintain a "can-do" attitude, especially when the going gets rough. Also, the board must be willing to take steps forward, even when the outcome is not known. Unfortunately, there are too many healthcare organizations where both the board and key leadership are risk averse.

I think Winston Churchill best sums it up when he said:

"Success is moving from failure to failure with no lack of enthusiasm."

WRIGHT

So what do you think is the biggest stumbling block for healthcare organizations in achieving success?

SHAHEEN

In my view, healthcare organizations often either lack or fail to commit the tools, knowledge, resources, and revenues required to manage change effectively so they can thrive in the years to come. Unfortunately, hospitals and other healthcare organizations often react to crises in their environment rather than thinking five to ten years out, and developing a strategy for getting from now to then.

Understanding these dynamics is what led me to develop my five core strategies change model, which we will discuss later.

WRIGHT

Healthcare organizations seem to be particularly challenged in reinventing themselves when compared to other industries such as the airline and telecommunications industries. Why is that?

SHAHEEN

Despite its perceived sophistication, healthcare is, in many ways, still a cottage industry. As one of my colleagues, Ian Morrison, a health futurist, once observed, "It is easier for me to use my computer to reserve dinner at a restaurant in England than to use it to make an appointment with my doctor." Yet healthcare is under tremendous pressure to change, given current changes and those on the horizon. Examples include:

- Consumers will take more responsibility for their own healthcare. This is beginning to happen now as savvy consumers come to their doctors offices armed with medical research downloaded from the Internet. In some instances they are more informed about their condition than the doctor is.

- Advances in genomics will lead to the development of "designer drugs" made especially to incorporate key characteristics of the consumer's genome.

- Advances in IT will mean that a physician can practice and work with other physicians anywhere in the world. Right now radiologists are having their scans read by physicians in India. That way they have their results back within twenty-four hours.

- Nanotechnology—the art of manipulating materials on a very small scale—will allow physicians to inject small machines into the human body to address complex problems. For example, to eliminate cancerous tumors.

- Non-invasive surgery provides opportunity for accelerated healing now and we are close to having better functioning artificial organs.

- Finally, the aging of Baby Boomers will have a significant effect on the cost of healthcare, how it will be delivered, and by whom.

Most importantly, all of these dynamic changes are happening at the same time!

Healthcare is a "helping" profession. By that I mean most individuals become MDs, nurses, etc. so they can care for and improve the lives of their patients. In many cases, it is hard for them to consider that, in the long run, they have to efficiently manage their organizations if they are to remain viable and robust.

In responding to today's challenges, healthcare executives can develop a siege mentality (i.e., keep their heads down, do their job, and hope whatever challenge they're facing will eventually disappear). Unfortunately, as Einstein once said:

"We can't solve problems by using the same kind of thinking we used when we created them."

WRIGHT

You're now working with healthcare executives, physicians, and health systems to help them effectively manage change—what prompted you to focus your professional efforts here?

SHAHEEN

The driving factor was my own experience. Like many of us, I personally resist change. I'm very comfortable in my own comfort zone! For example, once I arrange the furniture in a room, it never gets rearranged. It could be that change is especially hard for me because of my father's influence.

He was a product of the depression. Prior to it, his family was upper middle class and owned a successful heating and cooling business. The depression wiped it out and impoverished his family. This tragedy had a tremendous influence on my father and, as it relates to developing one's career, he was totally risk averse. He told me repeatedly that I should set my sights on working for a large organization (he worked for the federal government) and stay there.

In contrast, I learned early in my career that in order to grow and move up the career ladder, I had to change—both jobs and organizations. As such, over time I developed a set of skills and strategies that allowed me to embrace change and respond appropriately. However, Dad's influence is still strong. There are times, especially when I jumped off the cliff to start my own business, when I felt both guilty and scared because I was not taking my father's advice!

Not unlike you, David, throughout the course of my career, I've gone through several career iterations and worked for or with a variety of healthcare organizations. What I've learned from my experience is that each transition brings with it a mandate to change. To be successful you must address the changes and become "change resilient" or you will have no opportunity for growth.

Realizing that change is constant, I became intrigued with understanding its key "ingredients." I continue to do research on the topic. I believe I focused on this topic because it's a way for me to help healthcare organizations and individuals manage change.

My life experience is not unlike that of today's healthcare organizations. On one hand they are under tremendous pressure to stay put, while on the other they understand they have to have the foresight to embrace change and become resilient to survive.

WRIGHT

So why is organizational change so difficult?

SHAHEEN

Because it involves people.

WRIGHT

Right.

SHAHEEN

It's part of the human condition that, in the face of change, we like things the way they are. We have been conditioned to resist change, especially when it requires us to get out of our comfort zone, so it's a tough nut to crack. I don't know of anyone who gets out of bed in the morning excited about what new change he or she may have to adapt to during the day. Not many of us have mothers who, as we are setting off to grade school, sent us off by saying, "Have a good day at school dear. Go out and take a risk!" No, what is normally said is, "Be careful."

It is fascinating to me that so often, when I begin working with an organization, I run across employees who have chronically complained about their work circumstances and then suddenly announce that what they do and how they do it is absolutely perfect. I think the term "the good old days" reflects this perspective.

The cartoon that follows demonstrates this point perfectly. In a nutshell: If you can't motivate people to change, you can't change the organization. And if the organization can't change, there is no long-term success.

THE NEW YORKER

"Neither up nor down. I'm good here."

Reprinted with permission.

WRIGHT

Earlier in our conversation, you touched on your model consisting of five core strategies, which, if adopted, greatly enhances an organization's capacity to manage change effectively. What are these five core strategies?

The Five Core Strategies for Moving into the Future of Healthcare Delivery

SHAHEEN

They are:

1. Defining corporate destiny.
2. Clarifying values and vision.
3. Leading with authenticity.
4. Managing change effectively.
5. Balancing priorities.

It is important for readers to understand that all five are interconnected. You don't necessarily go through all five sequentially; you may start at number one and then skip to number three. Then you may have to circle back to number one before moving to numbers four or five. Thus the model's application is iterative rather than linear.

WRIGHT
Will you discuss them one at a time?

SHAHEEN
Certainly. Please understand that I am giving you the view "at thirty thousand feet." To enable healthcare organizations to rapidly integrate and execute these core strategies, I have developed a training program and integration plan for each of the five. The modules provide relevant reading, background research, tools, how-to's, and best practices. Through dialogue, we develop an approach for executing each strategy within the organization's unique environment.

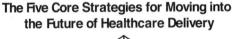

The Five Core Strategies for Moving into the Future of Healthcare Delivery

In module one, Defining Corporate Destiny, the key is using a proactive rather than reactive approach. Organizational leaders need to create a preferred future. Responding only to the immediate crises is a recipe for disaster.

To avoid this catch-22, I utilize an approach called "scenario planning"—a structured way for an organization's leaders to think about the future. Scenarios are tools that can help leaders take the long view in a world of great uncertainty. When used in an organizational context, scenarios are stories about how the world in which the organization operates might look tomorrow—in this case, the "tomorrow" being ten to fifteen years out.

In Peter Schwartz's book, *The Art of the Long View*, scenarios are described as stories that can help us recognize and adapt to the changing aspects of our present environment. They form a method for articulating the different pathways that might exist for the organization tomorrow.

Scenarios deal with two worlds: the world of facts and the world of perceptions. And, although they focus primarily on the exploration of facts, their primary aim is to alter and/or challenge the perceptions we hold as key decision-makers.

The idea is to identify five to ten plausible future scenarios reflecting expectable, challenging, and visionary futures. After a great deal of discussion and review of relevant research and other key findings, the field is narrowed to three to four strategies based on group consensus. Once identified, leaders then develop strategies for operating under each scenario.

Ultimately, the idea is to pick a "preferred future" from among the latter scenarios and use it as a basis for more in-depth planning. The exercise is important because the alternative scenarios can serve as contingency planning, where the preferred future may not be realized.

WRIGHT

I love the term, "preferred future." How do healthcare organizations that are mired in this cottage industry respond to this exercise?

SHAHEEN

Yes, the use of these words is very important. It changes people's mindset. In my experience in working with healthcare leaders, when we go from "what do we *have* to do" to "what do we *want* to do," there is a very powerful paradigm shift. Most importantly, these leaders are able to grasp the concept that they do have an ability to more positively address the challenges their organizations face.

WRIGHT

What is the second core strategy?

The Five Core Strategies for Moving into the Future of Healthcare Delivery

SHAHEEN

Clarifying Values and Vision.

I think this strategy is very important, especially given the role that ethics, framed in the espoused values, plays in healthcare delivery. Through my work with physicians, nurses, and other healthcare leaders, I have come to understand that to energize the change process, all members of the healthcare team—whether in leadership or staff positions—need to believe that values and vision are in alignment and reflected in organizational goals.

The purpose of establishing organizational values is to create a code of conduct—one that builds a cohesive culture and supports the vision of the organization.

Values are demonstrated through corporate behavior. The phrase "walking the talk" means there's no difference between corporate values and behaviors. Values "talk;" behaviors "walk."

One very clear example in healthcare of how physician leaders are "walking their talk" is the current emphasis being placed on developing and adhering to a code of conduct that governs physician behavior in the workplace. Behaviors seen as being normal before (e.g., surgeons acting out in the operating room, yelling, throwing implements, berating nurses, cowing interns) are no longer being tolerated.

Additionally, when the health system's values are made explicit, employees can assess the degree to which their values align with those of the organization. Where this is the case, research has identified some interesting findings. One is increased productivity, another reduced employee turnover, and the third increased employee satisfaction. Of most interest to me is the fact that under these circumstances, organizational change becomes easier.

Richard Barret, an executive coach, wrote *Liberating the Corporate Soul: Building a Visionary Organization*, a book I have found to be exceptionally useful in my work.

In his book, Barret defines organizational values as rules for living (i.e., deeply held beliefs that a certain way of "being" or a certain outcome is preferable to another). The purpose of establishing a set of values is to create a code of conduct that builds a cohesive culture and supports the organization's vision and mission statements.

One of my favorite quotes from his book is: "Through living their values, visionary organizations find a balance between organizational needs for survival and growth, employees needs for personal fulfillment, and the local communities" and society's needs for economical, social, and environmental stability."

Values, then, drive the corporate vision—a statement outlining what the organization wants to be in the world in which it operates. Bottom Line: values provide the framework within which every member of the organization can operate with *responsible* (the key word) freedom.

The Five Core Strategies for Moving into the Future of Healthcare Delivery

The third core strategy is Leading with Authenticity.

In this aspect of my work, three individuals have influenced me: Don Berwick, Robert Greenleaf, and Kevin Cashman. Don is a well-known and highly respected physician appointed earlier this year by President Obama to head the Centers for Medicare and Medicaid. In his new position, he is tasked with overseeing the massive healthcare reform effort that will roll out over the next four plus years. Robert, who was a business consultant, is considered the grandfather of the modern empowerment movement in business leadership. Kevin Cashman is a fellow coach. His book, *Leadership From the Inside Out*, is a must read, as are the articles and essays produced by the other two individuals.

I have integrated a number of their concepts and perspectives into the work I do, as I believe they define the authentic leader. Most importantly, this is the type of leadership required for success in the twenty-first century. Healthcare leaders can no longer be effective with the old "command and control" model—a model that has framed the behavior of many physicians throughout the past three decades.

Today's employees are not motivated primarily by money but rather by the degree to which their work environment meets their expectations for satisfaction and growth.

Ironically, in the long run, leaders are not judged by how well they have led, but rather by how well they have served their board of directors, customers, employees, and their community. In this context they are servant leaders—a term coined by Robert Greenleaf.

Anyone in the organization who is authentically self-expressing and creating value is a leader. The focus of the leader's leadership may be different—some create value through ideas, others through systems, and still others through people. In whatever way it's expressed, it's still leadership that needs to be nurtured by the healthcare organization.

To empower employees, authentic leaders provide them with needed information and give them authority to make relevant decisions. In recognition of the degree of leadership that permeates the organization, employees must be given the tools they need to work with and must be trained so they can incorporate into their leadership style the behaviors and capabilities needed to be good decision-makers.

Authentic leaders have no problem answering the important question: "How do I show up at the office every day?" They know who they are. This may sound trite, but many leaders know more about their favorite sport, restaurant, or vacation spot than they do about themselves!

The older physicians I work with often have an especially difficult time in today's environment in integrating these concepts into their leadership style. Much of this stems from the way they were trained in medical school (i.e., to be the "top dog"—the person giving orders and making the decisions, which often went unquestioned).

The challenge is further exacerbated by the multiple roles they now play in healthcare delivery. For example, through the course of the day, physicians may serve as clinicians, CFOs, team members, project managers, the people monitoring the quality of care provided, and administrators running major departments in the healthcare system. Given this situation, many physicians are currently struggling with self-identity, which confounds their ability to be authentic leaders. For the first time in their lives, they are being asked to look at themselves in an authentic way, which is no small feat.

The Five Core Strategies for Moving into the Future of Healthcare Delivery

The fourth core strategy is Managing Change Effectively.

To begin the dialogue with clients, I introduce the following observation made by a colleague of mine, Stu Altman, an economics professor at Brandeis University. According to Stu:

"Everyone is in favor of progress—it's change they don't like."

This expression has resonated with every CEO and team I have ever worked with. Truth be told, moving an organization from an old to a new paradigm is extremely hard work. Interestingly enough, the process of going about it is often given short shrift. Issuing a memo or having staff attend an informational meeting certainly does not accomplish it. It truly doesn't happen without creating a road map of where you want to go and how to get there. Most importantly, the organization must commit to using the road map as a tool for moving forward.

Although there are many approaches to managing change in the business world, the approach I use is based primarily on the work of Harvard professor John Kotter and business consultant William Bridges. I've enjoyed integrating the two models they have developed and believe the model I have created provides an effective way of dealing with both the intellectual and emotional aspects of change. Addressing both is very important. Unfortunately, most often, healthcare leaders managing the change process focus on the intellectual and not the emotional aspect of change.

For many healthcare leaders moving into the emotional aspects of change, the "warm and fuzzy" side of leadership is very difficult. Again, dealing openly with this topic is often very hard for physician leaders who have been trained to mask their emotions and often need to be given the tools to manage this aspect of the change process.

This is one of the reasons I introduced the topic of authentic leadership just prior to this one. The earlier discussion provides a context for dealing with the emotional aspects of the change process in a more comfortable way.

There are several maxims I have gleaned from working with healthcare leaders managing the change process in their institution. They are:

- There is no change for change sake. Remember our discussion on getting people out of their comfort zone—to really motivate people, you need to create a crisis.

- For example, one hospital I worked with found the number of patients contracting nosocomial (originating or taking place in a hospital, acquired in a hospital, especially in reference to an infection) infections in their institution was unacceptably high. Astutely, hospital leadership used this finding to galvanize physicians and nurses to develop a change strategy to reduce the infection rate.

- You can't work with everyone at once. Create a strategy group with members from across the organization. Include not only the usual cast of characters but all groups within the organization who will be significantly be affected by the change.

- I am always amazed at how creative non-traditional leaders can be if asked for input on the best way to manage change at their level in their organizations. They just need to be asked and then heard.

- Generate ideas and remember, any idea might be a new idea— even though you tried it ten years ago.

- Be especially mindful of the naysayers in the organization—they will definitely be there. Often naysayers have been there for years and experienced lots of change efforts. They often incorporated strategic plans that were only partially or never implemented. Given the frequency of past efforts that failed, they can be quite jaded about this round. If these individuals are given too much time to express their negative views, they can sabotage the process. Be aware of who these people are and develop a counter strategy to address their negativism.

- Throw a number of new ideas against the wall—follow through with those that stick. If possible, take the "sticky" ones out for a trial run. Most importantly, don't be afraid to fail. It's important to take a risk, something often very difficult for large-scale health systems whose various constituencies are often very conflicted on the change process as a whole.

- Once a strategy has been selected, honor employees" concerns. Most importantly, don't pretend they don't exist. Hold a wake to say goodbye to what is being left behind. This is one of those warm and fuzzy steps that's critical to maintaining employee morale and commitment to moving forward. Unfortunately, in major healthcare organizations, this is not often done. Where it's not, employee concerns will continue to fester.

- Most important, celebrate success. It's hard won and celebrating it will provide the needed momentum for the organization to move forward. And remember that to accomplish this takes patience, time, and tenacity on the part of leaders. It's not an easy job.

WRIGHT

And number five?

The Five Core Strategies for Moving into the Future of Healthcare Delivery

SHAHEEN

This core strategy—balancing priorities—is one of the most important, yet often the most frequently overlooked, especially by physicians. This becomes problematic, especially when physicians are asked to manage the institution's change process but not relieved of some of their other duties.

As we discussed earlier, David, managing change is an intense and difficult process. Many healthcare leaders, tasked with leading the effort, defer taking care of themselves—both physically and mentally—as well as dealing with other aspects of their personal lives.

As a coach, one of the things I communicate to healthcare leaders I am working with is that there is no separation between one's personal and professional life. We cannot compartmentalize them. What happens at work affects what happens at home and vice versa; *especially* in healthcare, where leaders are already used to working long hours. Thus, addressing issues on the personal side of their lives is either given short shrift or ignored. One of the quotes I use to make the point (by now you realize I love using quotes) makes this point perfectly:

"Take care of your body. It's the only place you have to live."

If leaders burn out, there's a good possibility the change process will flame out.

Change leaders need to take care of their physical health, invest in their personal life, and make sure there's a balance there. They need to remind themselves to disengage from their jobs and set aside time on a weekly basis to attend to their personal needs.

Early on in my work with healthcare leaders, I have them complete a "The Wheel of Life" exercise.

To complete the survey, clients are tasked with "grading" themselves on each component of their lives, as depicted on the circumference, for every piece of the pie. They must give themselves a grade on a score of zero to ten. A score of one for a given slice indicates clients believe they have not made any real progress on this particular aspect of life. A score of ten means they feel confident they have addressed it. As is depicted in the diagram, most people do not have a perfect score; as a result, the wheel provides a pretty bumpy ride.

When healthcare leaders complete the exercise, they often have an "A-ha" moment when they realize how far they are from addressing key aspects of their personal lives.

To further emphasize the point, I also ask them to take a long weekend and leave their BlackBerry, computer, and cell phone behind. You can imagine how difficult this is for them—it's like losing one's security blanket!

Although it might seem self-serving, I believe each change leader needs to work with a coach to achieve this balance. Without a work/life balance, change leaders are at high risk for health problems and if they are married, the possibility of divorce. We all know an executive, now in his or her late fifties or early sixties, who has regrets about how key aspects of personal life were handled or ignored during the course of his or her career. These individuals are often the ones who, either through the death of a spouse or a divorce, elect to remarry and raise a second family, primarily because they missed out on raising the children of their first marriage.

WRIGHT

So why is it necessary to address all of the core strategies as a part of the change process?

SHAHEEN

One of the reasons I labeled these components "core strategies" is because you have to look at all of them. Based on my experience, organizations significantly lower the probability they will succeed if they just attend to one or two of them. The core strategies all fit together like puzzle pieces and organizations must address *all* of them if they want to remain successful in an ever-changing business environment. To not do so is throwing money down the drain.

WRIGHT

With four decades of experience in working with healthcare organizations, you certainly have gained a number of insights. What bit of wisdom would you like to pass on to our readers, many of whom work in other industries?

SHAHEEN

First and most important is that you believe in what you're doing— that you are working on purpose. This is one of the most important concepts. And, if your readers remember nothing else from this chapter, I hope they remember this. Research has consistently shown that individuals working on purpose are peak performers. Working on purpose provides the energy needed to continue with the work you are doing. If you are not working on purpose, you need to find some other line of work.

Second, you must remain passionate about what you do and communicate it to your employees. Passion is critical in managing change. It catalyzes others to follow and to move forward, even though the path might not be entirely clear. Employees working for passionate leaders believe their allegiance to them will result in a positive outcome.

Third, you must remain committed to and believe in what you are doing. It's your commitment, even in the face of large obstacles, that allows employees to feel secure in what you are asking them to do and where you are leading them.

Probably one of the most important is that you remain tenacious. As I have said throughout our discussion, managing a change effort is often a difficult and sometimes thankless job. So personal tenacity, a belief in yourself, and confidence in where you are going, even though the way may be somewhat murky, are critical. There will be lots of times during the process, which may come to be viewed as interminable, when you are going to want to throw in the towel. That's when it's critical for personal tenacity to come into play. You have to be willing to go the distance and bring key constituencies (e.g., employees, board members, and patients) along with you.

WRIGHT

What you just said goes right along with something I heard years ago and nothing has happened in my life to make me change my mind. I remember hearing that 98 percent of all failure comes from quitting.

SHAHEEN

Absolutely. A good example of that is Edison's attempt to invent the light bulb. One of the biographies I read on his life depicted Edison's dedication to his work. His success in creating a working light bulb had behind it more than five hundred failures.

WRIGHT

Well, what an interesting conversation with such an interesting person. This has really been great for me. I've been taking copious notes. These are some interesting issues you have talked about, and I think our readers are going to learn from this chapter.

SHAHEEN

I hope so. Let me close our conversation with a quote I discussed earlier because it is so appropriate:

> *"Success is moving from failure to failure*
> *with no lack of enthusiasm."*
> —Winston Churchill.

WRIGHT

I appreciate all the time you've taken to answer these questions, Pamela; it's very gracious of you.

SHAHEEN

I appreciate your giving me the time; it's very gracious of you!

WRIGHT

Today I have been talking with Pamela Shaheen, Founder and President of the Delta Collaborative Consulting and Coaching firm. As we have found here today, her core passion is to help individuals and organizations learn to manage the changes they face now so that they can thrive in tomorrow's marketplace.

WRIGHT

Pamela, thank you so much for being with us today on *ROADMAP to Success*.

SHAHEEN

Again thanks for having me, David.

About the Author

Dr. Pamela Shaheen is President of the Delta Collaborative, a consulting and coaching firm specializing in change management. The firm works with healthcare clients who are wrestling with the multiple changes of declining reimbursement, healthcare reform, changing professional roles, and empowered patients. As a member of the Collaborative, Dr. Shaheen serves as a healthcare consultant and executive coach to organizations in the healthcare field. Her expertise is in the areas of change management, leadership development, policy formulation, strategic planning, and program development and implementation and has more than forty years of experience in the field.

Dr. Shaheen also directs a Program Office for The Kresge Foundation. Her responsibilities there include advising the Foundation's Health Team in strategic planning, program development and implementation, and evaluation and policy analysis. In this capacity, she also manages foundation grants and providing coaching and consulting services to grantees.

Dr. Shaheen is also an Adjunct Professor at the University of Michigan School of Public Health where she teaches a course on career management and serves on the Department of Health Management and Policy's Alumni Board.

Her earlier career has included holding a number of administrative positions within the Michigan Department of Public Health and serving as the Senior Health Policy Advisor to the Speaker of the House in Michigan's House of Representatives as well as serving as the Governor's health and human services advisor.

Dr. Shaheen earned her BS in Human Ecology and Communication Arts from Michigan State University, her MPH in Public Health Planning and Administration from the University of Michigan, and her DrPH as a Pew Scholar at the University of Michigan School of Public Health. She has contributed articles to the *Journal of Public Health Management and*

Practice, the *Journal of Health Politics, Policy and Law,* the *Indiana Law Journal, Medicine and Law,* and has served as a guest lecturer, both within Michigan and nationally on health policy issues.

Dr. Shaheen is a member of a number of national organizations and was recently invited to join Cambridge Who's Who.

Pamela Shaheen, President

The Delta Collaborative LLC

4241 Vanneter Rd

Williamston, MI 48895

517-655-5879

517-230-3895 (cell)

888-370-6421 (fax)

PPS@thedeltacollaborative.com

www.thedeltacollaborative.com

Chapter Eight

THE ESSENTIALS
OF SUCCESS

DR. DEFOREST B. SOARIES, JR.

"The only thing worse than not having what you need
is not using what you have."

DAVID WRIGHT (WRIGHT)

Today I am talking with the Reverend Dr. DeForest B. Soaries Jr. Dr. Soaries is the Senior Pastor of the First Baptist Church of Lincoln Gardens in Somerset, New Jersey. His pastoral ministry focuses on spiritual growth, educational excellence, economic empowerment, and faith-based community development. He is the author of *dfree® Breaking Free from Financial Slavery*, published in January of 2011 by Zondervan. The book is based on Dr. Soaries' dfree strategy to teach people how to be debt-free, deficit-free, and delinquency-free. Dr. Soaries' original goal was to use dfree as a tool to show his seven-thousand-member congregation how to be debt-free. He is now prepared to share this strategy throughout the country with a goal of helping one million families live a debt-free lifestyle. His dfree strategy was also the focus of the third installment of CNN's Black America documentary "Almighty Debt" hosted by Soledad O'Brien, which aired on October 21, 2010. The ninety-minute feature highlighted three families at First Baptist Church of Lincoln Gardens who were facing tough financial times as a result of the recession.

Serving from January 1999 to 2002, Dr. Soaries was New Jersey's first African American man appointed to Secretary of State of New Jersey. He earned a Bachelor of Arts degree from Fordham University, a Master of Divinity degree from Princeton Theological Seminary, and a Doctor of Ministry Degree from United Theological Seminary.

A passionate writer, his work has been featured in several publications including the *New York Times, The Wall Street Journal, Ebony Magazine, Black Enterprise,* and *Government Executive Magazine.*

He was born in New York and raised in New Jersey. He resides in Monmouth Junction, New Jersey, with his wife, Donna, and twin sons, Malcolm and Martin.

Dr. Soaries welcome to *ROADMAP to Success.*

DR. DEFOREST SOARIES (SOARIES)

Thank you so much.

WRIGHT

So how do you define success?

SOARIES

For me, success means mastering the art of becoming myself and using that mastery to the benefit of others. I believe that ultimately each of us should specialize in maximizing our own potential. We are successful when we do that and learn to use our accomplishments to be a blessing to other people. Of course, that means that success is a process and not an event. Success is staying the course and focusing on growing and developing who you are. Failure, then, is when a person strays from that path and pursues, for instance, a path of becoming an imitation of someone else. As a Christian, I believe that Jesus is the model for human existence and I can succeed in being my best by imitating Jesus.

WRIGHT

To whom or what do you attribute your success?

SOARIES

I attribute the foundation of my success to God, of course, who gave me the gifts I have and the life I have. I attribute my success to my parents. My dad was the most disciplined person I know and I think discipline is a key ingredient in discovering and mastering who you are. My mother is a perfectionist and she instilled in me the value of excellence. To strive for perfection is to commit to excellence.

Additionally, I had great teachers along the way from elementary school all the way through my doctorate program. I have been blessed to have great teachers who believed in me and helped me expand my imagination and my intellect. Last, but certainly not least of course, my wife, who keeps me focused, humbled, and encouraged. Those are all of the people who have contributed to the success I have enjoyed so far.

WRIGHT

Wives always seem to be the levelers in our lives right?

SOARIES

Yes, that's one way to describe it.

WRIGHT

What are your core values in business and in life?

SOARIES

The 3 P's: Practice, Preparation, and Prioritize. The value of practice—successful athletes practice as if it's game time. The same principle should be used in life; practice all activities as if it is the real thing. Next is the value of preparation—making sure you are prepared before you engage in any activity. The final value would be the establishment of priorities—doing what is most important first and not wasting any time.

WRIGHT

Motivation seems to be important in our culture; what drives you to be successful?

SOARIES

Scientists suggest that we have a lot more room in our cranium to fill. In other words, we are not even close to tapping into our full potential of brainpower. This was stunning to me and I don't think a day goes by when I am not challenged by the fact that there is a portion of my capacity that is yet unused. This alone keeps me motivated to continue to push further, try harder, to do better.

Knowing others have achieved even greater things than I'm attempting also motivates me. I remember when I was in college taking Classical Greek and felt as though it was just too difficult for me to learn. What really motivated me to hang in there was the fact that others had learned Greek, thus I concluded that if they had learned it, so can I. I apply that same principle to my entire life; when I think that my church responsibilities are overwhelming I think about people with churches three times the size of mine. So I use other people's achievements to keep me motivated as I attempt to manage my own. Then, of course, the belief that God made me for a purpose and has something very specific in mind for me. Therefore, I do not consider it an option to undermine what God has in mind for me.

So those are the things that keep me motivated.

WRIGHT

What is the importance of the "what" and the "how," and how do you distinguish between the two?

SOARIES

I often tell people the what is your destination and the how is the route you plan to take to get to your destination. I have found it is important to keep focus on the what because the how may change.

For example, if I were planning a trip to New York City, that would be my what—my destination. The route in which I take to get to New York City would be my how. In this situation, I may choose to take the New Jersey Turnpike as my route; however, I begin my travel on the New Jersey Turnpike and encounter major traffic. This is when it is important not to confuse your what with your how, as the traffic may cause some people to turn around and go home, leaving their what unattained. On the other hand, the person who remembers that their how can change will choose an alternate route because their focus is getting to where they are going—their destination, their what.

So I describe my what as my mission in other settings and the how is my project. My what is nonnegotiable, however my how can change.

When I teach goals and objectives, I often call my goals my "what," and my objectives my "how." Some people reverse that but the key thing is that the what is the big picture—it's the goal, it's where you want to end up and the how is a method. Even in leading team members and managing people, I challenge my staff to stay loyal to the what and to be creative in the how.

If you can get me to my what by a different how, then that's fine. You don't have to do it my way, as long as you get me to my destination.

WRIGHT

Let's talk about communication skills for a moment. How big a role do communication skills play in success?

SOARIES

I don't think there is any skill more important than communications, whether it's group, interpersonal, verbal, or written communications. I think communication is the paramount skill that we need to be successful. I don't know anyone who has been successful in business, government, religion, and/or politics, who was a poor communicator. Effective communication is more than oratory—it's style and substance and it's the ability to organize content, to translate subjective expectations into objective and quantifiable requirements, deliver content, and then match the content with some concrete life examples that reinforce that content. All of my accomplishments have had communications at the core of my skill.

WRIGHT

So how important is time management in being successful?

SOARIES

I do not use the term "time management" because humans cannot manage time. God made time, God owns time, and God is the proprietor of time. I think the concept of time management is a misnomer. I think we manage our lives and we use the gift of time that God gave us. To suggest that we can manage time suggests that we can control, stop, or restructure time. Time is just time and as the saying goes, "time marches on." I believe that we use time to pursue the goals we have in life and to contribute to the lives of others.

There is a specific system I use to organize my life and to assist me in utilizing my time wisely. The system is called GAP, which is an acronym and indicates the need to close any gaps that exist between where I am and where I want to be, or where I am and where I ought to be.

GAP has three parts:

G—Goals. I start by reducing my entire life into five goal categories: personal, intellectual, spiritual, vocational, financial. I then identify three key goals in each category for at least three years. By doing this, I can paint a comprehensive picture of my life for the next three years on one single sheet of paper. Another benefit in this system is it allows me to see if any of my goals contradict one another during that time period.

A—Agenda. Next I create a chart that shows all 168 hours for one week. I use that chart to write all of my intended activities. This process helps me to see what time I have committed to certain activities. It is very important to link all of my time commitments to each of my goals. This also helps me identify times that are uncommitted and therefore available for the things that I want to do but can never "find the time" to do.

P—Priorities. After establishing my goals and my agenda, I use a bracket system to establish priorities for the allocation of uncommitted time. By "bracket system" I mean that I treat my options as if they were competing teams in a tournament. As each item "wins" against another option and moves to the quarterfinals, semi-finals, and finals, there is a natural process of elimination and therefore prioritization of future activities.

I use this system when mentoring and coaching people who desire to maximize their potential and take control of their lives.

WRIGHT

So what do you think are the biggest obstacles people face in trying to become successful?

SOARIES

I think the biggest obstacle is the inability to distinguish between the what and the how. I think people often times will confuse their what with their how and when their how breaks down, they give up and undermine their potential to reach their what.

All of the great entrepreneurs report on successes they have after failures. Well, if you fail at your how and you have confused it with your what, then you'll give up and never reach your goal.

Babe Ruth was the homerun king *and* the strikeout king. Swinging the bat was not his what, swinging was his how. If he had given up on swinging every time he struck out, he'd never hit home runs. I think the biggest obstacle people have is letting failure with the how abort the possibility of achieving the what.

WRIGHT

Is the road to success a ride that one takes alone or is team-building a necessity?

SOARIES

Well, it's both. You have to have a team, but you also have to play your individual role on the team. You have to be on the team, but you have to be on the team on your own. As an individual, there is a personal responsibility component that says no one can do for you what you are not willing to do for yourself. The team component says there are things you cannot do for yourself that you need others to do with you and for you.

WRIGHT

When you consider all of the successes you have had, and I've read a lot of them, what leadership skills have been the most important to you?

SOARIES

The skill of communication, as I mentioned earlier. I call it a skill but it's broader than that—it's a passion, a capacity for vision. You must be able to see beyond the right now into the not yet to have successes tomorrow that you haven't enjoyed today. If all you can see is what is in front of you, then you are limited; you have to have imagination and vision.

Another skill would be courage—you must have the courage to be alone, to take a stand that is unpopular, and to try things that others think will fail. You have to have the courage to disagree with people whose relationships you cherish. You have to get up the courage to fail.

Finally you need the skill of honesty—you have to be willing to tell the truth whether it's popular or not, whether it's in season or not, whether it defies conventional wisdom or not.

WRIGHT

So it can be either way—they can start as a skill but the development of the skill is what is important.

So how do you stay relevant and at the top of your game?

SOARIES

I believe in surrounding myself with people who are not like me—people who think differently than I do and people who are younger than I am. It's important to have people who are more relevant than you are to help you stay relevant.

I believe in reading materials that are not necessarily a part of my normal life. In other words, I believe in reading things that relate to areas and industries and businesses that I have nothing to do with so I can find out what is happening in other people's worlds.

I think another way to stay relevant is to just observe. You have to be observant and interested in other venues, other locations, other cultures, other philosophies, other theologies and spend time observing and studying things that are different than you. Then adventure—you've got to venture out. I learned finance by serving on the board of directors of a small bank. I had ten years of formal education beyond high school, I had earned three degrees, received six honorary degrees, and I had never taken a course on finance. I didn't know how to do a budget, so I ventured out and joined a bank's board. I'd never been on a bank board before, I barely had a bank account, but I learned banking and finance by being on the board of a very small one-branch bank, $100 million in assets. Now I'm on the board of directors of a bank that has $135 billion in assets.

WRIGHT

So what kind of material do you regularly read?

SOARIES

I read the Bible every day, at least five different newspapers every day—the *New Jersey Star Ledger, New York Times, Huffington Post,*

Washington Post and *Wall Street Journal*—and I read some portion of a book on my reading list.

WRIGHT

A brilliant man once told me that if I were walking down the road and saw a turtle sitting up on a fence post that I could bet my bottom dollar he didn't get up there by himself. So who are your role models or who mentored you, and is mentorship important to becoming successful?

SOARIES

Yes, mentorship is key to becoming successful because it creates a sense of accountability and it also creates opportunities for encouragement. Mentorship is absolutely key. My chief mentor is Jesus. I use Jesus, not just in a spiritual way, but in terms of Jesus' lifestyle and His leadership style; His ministry instructs me on how to handle life's situations.

My dad was a mentor; however, he died when I was twenty-four so I didn't have much time with him as a mentor. I had a professor in undergraduate school who became my intellectual mentor. He was an Old Testament scholar and he helped me as I studied religion formally. My main mentor was Rev. Dr. Sam Proctor, who was Dr. King's mentor. He was the Pastor of Abyssinian Baptist Church in Harlem. Until he died in 1997, he was my chief mentor. He is more responsible for my speaking style, my leadership style, and my theological perspective than anyone other than Jesus.

WRIGHT

Well, what a great conversation. I have really enjoyed this, especially the different take you have on goal-setting. I really do appreciate all the time you've taken with me to answer these questions.

SOARIES

Thank you. I guess we're in this together. The questions helped me think through some thoughts that I need to be thinking anyway and the answers help me think more precisely about myself. I have a passion about the time issue because I have a lot of people asking me about time management. I think the concept of time management, in my view, represents the arrogance of humanity—the idea that we could manage something that truly belongs to God. We can't manage time any more than we can make blood. Time is a gift.

I tell my staff all the time that I'd rather give them money than give them time—I'd rather lose money than waste time. Time won't stand still, time won't wait for you, and the best thing we can do is use time wisely. So I don't even use the term time management because I think it's too arrogant a term.

WRIGHT

Well, I think that we have both won here today. I'm glad this chapter will be in the book because you have given some excellent advice.

SOARIES

Well, thank you.

WRIGHT

I have been talking with the Reverend Dr. DeForest B. Soaries Jr. Dr. Soaries is the Senior Pastor of the First Baptist Church of Lincoln Gardens in Somerset, New Jersey. His pastoral ministry focuses on spiritual growth, educational excellence, economic empowerment, and faith-based community development. I've listened to him today and I think he knows what he's talking about.

Dr. Soaries, thank you so much for being with us today on *ROADMAP to Success*.

SOARIES

Thank you for having me.

About the Author

Dr. DeForest B. Soaries, Jr. is the Senior Pastor of the First Baptist Church of Lincoln Gardens in Somerset, New Jersey. He is the author of *dfree® Breaking Free from Financial Slavery*. Founded in 2005, his dfree campaign is the linchpin of a successful strategy to lead people, families, and organizations out of debt to attain financial independence. Dr. Soaries and his dfree strategy were the focus of the third installment of CNN's Black in America documentary "Almighty Debt." Dr. Soaries served as New Jersey's thirtieth Secretary of State and is a popular speaker at colleges, universities, conferences, and churches around the world as well as a frequent advisor to major corporations in the areas of diversity, philanthropy, and community relations. It is his goal for his seven-thousand-member congregation to be debt-free and to train and encourage other churches and community-based organizations to follow suit.

Dr. DeForest B. Soaries, Jr.

dfre e ®
PO Box 561
Kingston, NJ 08528
Fax: 609-430-1715
info@mydfree.org
www.mydfree.org

Chapter Nine

THE BEST YOU: SEEN, HEARD, AND VALUED

BOB ROSEN

DAVID WRIGHT (WRIGHT)

I'm excited today to talk with Bob Rosen, board certified coach and nationally certified counselor. As a contributing author for our discussions of life planning and the construction of a personal road map for living from your best self, Bob brings lessons learned from hundreds of clients, pinpointing just what it takes to turn down the volume of the unhelpful programs you've been rehearsing for decades and letting your brilliance shine. With decades of experience in private practice, government, corporate, and not-for-profit executive and team coaching, Bob can show you how to tap the courage and skills for living from your best self.

Bob, welcome to *ROADMAP to Success.*

What can you promise the reader will get from investing his or her time in what we say today?

BOB ROSEN (ROSEN)

David, I'm coming up on thirty-five years of a career devoted to assisting others successfully create a life they really love. I was able to become the architect and builder of the life I'm called to only when I learned how to get seen, heard, and valued.

My promise to you and to those joining us is to share what my clients have reported as most important in creating the life they *wanted* to live.

WRIGHT

I'm looking forward to finding out about their challenges and successes. We'll get into more details as we go along, but first, would you summarize what brings someone to Life Management Coaching with you?

ROSEN

I went looking for a coach to help me manage my life when I started waking up asking, "Is this all there is?"

Budget cuts eliminated what I thought was the best job in the world— Team Effectiveness Coach at Ford Motor Company in Dearborn, Michigan. I met my wife while I was there coaching the team that created the Lincoln Aviator. I was really struggling. It seemed that I could be a better partner to my wife than I could to me. I got to the point where my focus was on how my death insurance would provide greater value to my family than I was able to provide.

I had been living the life of my dreams, and just as though someone had pressed the "delete" key, my work life was gone.

WRIGHT

What's it like to remember that time in your life?

ROSEN

You sound like my coaches now.

Looking back at those dark days and nights from where I am now stimulates a lot of compassion and empathy. I have so much for which I'm grateful and a truly endless gratitude list. Not only do I love what I have and know what else I want, I know how I got the life I have. If, or when, some part of it is taken away, I have great confidence in being able to create something as wonderful or better in its place. That gives me control and courage.

WRIGHT

Interesting. Will you say more about what it was like for you?

ROSEN

Movies started playing in my mind, as I talked to you just now about another set of experiences in my life. They showed how different my experience of surgery was before and after I could hear what I needed and prize getting those needs met.

In 1990, my gall bladder decided it wanted to be donated to science. The night before surgery was one long panic attack. I wasn't doing a very good job of hearing or supporting myself.

Fast forward to 2008 and I was in great health except for the cancer in my prostate. The night before surgery (as well as the prognosis) was wonderful. I could hear the part of me that is best connected to who I've come to know God to be. I could hear what I needed and could ask for it from the people caring for me. I was my best friend and surrounded by people who cared.

WRIGHT

I'm delighted you're healthy and it sounds like you're thriving not just surviving your cancer.

ROSEN

Thank you. I agree.

WRIGHT

From your experiences and growth, what have you distilled as key that you now offer your clients?

ROSEN

The four keys are: *Normalize, Simplify, Restore Resources,* and *Add Resources.* The immediate result is that we *experience* the challenges to being understood and valued getting smaller, and our abilities increasing. Moving from feeling out of control to expert feels wonderful and doable.

WRIGHT

Let's dive deeper into each one of those keys. Mastering these skills sounds about as easy as changing a SIMM card in a cell phone. Is it?

ROSEN

Assuming you're a techy-type for whom that's easy. Most of us are at the "I don't even know what a SIMM card is, and wouldn't know one if it bit me in the butt" stage.

Becoming heard and valued may not mean more than a "SIMM card" in the beginning, either. What potential clients are aware of is the frustration or emptiness of seeing other people have the relationships, job, car, home, and social and spiritual life that they wish were theirs. Learning what it takes to have what you want and want what you have is simple but not easy. Over the years we have learned something about speeding up the process, but when humans use their brilliance to avoid being seen, heard, or understood, we come up with some very tricky habits.

Declaring an intention to see, hear, and value all of who we are and our calling is a perfect place to start. Like the story about getting to Carnegie Hall, however, we've got to do a lot of practicing. Normalizing begins when we find a non-judgmental way to say, "Okay, I have some habits I want to change." I have a set of habits that I was smart enough to create. Those habits are no longer helpful. I'm going to try something else.

WRIGHT

Are you starting to touch on the challenges of communicating?

ROSEN

Yes. Communication is the main ingredient of Normalizing, Simplifying, Restoring Resources, and Adding Resources.

WRIGHT

Before we go there, you said I sounded like your coaches. Are you still are being coached?

ROSEN

Oh yes! I am consistently remodeling or adding on to my life. I get a lot out of being coached by those who have understood, valued, and helped me over the years. Let me tell you about three men and one woman I talk to regularly:

Dave Ellis (www.daveellisleadership.com) is a mega-successful author and coach. When he's not working with clients or traveling the world to connect with his family, he's committed his time and money to ending death by starvation on the planet. A long-time member of Dave's coaching team is JoAnne Bangs (joanne@daveellisleadership.com). I work with her twice a month. It's so helpful to have a woman's view of the world.

T. Falcon Napier (www.tensionmanagementinstitute.org) created the MasterStream® Process and the ChangeGrid®, which is an assessment tool I use regularly. T can do just about anything (I had a coaching session one time as he was designing and sewing a duvet cover after just finishing a training program for a U.S. company's European executives). T is dedicated to merging brilliance into effective training and certification programs.

Mike Jay (www.mikejay.com) is also a world-class traveler, consultant, and coach. He's trained hundreds of coaches to help clients obtain happiness and success. Mike is currently immersed in a project in the Philippines, educating and training groups who had little hope of doing more that surviving.

So I've been attracted to coaches and am growing more and more into a coach with a world-centric view, valuing, appreciating, and celebrating the brilliance each client brings to our coaching time. It's magnificent, David.

WRIGHT

You've got me excited. There's a lot I want to talk about, including how life management coaching is different than psychotherapy, and how long it's been since you had to think in terms of diagnosing anyone's pathology.

But I want to go back to this key point about communication being such a challenge.

ROSEN

Imagine that I'm looking at a picture and tell you, "Dennis must have just been shot. He was right in front of Donna. Donna is pale and doing nothing. Another woman seems totally unconcerned and continues with her work." What's it like for you to hear that, David?

WRIGHT

I'm seeing the scene. Dennis is lying on a sidewalk bleeding. Donna is paralyzed and pale. A bystander is paying no attention. I feel a little anxious and have concern about a nut with a gun still being on the loose. I can see it pretty vividly. So we've communicated, is that right?

ROSEN

Well, not exactly. I see I forgot to tell you the piece that they were all around a table.

WRIGHT

Oh, okay. So I have the scene wrong. Was it at a restaurant or in an office conference room? The work of changing things in my mind has also changed how I feel. I'm more separate from the experience—more like a set designer than a witness to a shooting.

ROSEN

That's very interesting. Let me add one more piece that I haven't mentioned. Behind the group of people there is a sign on the wall. It says, "Flu Shots Today."

WRIGHT

Well, that changes everything, doesn't it? My initial reaction was a mixture of surprise, humor, and frustration. I thought, "Why didn't you just tell me that!"

ROSEN

Exactly. "Why didn't you just tell me that" is the caption underneath every picture of frustrated communicators. Some pieces of my experience stand out for me; some are assumed or left out. When I share my story with you or you share your story with me, we have lots of room for creating at least two very different scenarios in our minds.

Are you up for me telling you another story? Please keep in mind that this is normal and healthy. Whether I want me to understand a need or reaction, or I want you to understand my request or response, let's practice normalizing the idea that meaning contains ambiguity and needs to be dialoged out. We start with a "sense" about it and develop as much detail as we need.

WRIGHT

Sure, but I have to warn you, you're credibility for accuracy is now pretty low.

ROSEN

Thanks for telling me that. If you were going to hear me tell another story, you have added a layer of complexity in that some of your energy is now going into wondering how much of what I'm about to tell you is the truth, the whole truth, and nothing but the truth. That takes some energy away from listening to what I'm saying.

WRIGHT

Yes, that's true, but I don't think you're lying.

ROSEN

I'm sure glad of that. The point is energy that was needed for listening is now going into evaluation as you sort what's likely to be true from what's likely to be "not the whole story." With each additional task added to listening, communication gets more challenging. To *Simplify*, we want to reduce the number of processes going on at any one time. By filtering out "judging" and focusing on "capturing the information," we're making the process less complex.

WRIGHT

So you're saying that if my energy is divided—whether it's because I'm protecting myself or preoccupied because I'm still worrying about Dennis dying—that I can't listen as well?

ROSEN

Right. And listening is essential but not sufficient for good communication.

WRIGHT

What else does it take?

ROSEN

There are two additional steps: "Hearing" and "Getting it."

WRIGHT

What's the difference between listening and hearing?

ROSEN

Well, listening is the act of giving the speaker as much of our undivided attention as possible. The more completely we're attending to the person speaking, we're actually *Simplifying* the process. If we give enough attention—if we're not trying to multi-task—we can hear. We can capture what the other is saying, and say the words back.

Listening fully is an example of *Restoring Resources*. Paying attention to the person speaking is not something people do regularly. More often, we're waiting for the other person to stop so we can say what we want to contribute. Let's restore the resource of full listening.

WRIGHT

Got it. Listening is paying attention. Hearing is being able to accurately say back what I'm being told. And "getting it?"

ROSEN

Moving from listening to hearing is almost mechanical, we're doing it or not. "Getting it" requires the ability to be able to separate from your own point of view and "step into" the other person's world, temporarily taking on their perspective. Getting it happens when we have a "felt sense" or a visceral understanding of what it's like for the other person. We're not even equipped to be able to do that until sometime in adolescence.

WRIGHT

That may explain a lot about why communicating with my teenagers is so challenging. I can tell we're moving to *Adding Resources* now. Do you have an example to help me better understand the concept of "getting it"?

ROSEN

Have you had the experience of calling a customer service representative to get help with an account or product?

WRIGHT

Sure, lots of times. It's been awful.

ROSEN

What's been awful about it?

WRIGHT

In addition to horrendous wait times, the person I'm talking to is at best just reading from a script on his or her computer screen. Sometimes the person gives me what I want; mostly, though, I have to try several different people and options. Not my favorite way to spend my time.

ROSEN

Ever had a good experience?

WRIGHT

There have been a few memorable times when the person seemed genuinely interested in my getting what I needed. The customer service person was able to ask good questions and could restate my answers in his or her own words but in a way that let me know I was understood. It felt like a miracle. I almost felt glad to have had a problem just to be able to experience this conversation, and I wanted to tell someone like the supervisor or president about what a good experience I'd had.

ROSEN

Those times *are* great, and that's exactly the positive response that people share when someone "gets it." What started out as a problem, turned into a celebration. Getting to have those experiences with my clients is part of why I love my work.

WRIGHT

It is amazing. It happens so infrequently because the person I'm talking to may not be listening or listening only partially, so he or she can't hold on to what I'm saying. The person can't let go of his or her own point of view to step into mine. Don't the odds of the person "getting it" seem pretty low? How does your coaching help?

ROSEN

My clients get to experience some immediate relief when they find that I get what it's like for them, and they learn that "getting it" is not an inborn ability but a skill that is learned. We add resources through focused experience.

Lily and Peter had reached the point of knowing they wanted to be together for a lifetime, and used my coaching to help design and create the life they wanted to share. They loved the design process with the end product reflecting a great collaboration.

Early on, the fun of envisioning a future was blocked by the pain of miscommunication in the present. We created a safe space to listen, hear, and "get" how their passionate energy could become hurtful when used defensively. Peter and Lilly became ideal co-creators of a shared future, and proved to have the love and support so prized by the other.

WRIGHT

You've been coaching individuals and work teams for more than thirty years. That means you've been able to watch the effects of your clients' work over a long period of time. What else has happened for your clients over these decades?

ROSEN

Thanks to FaceBook and LinkedIn, people are finding me and sharing how they are experiencing both success and happiness using the processes they learned in our work.

WRIGHT

Tell me more about that, will you?

ROSEN

Peter Drucker said, "We don't know who discovered water, but we know it wasn't fish." One of the reasons having a coach is important is the help I can be in making automatic or transparent thinking much more conscious and much more in our control.

WRIGHT

Are you saying that we get so used to what and how we think that we don't notice our thinking the same way that fish probably don't notice the water in which they swim?

ROSEN

That's right. We may or may not notice the content of our thoughts, or the collections of thoughts called beliefs, but until we move past noticing (a restored resource) and learn to question our beliefs (an added resource), we are likely to keep following old habits even though we really want to be, have, or do something different.

In our culture we're so focused on doing. Many have heard the maxim, "If we keep doing what we've always done, we'll keep getting what we have always gotten." I think the idea could be more accurately stated, "If we keep thinking what we've always thought, we will keep doing what we've always done."

WRIGHT

Most of us finish high school and go on for more schooling or training. Why aren't we taught things like communicating and thinking about our thinking? It seems to me that we still have lots to learn as we get into our twenties, thirties, forties, and older.

ROSEN

Unfortunately, most school systems aren't designed to help us know about the stages of growing, or provide us with maps to navigate those stages. There are some educators who "get it" and are working to get the curriculum changed. Until then, there are therapists and spiritual directors and teachers to help us as we wake up and grow up.

WRIGHT

And coaches like you.

ROSEN

Yes, and coaches like me.

WRIGHT

Perhaps we can look at how coaching is different than psychotherapy or spiritual direction in a bit, but let's get back to thinking about our thinking.

ROSEN

There's the story of the Zen master whose guest wanted wisdom. The Zen master brought a full teapot to the table and began pouring the tea into cups. He didn't stop pouring when the guest's cup was filled, and tea was overflowing the cup and the saucer and onto the tray. "Stop!" yelled the guest. "The cup can't hold any more tea!"

"And you can't hold any new learning," taught the master, "until you empty your head of all that you are carrying around."

WRIGHT

The moral of the story isn't to stop thinking, is it?

ROSEN

No it's not. The moral is that if we don't have any room to grow, we're going to be in trouble as life continues to bring us more and more to deal with.

My clients are supported as they focus on identifying the thoughts, beliefs, and attitudes that support the life they want to create. Sometimes it's like cleaning out a closet or the garage—creating areas for thoughts and beliefs the client wants continue using, and changing or trashing others.

WRIGHT

What do you mean when you say, "preserve a belief"?

ROSEN

Many people decide to start coaching with me when they feel that their life no longer "fits." "Growth spurts" aren't just for pre-teens. We have them throughout our life; hopefully it's our self-awareness that's growing more than our bodies. With each new stage of awareness or consciousness, some beliefs just don't fit what we truly value. And usually, we're aware of what doesn't fit before we've found the thoughts for what resonates or does fit.

WRIGHT

So I can imagine someone who believes that contributing to the family's financial success is the most important thing becomes very busy—maybe too busy—doing what it takes to be successful. Even if he or she is getting more and more responsibility and pay and climbing the ladder at a good clip, life could start to feel as though it doesn't fit. In my own life, there have been times when I needed to get my life back in balance—more in line with what was important to me.

ROSEN

That's exactly it. Most of us don't go deep enough to learn what makes us happy—truly happy—and instead, sacrifice a lot in the name of pursuing success. Sometimes we're faced with a crisis—loss of a job, a major illness or injury, or dissolution of an intimate relationship. Sometimes we're like the overflowing tea cup, and just feel that what used to get us up early and excited is now what is waking us up in with anxiety in the middle of the night. The cost of living a life that doesn't fit is like an unpaid credit card. In time, all our time and money is going into just paying down the interest.

WRIGHT

Connect that with "preserving" old thoughts.

ROSEN

The preserving comes at the end of the process. Because each stage takes all that was before and goes beyond, we say a new stage of life transcends and includes all the previous stages. Like footy pajamas outgrown so fast they barely had time to lose their sheen, we decide we will keep them for the next baby in the family. Our old thoughts and beliefs aren't bad or necessarily wrong for the stage we were in, so we might keep some memento or memory to signal the time we spent together and our transition into a new life.

WRIGHT

Okay. Somewhere I have some pictures of different co-workers at my old jobs. It's fun to find them again every few years and remember what was good about those days. Is that what you mean?

ROSEN

That's a great example. "Remembering what was good" is a mindset that supports life in an important way. Appreciation and gratitude can play a huge part in our ability to create and in our capacities to accept what is. They are two critical pieces in bringing into existence a life that is fulfilling and successful.

WRIGHT

Coaching seems to be about helping people decide what kind of life would best fit for them and then making it happen. Is that what you do with your clients?

ROSEN

That's a great way of describing what Life Coaching with me is about. I coach people in winning the game of life like an athletic coach works with an Olympic contender. Life is one game in which there can be lots of winners. Sometimes we're focused on getting an area back in balance, like renegotiating a client's work life allowing investment in personal needs, job deliverables, and family intimacy

Sometimes we're focused on a major life redesign—new career or beginning retirement, life as a single person after being in a long-term relationship, or deciding how I want to make the world a better place when children and parents are gone. Are you getting a sense of why I love what I do? I witness and support the processes of creation, helping people bring new life and with it a new level of happiness into their world.

WRIGHT

Maybe this would be a good time to ask about the difference between counseling, spiritual direction, and coaching. You've done all three in your career. How has life coaching evolved as your current calling?

ROSEN

Now I'm the one looking at photographs and remembering the good. After the Navy and working as a career counselor, I was ordained and became the Minister of Counseling in a church that valued both spiritual growth and mental health. As psychotherapist and professional counselor, I focused on helping clients heal from childhood trauma that was still getting in their way of loving self, God, and others. For me, both counseling and spiritual directing, which focuses on guiding someone along the path of living their spiritual story, involved taking significant responsibility for the welfare of the one in the "client" role.

WRIGHT

In Life Coaching, then, one of the benefits to you is a mutual relationship rather than a care-taker role?

ROSEN

Yes, and I hope the benefit extends to the client as well, who is free to design and implement a life for his or her happiness and success without concern about a psychological diagnosis or an imposed moral code. I see it as the co-laboring of two experts. I am skilled in suggesting structures and processes that will get a client what she or he wants. The client is the recognized expert and designer-in-chief of her or his life.

WRIGHT

People seeking coaching can still have problems, need advice, and get help figuring out what they want, can't they?

ROSEN

Yes, absolutely. My happiness increases when I can work with people solving problems, defining new life-giving beliefs and values, and discovering what in life delights them. Both of us realize, however, that my opinion and a couple of dollars will get them a ride on a bus in a city of their choice. I focus on finding the most powerful questions and collecting their ideas from different perspectives. The client comes to know what it feels like to go in the right direction and when it's time to get his or her bearings, just like someone walking along the beach with a metal detector learns to know when he or she is moving closer to some treasure.

WRIGHT

I've heard you say that it's important to "love what is," and now we're talking about creating a preferred future, or clients coming to you when something about their current life no long fits them. How do you see loving what is and wanting to change what is as compatible?

ROSEN

"Loving what is" means completely accepting what is happening. Blaming, "should-ing" on oneself, whining, or defending against a self-generated criminal indictment suggest being stuck and wasting lots of resources.

WRIGHT

Being a victim, in other words?

ROSEN

Right. I help my clients stay off the victim, persecutor, and rescuer triangle of roles. Although, I will admit to being an expert at pouting on occasion. My son will tell you that I still use the phony excuse that I'm healing from surgery I had twelve years ago when I need him to do most of the heavy lifting.

WRIGHT

Do your clients ever complain when you introducing something very interesting in the middle of an already interesting conversation? I want to go down the path we started about "loving what is" and "wanting to change." I also want to ask you more about the "victim, persecutor, and rescuer" in me. It feels like I'm at a great buffet and can't possibly have everything!

ROSEN

Can you see why I love coaching! There is so much good stuff. Here's where I suggest we follow Yogi Berra's advice, "When you come to a fork in the road, take it."

I like the idea suggested by the thirteenth century Sufi poet, Rumi. He wrote about welcoming our feelings as if they were visiting guests. Anytime feelings—from irritation to rage, worry to terror, hysterics to paralysis—"pay a visit," we have an opportunity to either welcome or love what is, by exploring the unmet need they signal, or to fight reality or to jump on Taibi Kahler's Drama Triangle entering the energy-draining path of the three roles that fight with reality: Victim, Persecutor, and Rescuer.

WRIGHT

How can you win in a fight with reality?

ROSEN

Exactly. To quote Byron Katie, who first called my attention to "Loving What Is," "Any time you fight with reality, you'll lose, but only 100 percent of the time."

WRIGHT

Let me see if I'm getting it. If I'm paying attention, there are probably dozens of times each day that give me the opportunity to learn about something I need to know. Instead of discovering what I need and getting it for me, I use my energy to react against what I think shouldn't be happening. Is that right?

ROSEN

Yes, I agree completely.

WRIGHT

But isn't it normal to react to what's happening?

ROSEN

If by "normal" you mean, "what most of us do most of the time," yes that's normal. But normal isn't necessarily helpful. In fact, we can create more trouble for ourselves that way.

WRIGHT

Will you give me a specific example?

ROSEN

Bill was focused on not disappointing people. As a result, he routinely over-committed himself and that stimulated a lot of resentment and anxiety.

WRIGHT

Because that set him up to keep disappointing folks?

ROSEN

Right, and just as important, not leaving any time or energy to take good care of himself.

WRIGHT

I see that.

ROSEN

To keep the anxiety from taking over and the anger from exploding, Bill would treat himself to large, expensive meals. He really enjoyed eating, at least the first few bites.

WRIGHT

That's really interesting. He was literally, "Biting off more than he could chew," just as he did in other ways in his life. So instead of getting himself what he really needs, he is bribing himself with food, or being an overindulging rescuer.

ROSEN

Exactly. And by the time he left the restaurant, he was beating himself up for "stuffing" himself, worrying about his growing waistline and credit card balance, and then taking in extra caffeine to keep from nodding off at his desk. To keep something he didn't want from happening—feeling the anxiety and the resentment—he was actually creating suffering, not happiness.

WRIGHT

This is helping me understand what you were talking about. Here's Bill, who could be looking at how much he's taken on and getting what he needs to be able to set limits and balance his self-care with his want to care for other people. He might see that more clearly if he "opened the door" and welcomed his feelings instead of avoiding or ignoring them. Bill's trying to make things better by switching between the rescuer when he bribes himself with too much food, and the victim when he eats it and is stuffed, getting fat, and going into debt.

I have the sense that he's headed for a train wreck.

ROSEN

The good news is that so did he. His therapist referred him to me for coaching when it became clear that Bill was using his counseling to explore all the dynamics that have led him to feel like a victim of others and himself, and could be fired, divorced, and dealing with diabetes before he could figure everything out.

WRIGHT

How did coaching with you speed things up for him?

ROSEN

Bill's problems started "solving themselves" as we focused on what was really important to him. We created powerful questions about what he admired in other people, what he wanted in his day, and what was working well for him. The path of least resistance was now "pulling" Bill to identify the many pieces that all of him wanted.

That led to Bill mapping out an action plan to make it happen. We had many conversations over several months. Between conversations with me, Bill completed some important projects including completing a weekly ChangeGrid™.

WRIGHT

That's like the chart we'd put up on the refrigerator to track the kids getting their chores done with stars and stickers, right?

ROSEN

Way more. The ChangeGrid is an instrument created by T. Falcon Napier at the Tension Management Institute. I can custom design it to fit each client at each point in his or her coaching.

Bill and I would talk through the patterns of his scores on the grid, as they revealed his levels of productive tension. We had an important and accurate way to gauge the conversations he was having with himself about the challenges he was facing during the week.

WRIGHT

Wow. So as Bill shifted his attitude and mind-set from victim of life to creating his life, the ChangeGrid validated his progress, and he could use it to alert himself about potential traps *before* he got into trouble! That reinforces the positive and lets him know what to do in case he found himself in trouble.

ROSEN

Bill discovered that deep down, he valued honesty more than anything. For a while Panic wasn't just "visiting," it had moved in and taken over Bill's space. Bill had his hands full practicing saying "I will" when he could, and "I can't, unless—" when he couldn't find a way to say yes to other's requests. He used a lot of creativity in devising maneuvers to keep from identifying with the panic.

WRIGHT

What do you mean by that?

ROSEN

Honesty became the lens through which Bill tried to look at everything. He concluded that "I am panicked," wasn't as true as, "the feeling of panic is getting a whole lot of my attention." That separation—being able to see that the panic was an "it"—kept him from being consumed or giving up on himself.

WRIGHT

Okay, I get that. It's true for me, too, that it's so much harder to deal with who I am than some *thing*, even if it's something stinky that I stepped in.

ROSEN

The more time and energy Bill was devoting to pursuing what he truly wanted, his relationship with pleasing people, food, money, his body, and his anxiety changed dramatically. We didn't spend lots of time and energy exploring the root causes of his problems and trying to change his personality or his relationship with his parents. Bill focused on identifying what was important to him and how to get it. As his situation in one area of his life got better, he designed and worked on another until he did have the pieces in place for a healthy and fulfilling life.

WRIGHT

Did that take years?

ROSEN

It did take a couple of years before Bill had remodeled key areas—his participation in his marriage, becoming a trusted and value-adding employee, relating to his children, his role as his parents moved into the last stages of their lives, building deeper friendships, avenues for play and recreation, his mental, physical, and spiritual health, and where he'd invest his energy as a volunteer in his community. The time between our conversations increased, but we still talk at least once a year, because doing an annual review is as important to him as getting a physical.

WRIGHT

I suspect Bill represents a composite of many clients. It's easy to see the victories and I have to keep reminding myself that we're talking about a lot of hard work. Is there an essential strength or competency that makes success more likely?

ROSEN

I think you'd enjoy a video Dr. Brené Brown, researcher and storyteller, that is on my Web site. Brené's research shows that the key ingredient for success is experiencing one's worth and knowing that "who I am" is enough.

WRIGHT

Is that something we either have or don't have?

ROSEN

Yes and no. Most of us grew up on a diet of "you can be, have, and do anything you want."

WRIGHT

That's empowering, right? Sounds like a good permission for succeeding.

ROSEN

It was meant to be by the people who love us, but when advertisers and marketers bombard us with it, not so much.

WRIGHT

Is your point that when it was intended for good, it is empowering and when it's manipulation, it's not?

ROSEN

Not exactly. My point is that well-intended or not, it is permission to succeed, but success at the expense of happiness.

WRIGHT

I don't think I agree with you, Bob. If I've heard it once, I've heard it thousands of times, "all I want is for you to be happy!"

ROSEN

Exactly!

WRIGHT

Please don't *do* that, you're making me crazy!

ROSEN

Okay, sorry. But you're absolutely correct.

WRIGHT

Great. Explain that.

ROSEN

The messages from those who care about you are combined with the messages saturating our culture—the water we swim in—so that success *is* equated with happiness. *And* success is defined by what is valued in the culture—what is being marketed and advertised on our cell phones, the internet, television, from the pulpit and podium, and now on an electronic billboard at the street corner indicating when you can safely cross the street and when you can't.

WRIGHT

What's wrong with that?

ROSEN

Two lies. First, it isn't true that I can be, have, or do anything. I have limitations and strengths and weaknesses. There is less in my control than I want, even if there is always some action I can take. The second is that success is not the same as happiness. It doesn't even lead to happiness. At the very most, success can free time and energy to pursue something that leads to happiness, although most of the time, our success consumes more and more of our time and energy.

WRIGHT

What about people like Oprah, Bill Gates, and Warren Buffet?

ROSEN

They are wonderful examples of people whose extraordinary success came from finding ways to create, package, and sell what made them happy! I cannot have their success because no matter how much I imitate their behaviors, what makes them happy isn't what makes me happy.

WRIGHT

Okay. So how about we shoot for success first and use it to fund what makes us happy?

ROSEN

That was the "good life" for our parents and grandparents. They worked, and work didn't have to be (and generally wasn't) something you liked. It was something you did to earn money or get credit. Then you retired and were free to do whatever made you happy.

WRIGHT

Sounds good to me.

ROSEN

But that model doesn't fit our world anymore. There are dozens of people competing for one job opening or you're in a job where a hiring freeze means you're expected to do the work previously done by two or three people. And another thing, when you've grown up on a diet of "you can be, have, or do anything," we get picky about what we do, and struggle with feelings of entitlement to being well-treated and well-rewarded.

WRIGHT

And this is related to feeling a sense of worthiness, how?

ROSEN

It's directly related to why I had to (and why I help my clients) unlearn unworthiness and to remember that who I am (and who they are) is enough. The more that success eludes me, or the more the pursuit of success uses me up, the more I'm invited to feel defective or ashamed. That brings us back to Bill and the extremes he had to go through to avoid the anxiety and pain of not being "enough."

WRIGHT

I'm starting to understand. Do you have another example?

ROSEN

Many of my clients have been business owners. They are people who either fell in love with an idea of being able to earn a living by offering something they loved and believed in, or grew up in a family business in which a parent, grandparent, or someone generations earlier had the idea and started a business.

WRIGHT

And now they're competing with Wal-Mart or with other people to get their stuff into Wal-Mart.

ROSEN

Even Wal-Mart started out as an idea in the head of Sam Walton. Sam is another great example of someone who was able to channel what made him happy into a money-making machine. And what seems true for Sam and the others we've talked about is that money never became more important than what they were doing to express their happiness. Money was always a "means" to do more of what made them happy. Ultimately for each of them, the greatest joy came from using their resources to meet the needs of others.

WRIGHT

I get that.

ROSEN

The discovery my clients make is that they have left the path of what makes them happy, and are being consumed by activities for getting or not losing their success.

WRIGHT

Well, even if they are the boss, they can't just decide to play instead of going to work. It's like a baby—you have to take care of it or it will get sick or hurt.

ROSEN

You're right. In fact, the road map to success they create is never grounded in "either/or." In our work together, my clients create the "both/and," learning to manage and tap into the positive outcomes of both happiness and success.

WRIGHT

That suggests another conversation I want to have with you soon. But for right now, just tell me, where does the time and energy come from to get there? It sounds like alchemy is involved, you know, turning lead into gold.

ROSEN

I bet you will "get it" when you think of a time you were doing something you loved—something you enjoyed for its own sake.

WRIGHT

Well, the most obvious is what I'm doing right now.

ROSEN

Talking to me?

WRIGHT

Yes, although I have to caution you about the dangers of breaking your arm if you rush to pat yourself on the back. While I'm getting some really good stuff from our conversation, what I was referring to was I'm doing two things I love: interviewing an interesting person, *and* getting to be in the studio pushing the buttons and engineering the recording of our interview. When we're finished, I'll lose myself in the editing processes. Sometimes I just lose track of time because it's so much fun.

ROSEN

Say that last part again, will you?

WRIGHT

I said, "I lose myself in the editing process and forget about time because I'm having so much fun."

Wow! I just discovered where energy and time comes from! That's really amazing.

ROSEN

So what is it like for you right now, in this moment?

WRIGHT

I think I'm back where we started. I "get it"—I hear what I said. I create energy and time when I'm doing what I know makes me happy.

ROSEN

Yes! Enjoy that. You've *Normalized* the process, *Simplified* the meaning and have a visceral sense of knowing, *Restored the Resource* of finding your "flow" state, and *Added the Resource of* new learning and more efficient use of your energy.

WRIGHT

It's funny, though, I don't exactly feel what I think "happy" should feel like. I feel something bigger. Maybe "grateful" is a better word to describe it.

ROSEN

That's my experience, too. And I feel grateful getting to share your experience. Thank you.

WRIGHT

How about we stop here and look for another time to talk. I'd like to sit with this for a while, and then I have some great work to get into.

ROSEN

I'm looking forward to hearing the fruit of your labor. Let's talk again soon.

ABOUT THE AUTHOR

Bob was very young when he was born and quite old when he grew up. Helping others has always been important to him. He created an employment agency and helped his fellow high school students get summer jobs. He was an assistant to the Dean of Students and the founding president of Lambda Psi Omega Service Fraternity in college. During his Vietnam Era service in the Navy, he was the designated "go-to" guy for sailors mixing drug problems and security clearances so they could get help instead of jail time. Since 1975, he's been a mental health professional, minister of counseling, life coach, and consultant helping individuals, families, and work teams in the public and private sectors experience greater happiness, health, security, and safety as they learn to make higher quality decisions and take more effective actions. Bob is a member of the International Coach Federation. Home base became Savannah, Georgia, in 2006 when his wife, Dr. Mary Lou Davis, joined the Liberal Arts faculty of the Savannah College of Art and Design.

Bob is a member of Rotary International serving on the Board, teaching Junior Achievement, and working on the Medical Equipment Transport Service project. Bob also volunteers at Hospice Savannah serving patient families and staff as a photographer. Bob is a Disaster Mental Health Supervisor and past Board Member for the American Red Cross, traveling to Texas after Hurricane Ike, and helping people cope in disaster relief operations in Fargo, North Dakota, and Blackshear and Atlanta, Georgia.

Bob Rosen

Robert P. Rosen & Associates
PO Box 13124
Savannah, GA 31416
912-344-9862
877-355-7019
Fax: 912-335-3418
Bob@RobertPRosen.org
www.RobertPRosen.org

Chapter Ten

THE ONE WHO KNOWS PROCESS: USING YOUR DIET AS A DOORWAY TO DISCOVERY

LISA WALDREP, JD, CPC

DAVID WRIGHT (WRIGHT)

Today I am talking with Lisa Waldrep, attorney, advocate, and Certified Professional Coach. Lisa completed her undergraduate studies at the University of San Diego (USD) where she graduated magna cum laude. She obtained her law degree from The Law Center at the University of Southern California (USC) and graduated with honors. She then became a Certified Professional Coach and pursued her lifelong dream of helping others. "Remember, Reunite, Recreate"—these are three powerful words Lisa uses each day as she forms a multidimensional career as a wellness coach, inspirational speaker, advocacy attorney, and philanthropist. She has pioneered one of the most practical, personal techniques to transform lives.

Unlike any other wellness program of its kind, Lisa's process has motivated thousands of clients to use The One Who Knows™, as she says, to help them find the inner power and wisdom already within them. She has developed many tools and programs to help others, including her online e-course, "RX for Renewal," a workbook series, and several customized empowerment programs, such as "Thriving Through Tough Times." She has also presented motivational and keynote speeches and offers a monthly inspirational column titled, "Dreams Have Wings."

Through her many endeavors Lisa's dream remains consistent—to be of service to others and facilitate healing, wellness, and abundance in her client's lives. She resides in Southern California with her husband, Dr. Donald Waldrep, a renowned laparoscopic and weight loss surgeon, and her miracle twins, Sophie Grace and Carson James.

Lisa Waldrep, welcome to *ROADMAP to Success*.

LISA WALDREP (WALDREP)

Thank you; it's great to be speaking with you today.

WRIGHT

So if you could condense your teaching philosophy as a Certified Professional Coach into a few sentences, what would you say?

WALDREP

If we can break through our ordinary perception of reality we can actually directly access the empowering solutions that are inside of us. So my work is about developing these very simple and powerful techniques to allow people to come into contact with their true inner wisdom. Call it instinct or intuition; some people call it soul. I like to call it "the voice inside, that is on your side." You can learn more about this exciting concept by visiting www.TheOneWhoKnows.com.

WRIGHT

Would you tell our readers about yourself and one of your first inspirational coaching projects?

WALDREP

Absolutely, I would love to. I believe that I was forging a multidimensional career as a certified life coach before I was actually professionally labeled as a coach. I found, as an attorney, that I was often profoundly engaged and touched by the stories of my clients. When I worked in law that I was practicing law, but was engrossed in coaching, so I decided to officially shift gears. I left law in order to pursue a certified professional degree in coaching and that opened up some great opportunities to create some new organizations.

I feel that the one company that speaks most to my truth is The One Who Knows. It focuses on developing life-changing, personal coaching programs. We use journaling, art therapy, affirmation techniques, and more; we really have a wide variety. It's a twelve-part program and it's life-transforming, oftentimes for me as much as my clients!

In the process, The One Who Knows helps thousands of people understand that inner power I talked about. The voice inside that is on your side is accessible. It is there for you and it can be harnessed to change your life, especially in a world that seems uncertain at times.

WRIGHT

Elaborate more on how your career as a lawyer acted as a segue to your coaching career and led you to the development of The One Who Knows.

WALDREP

After graduating from The Law Center at the University of Southern California Law School, I built a successful law practice. I eventually decided to shift my life focus to help clients directly empower themselves. A lawyer usually represents someone in order to help them. But I helped my clients realize that the best representative was, in fact, themselves. So I founded The One Who Knows in order to provide that personal development program for individuals and corporations across the nation. I gathered all the information from my legal and nonprofit work with hundreds of men, women, and children. I used my own instincts and life experiences to guide people to work from their core strengths and activate their own inner knowing.

WRIGHT

What tools do you provide your coaching clients from The One Who Knows?

WALDREP

I've developed an entire line of products that I've created in response to my clients' needs and successes. My favorite is a visionary workshop, or, as I prefer to call it, a "playground" called "RX for Renewal." We've also developed a series of workbooks, motivational and keynote speeches I've given, and I have a line of dietary supplements. I've been able to utilize a lot of the knowledge I have gained from my own life to help people bridge their inner and outer life to create some amazing results.

I truly believe that my personal approach and the intimacy I have in my personal and professional relationship-building have allowed me to connect to and forge business alliances with professionals in every field.

The One Who Knows is a multidimensional, personal coaching and empowering program focused on the concept of that inner knowing. The One Who Knows refers to the inner voice that guides us from our past to our present and into our future. It teaches individuals that within them there is a foundation and a potential for this ideal destiny. The important resources are both within their physical cellular memory and the internal, non-tangible whisperings of their own heart. By learning to listen to The One Who Knows, people find they are no longer victims of chance or circumstance, but they can transcend their negative conditioning and their limitations in order to experience the joy and freedom of living by choice.

WRIGHT

What is your next coaching project?

WALDREP

Oh I'm very excited about it. I am working on it with my husband, Dr. Donald Waldrep, who is a pioneering, nationally-renowned weight loss surgeon. We are currently developing a supportive product line. This includes a joint curriculum to help people deal with issues of weight loss and weight wellness, utilizing The One Who Knows programs. We're making the twelve pieces of the program very specific to weight loss. We've created the RX for Renewal System, which can be accessed at www.RxForRenewal.com. The program is designed for overweight clients of CURE Centers. (CURE is an acronym for Compassion, Understanding, Renewal, and Empowerment). CURE Centers, our jointly owned business, are state-of-the-art medical clinics that stress the unity of body, mind, and soul. These are innovative health centers that are integrating The One Who Knows life coaching method into an overall wellness plan. We've seen great results so far.

WRIGHT

How do you keep yourself involved as a personal coach in your community?

WALDREP

I'm very committed to providing quite a bit of pro bono personal coaching in my community. In fact, part of The One Who Knows Program, involves the importance of giving back. An important aspect of true abundance, wealth, and truth is being able to share what you have. The whole purpose of having abundance and excess in your life is that you have more to give. So I've worked with a variety of different projects, but of course my favorite is the nonprofit group Dr. Waldrep and I founded, The Step Ladder Initiative.

The Step Ladder Initiative donates a portion of the profit from our CURE Center businesses to families in need. So throughout my personal and professional endeavors I have tried to keep my dreams very consistent, to look at life from an empowered perspective of service to others, and to facilitate that same healing and wellness in my own and my clients' lives.

WRIGHT

What makes your mission as a personal life coach different than any other coach's?

WALDREP

My mission is to help people worldwide hear that inner voice within them—the voice I call "The One Who Knows." I have personally experienced, and I want to help others experience, the joy and freedom of living in choice. It's funny because people actually hear the word "responsibility" and think of it as an onus, something they have to avoid. If asked, most people will admit that they work very hard at times to avoid their responsibilities, but I choose to see "responsibility" as more of a "free-sponsibility"—the ability to respond *in conscious choice* when you have a situation arise.

I've been able to teach and illustrate, through many of my client interactions, that through having choices we can become self-empowered. Through self-empowerment we can have transformative abundance. Both my personal story and my life's work have taught thousands of people that they have the wisdom within them to make those empowering choices. They have the power to actually create certainty, joy, and service. They can take their past and present pain and their shortcomings and all of those negative tapes that run through their minds and actually transform them into powerful, meaningful experiences through a shift in perspective.

I've been motivated to help clients understand that while they might not be able to immediately change the events in their life, they always have the choice of how to respond to the events. That response can be done with integrity, through wholeness. This understanding transports you out of the victim mentality. This newfound self-empowerment can lead to re-found self-love. I find that as people fall back in love with themselves, they not only affect others around them but they experience true transformative abundance. This means that they see life-changing, positive results in their personal lives, their core relationships, their communities, and even in the world at large. It's an amazing program and I'm very proud of it.

WRIGHT

Will you elaborate on how you incorporate your personal experiences into your coaching practices?

WALDREP

I consistently describe my own life as a quest. Philosophically, I believe that we're in a very important transformational era in humanity's development. In 1998, I experienced an event that I like to describe as a "wake-up call." In the middle of that event, I went through what many people would consider to be a dark night of the soul. I will often say that in the process of my world collapsing, I lost my mind and found my heart. You see, sometimes lawyers can get a little bit stuck in their head. I had been a young lawyer practicing in a very well-known law firm and I had fallen into that trap. But when this event happened, I realized that the most effective way to take an integrative approach to life and to be successful in life is to make sure that the heart has evolved and that the inner instinct, inner wisdom, and inner voice is given a role.

Working as a conflict resolution specialist for more than eighteen years, I saw how important it was to not only recognize what people wanted, but to realize that there are always certain commonalities between different people. Rather than stressing the differences between people, we can see those commonalities and then witness transformative results. We can always look at a situation and say, "Oh, this person seems very different from the next," but a truly wise individual would search for those commonalities. One of the techniques we use is to show people how to look at a situation that seems to involve a lot of different aspects and find the similarities between them. This enables people to come together and create dynamic results that speak to everyone.

I emphasize that what I coach isn't an exclusive message; it's one that we can translate through our own filter of our own life experiences. My personal experiences have of course influenced me, but they resonate with so many other people that I feel it is a tremendous blessing.

I think we all have the ability and responsibility to speak our unique truth and that's my mission and my purpose—to help people do that.

WRIGHT

If you could give each of your clients a short paragraph to sum up your message, what would that be?

WALDREP

Remember. Reunite. Recreate. A permanent approach to weight loss and healing is a transformative journey that culminates in self-respect, unconditional love, and self-esteem. In three stages: you remember who you really are, reunite with different aspects of yourself and others, and Recreate a new life story, the One Who Knows guiding you along the way. As you go about the process of healthy, natural weight loss, you develop a permanent skill set of empowerment and wellness.

WRIGHT

Would you tell us a bit about the role of intuition in success?

WALDREP

The minute we started this interview, the mind and intuitive process are engaged. Unfortunately, the signals that are sent by our intuition usually are completely unnoticed in the everyday world when we're struggling for success. In this economy, people are very easily distracted and very often they want to be told what to do. But the truth is that we don't need to be told what to do. What I teach is that we already know within us what those answers are and we can take advantage of the information that is coming to us through intuition. This is how you begin the unparalled journey into releasing your extraordinary capabilities, which helps you succeed in almost anything you set out to accomplish in life.

My work helps people learn to access and use their innate, powerful intuitive powers for success in not one or two, but all aspects of their life.

WRIGHT

How does your One Who Knows process come into play here?

WALDREP

People do best with simple techniques, so I created a short and practical twelve-part process. These techniques are what I call The One Who Knows process. It's very specific and it's a program that allows us to unlock that inner One Who Knows so that we have greater success. The One Who Knows is a natural capability that everyone has, but it needs to be developed like any other skill—with an open mind, some guidance, and a little practice. All you really have to do is remove some unfounded and self-imposed limitations and then The One Who Knows is free to shine and to guide you to unlimited possibilities.

WRIGHT

How did you discover The One Who Knows process?

WALDREP

It's funny—the One Who Knows process discovered me in some ways. Because it's based on my twenty years of searching for ways to predictably increase my clients' success. My extensive background in communication, law, and healthcare that really helped, but it wasn't enough; it didn't fill the need I had to give something of myself to this world. I think we all have to have a mission and a truth that is overarching in our lives. So in my own struggle to be successful as a high profile Los Angeles attorney, I aggressively sought the advice and insights of other successful people.

That life-changing breakthrough came when in desperation I left my mainstream career path to pursue a direction that just felt right in my body. That's what happened in 1998—it just felt right that I leave this very high-paying, powerful job and follow my heart. That's when I became a Certified Professional Coach; I walked away from an extremely high salary. It was a very difficult decision in my business career, and everyone, including myself, thought that the new direction could actually be self-destructive. That decision turned out to be the genesis for my development of a new success tool that has generated positive results in my life and in the lives of others. It turns out that, in truth, I hadn't walked away from anything. My success, and the corresponding salary, followed me!

WRIGHT

Why focus on the problem of obesity?

WALDREP

While working with my husband, we found that Americans spend more than *fifty billion* dollars a year on diets and diet-related products, yet the United States continues to be the fattest nation in the world. And worldwide, the problem of obesity is increasing. Part of that problem is the process of dieting itself. Research shows that diets don't work in the long-term; only 2 to 3 percent of dieters can expect to maintain their weight loss long-term. Chronic dieters may add five to ten pounds to their weight every time they diet.

Dr. Waldrep and I believe that the answer to reaching and maintaining an optimal body weight lies in developing a totally new mentality—one that utilizes inner wisdom and the voice that is on your side. We all know how to eat. When we were children we knew how to eat. We knew what to do. We knew that when we were thirsty we needed to drink. But we've lost our connection to that inner wisdom. So The One Who Knows process and the work that Dr. Waldrep and I do together help reunite people with that inner knowledge.

WRIGHT

What does The One Who Knows have to do with obesity?

WALDREP

The new mentality I mentioned is based on a system designed by Dr. Waldrep and me. We call it Rx for Renewal. Rx for Renewal takes The One Who Knows process and applies it directly to the issue of weight wellness. The program is based on the fact that every one of us was born with natural instincts that tell us when, where, what, and how much to do to maintain our body at our optimal weight. The problem for many people is that, as they grow up, they adopt a belief system that sabotages their natural instinct. These are beliefs that are gathered from parents, media, teachers, and others. These beliefs block our ability to access our own inner knowing. It seems that naturally slim people remain in touch with their own innate wisdom in the areas of self-love, self-nurturing, food, water, hunger, thirst, satiety, and exercise.

In order for overweight men and women to return to their naturally slim states, they need to develop new attitudes and skills; this is where The One Who Knows comes into play. People who are successful don't fight their body, they work with it. They work with their body, mind, and soul acting in concert together as allies. There are thoughts and beliefs and natural eating and exercise instincts that all people are born with. Utilizing them can help people to become naturally slim in an educated and gentle and loving manner. It's easy to develop body intuition once we take the mystery out of the process. That's what The One Who Knows does.

WRIGHT

So why aren't traditional weight loss methods working?

WALDREP

Too often, people are taught that success and weight loss is this simple, easy process where you need to do nothing more complicated than lowering calories and increasing exercise. The fact is if it were that simple, everyone would successfully lose weight, wouldn't they? Something else is obviously going on here. There is a self-defeating diet mentality made up of a series of destructive beliefs, thoughts, and actions that are embedded in people's behaviors. A new understanding of the bond between mind and body will lead clients away from the concept of dieting as a means of weight management and back to a true understanding and connection with their innate body wisdom.

Very often when we feel things that cause us to see ourselves as out of control, especially in today's economic climate; we can turn to food to ground ourselves rather than listening to our inner voice. We have to be aware that there are deeper solutions needed than, "Oh, I just need to eat less." If people could just eat less and lose weight they would do it, however, there is something else going on, and we need to be gentle and loving and compassionate enough to try to figure out what it is and work with it.

WRIGHT

Will you describe for our readers an intuitive eating program and explain why it's important?

WALDREP

An intuitive eating program is one of the things we've developed through our Rx for Renewal Program. You trust your body to make the right food choices and maintain your healthy weight. You listen to your body and its signals. Its focus is on nurturing your body rather than starving it or whipping it into shape. It helps you find the ways you were naturally meant to be. The concept is actually based on the belief that when you truly feel free in your food choices, without any hidden agenda of restricting those choices in the future, you eliminate the urgent need to overeat. You no longer have this instinct that says "there is scarcity," which you have to heed, so you go and hurry up and gobble up some food.

Often, as young children, we learn to use food as a substitute for love, attention, and security. An intuitive eating program replaces that learning with more healthy means of getting those needs met.

WRIGHT

Will you give us an example of one of the Rx for Renewal steps to help us better understand how the system works?

WALDREP

Sure. One of the most powerful steps is actually the tenth section in the program for Rx for Renewal and it deals with how you actually make contact with that wise knowing within you.

I had a client who wanted to lose weight; it just wasn't working for her and she was very frustrated. In order to try to break through the barriers blocking her, I had tried many of the techniques that had worked with other clients in the past to no avail. In frustration, I decided to make sure I was using *all* my resources. It occurred to me to close my eyes and connect with my own One Who Knows.

So I closed my eyes and I asked my heart, how I could help her. An idea came to me that, at first, seemed unrelated to any type of weight loss that I could think of. I felt inspired to ask her how she perceived her own One Who Knows. I asked, "What does it look like? What does it sound like?" I wondered if she was going to think I was crazy, but instead she related to the questions very well.

"You know," she said, "I thought about this many times but when I close my eyes and I try to give a voice or a feeling or a picture to The One Who Knows, I often can't see anything. I can't visualize anything. If I am lucky, I can somewhat see The One Who Knows off in the distance, but that is about it."

This was surprising to me. I was convinced that the distance had a lot to do with the fact that she felt very disconnected from her inner knowing.

So I asked next that she close her eyes and envision The One Who Knows. I asked her to try to imagine holding the hand of her One Who Knows. I explained that, whether it was a woman or a man, it didn't really make a difference, just that she was close enough to connect to it in some way.

I am proud to say that she is now almost one hundred pounds lighter. She sometimes makes mistakes and falls flat on her back, but she gets right back up again and reaches out her hand for The One Who Knows. Together she and her natural instincts and her body wisdom are working to make sure that she is living a healthier lifestyle.

WRIGHT

So what is the message you want people to hear so they can learn from your successes, and perhaps from those of your clients?

WALDREP

The most important message is that there never is a time when we're without hope; we always have this ally within us. I call it The One Who Knows, other people call it by different names. It doesn't really matter what you call it. But you are never alone, and things are never hopeless.

This incredible ally can help you remember why you came here and what you are here to do. It can help you reunite with your true self and with people who share a quest or a desire to know who they are in a healthy way. It can help you recreate your life so that you're living a healthy life in body, mind, and soul. If I had the choice to show them one thing, that's what it would be.

WRIGHT

Well, what an interesting concept. I'm fascinated by it. I would, like a lot of our readers, want to know a whole lot more about it. I have tried dieting all these years and, just as you say, most people tell you, "All you've got to do is quit eating so much and start exercising more!" Well, it doesn't seem to work does it?

WALDREP

No it doesn't and it's really unfair because if that were all that there was to it then weight loss should be easy. The lie says people are failing because they're not doing something right, which is just not the truth. The important part of this is that this isn't just all philosophical. There is an element of the mind, and the soul, or the heart that is involved in this work.

What is really amazing is that Dr. Waldrep has incorporated the physical (or body) aspect of this whole concept and he has created what we call "The Waldrep WRAP." This is a way to help people lose weight without cutting off half their stomach, without redirecting their intestines, or putting a foreign body inside them. It's something he's designed that is less invasive for people so they can access this surgery as a bridge, a leg up. It allows them to worry less about their physical weight so they can start dealing with those self-sabotaging belief systems created when we were kids. We are so very proud of the Waldrep WRAP and we are hoping more people will learn more about it. You can do that by visiting: www.WaldrepWRAP.com.

WRIGHT

Well, what a great conversation. I appreciate all this time you've taken with me to answer these questions. It has been informative.

WALDREP

Thank you. I've enjoyed it too, tremendously.

WRIGHT

Today I have been talking with Lisa Waldrep. Lisa is a Certified Coach and she is pursuing her lifelong dream of helping others: "Remember." "Reunite." "Recreate." She has pioneered one of the most inspirational and imaginative coaching programs today using simple and practical techniques to transform lives. Her process has motivated thousands of clients who use The One Who Knows method to find the inner power and wisdom already within them.

Lisa, thank you so much for being with us today on *ROADMAP to Success.*

WALDREP

Thank you so much. It has been my pleasure.

About the Author

For more than twenty years, Lisa Janks Waldrep has enjoyed a successful career as an inspirational speaker, workshop facilitator, Certified Professional Coach, accomplished advocate, as well as the founder of charitable organizations that meet the needs of at-risk adults and children. Her interactive, goal-driven The One Who Knows, Catalyst Coaching, and Thriving Through Tough Times workshops have transformed the lives of many individuals.

Lisa's background includes a BA with honors from The University of San Diego. She also holds a Juris Doctorate degree from The Law Center at the University of Southern California, where she also graduated with honors. During the past twenty years, she has been an attorney advocate, negotiation and conflict resolution specialist, an educational consultant, Catalyst Coach, and leading expert in the areas of self-esteem, achievement, inspiration, and peak performance.

Lisa Waldrep, JD, CPC

The One Who Knows
1012 Candlecrest Drive
Westlake Village, CA 91362
805-497-1771
www.LisaWaldrep.com

Chapter Eleven

WHAT'S IN YOUR CLOSET?

CYNDI SAVAGE RICE

POLONIUS:
This above all: to thine own self be true,
And it must follow, as the night the day,
Thou canst not then be false to any man.
Farewell, my blessing season this in thee!

Shakespeare's *Hamlet*

DAVID WRIGHT (WRIGHT)

Today I am talking with Cyndi Savage Rice. Cyndi owes her success to her passion for truth within herself and others. Her recent book, *Don't Conform, Connect*, speaks to this concept, as do most of her speeches and seminars. Cyndi has enjoyed more than thirty-eight years as a management and sales consultant, business developer, and speaker. Some of her successes include hosting a radio talk show, being named a Distinguished Toastmaster, winning an International Speech contest, and working as a Certified Cemetery Executive. She is also a recipient of both the Stephen Covey Effectiveness Award and the Dale Carnegie Human Relations Award. She is an authorized partner with Profiles International, Inc., and a performance coach. Her full life includes a variety of adventures and experiences. She is married to a handsome firefighter and has one awesome son and two beautiful granddaughters who reside in North Florida.

Cyndi, welcome to *ROADMAP to Success.*

CYNDI RICE (RICE)

Thank you, David; I'm excited to be with you today.

WRIGHT

So you provide great coaching tips to people. Where do these come from?

RICE

Good coaching comes from experience and knowledge. Great coaching comes from one's ability to listen with empathy. We all have a still, small voice within us waiting to be recognized. We are all wise beyond our understanding. We just don't believe that we are. We search to learn everything we can from written material, schools, and others because we believe that answers are found only outside ourselves. My goal is not to discount these sources of information; rather, it is to encourage people to look inside themselves for answers. In our technologically advanced world, we look for answers in external sources because they are neatly organized, easy to come by, and deemed trustworthy.

Few people realize the wealth that lies beneath their surface because they don't take the time or spend the energy to journey into their own resources. Yet the word "educate" comes from the Latin word *educare*, which means to draw from within.

> *That inner voice has both gentleness and clarity. So to get to authenticity, you really keep going down to the bone, to the honesty, and the inevitability of something.*
> —*Meredith Monk*

We seek help from counselors, psychiatrists, psychics, and doctors and expect them to fix us. While professionals can help to unlock the answers, great counselors understand that their role is to help the client uncover and discover what has been available to them the entire time.

Great coaching comes from a coach's ability to listen passionately and without judgment to the individual matter before them. A coach's undivided attention and empathy silently communicates that the client is important—that the client matters. When the one in need begins to feel appreciated and understood, he or she feels safe. This is when healing takes place. The client unfolds layer by layer like an onion revealing the soft, opaque inner core of his or her being where all truth becomes available. A sacred relationship begins to form.

Great coaching comes from a commitment to the process of uncovering one's innermost hurts, fears, dreams, and desires. Great counseling takes hard work. Anyone who has tried meditation knows the difficulty of shutting the world out in order to access his or her inner resources. Our ability to lend ourselves completely to another, because of the truth within us, provides the atmosphere necessary to induce personal growth and healing.

Proverbs 23:23 instructs us to "buy the truth and sell it not." There is a cost associated with finding the truth. Many of us assume that we know the truth about ourselves and others by the time we reach adulthood. Do you know anyone who married the wrong person? Do you know anyone who worked years at jobs they hated? By looking diligently inside ourselves for direction, we can avoid these mistakes while making the most of precious time.

I liken discovering our truth to cleaning out a closet. We all have closets full of "stuff." There we store valuables and things we don't know what to do with. Over time, the closet becomes full and unusable. Inside the closet there are important things, but it takes too much work to dig them out. Home decorating magazines are full of pictures of neatly organized storage areas. We look at these pictures and vow that someday our closet will look like the photos. Until we are willing to empty the closet, we won't ever have full access to the valuables inside.

Just as we store things in a closet, we store messages internally. Our mind is like a computer that needs to be cleaned and defragmented. It's 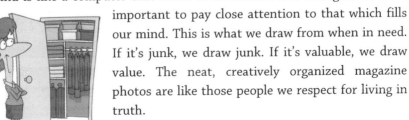 important to pay close attention to that which fills our mind. This is what we draw from when in need. If it's junk, we draw junk. If it's valuable, we draw value. The neat, creatively organized magazine photos are like those people we respect for living in truth.

Back to the closet: Making the decision that the

closet is worth cleaning is the first step. One day, we gather the courage to face the challenge. We lock the front door, open the closet wide, and start tossing. At first we are overwhelmed with unorganized piles that look bigger than the closet. Deciding what to keep, what to give away, and what to commit to garbage is a difficult process requiring time, energy, and self-questioning. We've all heard the phrase "stinkin' thinkin'." Stinkin' thinkin', like stored garbage, would be easier to get rid of if it really stank.

Is it worth fixing, returning, saving? Should it be recycled, tossed, cleaned up? Should we store it for later use or will it serve someone else's needs better than ours? As we empty the closet, the piles get bigger. The job is overwhelming. Our commitment tested, we are tempted to slam the door, but we resolve to keep going.

Finally, the closet is empty. The clean, open, available space gives us a new sense of control.

> *Healing takes courage,*
> *and we all have courage,*
> *even if we have to dig a little to find it.*
> —Tori Amos

We have the power to choose what goes in that closet. We, the masters, decide what we will keep and how we will use it. We shine up what is of value to us and dust off the treasures uncovered, vowing to share them with those around us. Refreshed and revived, we find inner strength for having endured the process. As we haul out the stuff we don't need or want, a new sense of knowledge comes to us—a renewed sense of what is important and why we are here. Our valuables have been identified and restored from the dust and clutter of the world.

A great coach knows how to provide a safe environment for cleaning out the closet. A great coach listens as we question, test, sort, and revive. A great coach watches and stands by us as we journey into the depth of our truth while honoring the process that readies us for success.

WRIGHT

I've asked this question probably thousands of times by now: how do you define success?

RICE

For years, I wondered what "success" really meant, David.

In the early 1970s, I took a job as a bookkeeper. Interestingly, it was in the cemetery and funeral industry. I happen to believe that everything has a purpose. This position

> To laugh often and much;
> To win the respect of intelligent people
> and the affection of children;
> To earn the appreciation of honest critics
> and endure the betrayal of false friends;
> To appreciate beauty,
> to find the best in others;
> To leave the world a bit better,
> whether by a healthy child,
> a garden patch
> or a redeemed social condition;
> To know even one life has breathed easier
> because you have lived.
> This is to have succeeded.
>
> —Ralph Waldo Emerson

certainly did for me. My sixteen-year-old brother had just died of a brain tumor and my husband had joined the service and married another woman while he was still married to me! I was devastated with loss. I threw myself into work and quickly moved up the ladder, eventually ending up as a sales consultant and family counselor. That was the beginning of my education in death.

Through the years, success found me as I worked hard and dedicated myself to others at a difficult time in their lives. I read Elizabeth Kübler Ross and Bernie Siegel. I studied the Bible frantically, trying to find answers for people in grief.

I was careful to keep in close touch with those dying and their families at the time of death, asking questions that would allow them to sort out their lives. What in your life makes you feel proud? What do you regret? Time after time, people who had nothing to lose by " 'fessing up" told me that they had regret. They were sorry that they hadn't started their own business. They were sorry that they hadn't taken that trip or told someone special that they loved them. They were sorry that they hadn't forgiven—or asked for forgiveness.

These experiences changed me. Each family who shared opened my eyes to what lies within each of us. They taught me the most valuable lessons of life. We are responsible for what we leave behind when we die. We are also responsible for what we fail to leave behind.

Success to me is daring to be real, whether it means following our own drummer or confronting the fears within. Success to me requires courage and compassion. Courage is necessary for embracing all the opportunities that come our way. Compassion is necessary for accepting others and allowing them to accept us. We must commit to live in the fullness of purpose within us, whatever that may be. This honors our lives, the lives of others, and our Creator. This is success; this is abundance.

WRIGHT

So what do you think are the biggest obstacles people face in trying to become successful?

RICE

Do you remember the balls, called "Shape O Toys" that Tupperware used to make for children? The hollow balls had holes in different shapes all around. The ball came with blocks in each of those shapes. Children would learn by trying to put a block into a hole in the ball.

Many of us live by trying to squeeze ourselves into the molds designed by the expectations of others. Unless we clearly understand who we are, what we value, and where we are going, we spend days of our lives trying to fit into the world's standards. We allow others to decide what we like, how we dress, what we wear, and what we believe. We settle for being cool rather than real. After all, cool is acceptable, real may not be.

I remember that old television game show called *To Tell the Truth*. Contestants would work to convince the players that they were someone else. In the end, the host would ask, for example, "Will the real Cyndi Rice please stand up!" That is what our journey is really all about—identifying the real person we are and standing up. Many of us, particularly women, spend our lives trying to be all things to all people.

I've hosted a number of women's groups throughout the years. My objective has been to gather professional women to help each other by freely sharing their skills, gifts, experience, and knowledge. A survey of the members found that the number one quality missing in their lives was "balance." Each struggled to be the best parent, the best housekeeper, the best wife, the best professional, and the best friend. None of them ever achieved any acceptable level of success in finding balance. Obsessed with becoming all things to all people, their struggle for balance was never achieved. In the surveys, no one ever voiced a desire to be the best "me" they could be.

It isn't necessary, or possible, to be all things to all people. We aren't here to please our parents, our children, our employers, or our friends. We are here to realize, honor, and give the amazing individuals we are to others. When we do begin to honor what is inside of us dying to get out, we become passionate about being us! We are meant to be exceptional at being us; that alone is a job big enough for a lifetime.

The Bible talks about the body of Christ as many members with one head. If I am created to be a liver, I cannot be an ankle, no matter how hard I try. There is a reason for this—each of us was created to be awesome at something, not an expert at everything. We are meant to be outstanding in being authentic. When I am authentic, and you are, and others are, the complete body begins to form and the many parts make a beautiful whole that works perfectly together.

I just saw the movie, *Black Swan*. Excited to see it because I love ballet, I came away with much more than the beauty of dance. We cannot be who we aren't unless who we are dies in the process. We don't have problems with other people, we have problems with ourselves. We cannot please others until we are at peace with ourselves.

The more I think about it, David, the more decided I am that balance is really unachievable and, just maybe, it's not all it's cracked up to be. My most productive, satisfying, and exciting times have been times when I am least balanced. Balanced is actually pretty darn boring if you ask me! When I am passionate and excited about anything, I throw myself into it. I live it, breathe it, and embrace it with all I am. This passion has provided me with excellence in areas of my life.

As I look to my heroes, I find that none of them had balance. They were driven and consumed with whatever seed was being birthed within them. Think about the world's heroes. I have many personal heroes in my life; there are many who have touched my life deeply. These are people I look up to for their passion and success. I don't look up to any of them for balance!

When we struggle to find balance, we are frustrated, and when we fail, we are discouraged. We are setting out to accomplish the unaccomplishable. This consumes some of us until we lose sight of what is really important. Michelangelo would not have given us such beauty if his focus had been balance.

Perhaps balance should come about as a result of a lifetime of effectiveness rather than a life of balance. Isn't effectiveness what we really crave? There are periods when we are better parents than professionals, periods when we are better lovers than housekeepers, periods when we reap, and periods when we sow.

"To everything there is a season, and a time to every purpose under the heaven: A time to be born, and a time to die; a time to sow; a time to reap" (from Ecclesiastes 3, written by King Solomon, a very wise man).

Might this "pie in the sky" goal of balance be the enemy of passion? When we focus on the things that naturally keep our attention, other things naturally take a back seat—we are out of balance. While enveloped in the process of accomplishment, when living in the truth to that desire and purpose within us, life is good. As each dream is fulfilled, another passion is ignited and we begin to round out into the perfect specimen of who we were created to be.

I don't mean to communicate that we should throw our responsibilities out the door for passion. Not at all. I do mean that we should make our life choices carefully in line with that truth within us so we don't end up living someone else's life or a life that ends in regret. We cannot be happy when we are not being true to ourselves. Whether we know it or not, this unhappiness is expressed to others and robs our relationships.

I've been accused of being impractical, David. Many have not had the opportunity to live as closely to death as I have. This intimacy with death has given me an incredible passion for life and its one-time appointment. Impractical to me is taking the only opportunity we have at life and prostituting it for anything but the truth. Is it practical to work your entire life at a job you hate when you may never have another chance to live the life you love? It makes my heart ache to see people out there every day trying to please others, working only for money, giving no thought for the value of their days, as if they could get another chance to live authentically.

What example do we send to our children when we settle for mediocrity? What messages do we convey when we live miserably, never satisfied, always trying to keep up with society, pleasing others at the expense of our one and only opportunity to live fully in truth to who we are? The real truth is that when we think we are living for others, we are not really doing that at all. The vitality that is missing from our lives, as well as the resentment we harbor, really robs them of what they need from us.

Maybe what we really crave is reconciliation in the big picture. When the sun goes down on my life, I want to know that I was true to myself, my loved ones, and the world I lived in. I want to look back and know that I invested all I had, that I lived with enthusiasm, and that I made a difference.

We will be reconciled to our lives by honoring the gifts within us. We do this by using our gifts effectively to nurture those we are given to love, while being true to that which we believe.

WRIGHT

So what would you say would be the biggest contribution to your professional success?

RICE

Two God-given qualities that I've enjoyed nurturing are thinking outside the box and being resourceful.

In the early 1980s, I was determined to help families who were grieving through the holidays. One night I had a vivid dream of having a huge Christmas celebration at the cemetery and funeral home. A little crazy, right? Nevertheless, I shared my vision with my staff the next day. We decided to hold a huge Christmas candlelight service in the middle of the cemetery.

We lit the entire cemetery with twinkle lights and lined the roads with luminaries. We found a forty-foot Christmas tree and set it up near a bonfire. Local choirs sang as we served hot chocolate and cider. Families came in droves. We all prayed, sang, hugged, and shared together. Special ornaments created by family members in honor of their loved ones were hung on the tree in a special dedication ceremony. It was the most touching, poignant night. We lit tiny candles and together we healed as we made it through the holidays. Stories, memories, and poems were offered by those who realized that night that they were not alone.

I later shared the experience and details of our success at the International Cemetery and Funeral Association annual meeting. I offered a workbook helping other cemeteries and funeral homes around the world to do the same. I am so touched and encouraged when I think about the families who have found hope and healing just because my team and I dared to listen and use what we heard in order to give.

It's all inside us, David. It's all there. We just have to find ourselves first so that we recognize the wisdom we came equipped with when we need it. How often we fail to speak up for fear that we are wrong or that we will be laughed at. I've been laughed at more than most, and I've usually had the last laugh because of the opportunities that were made available to me as a result of being courageous enough to step out of my comfort zone.

There is a scripture verse that reminds us that all things work for the good of those who love God and are called according to His purpose (Romans 8:28). This promise keeps me going when I feel like quitting. I am passionate for truth in everything and everybody. I think that once we find truth, our judgment of others and our criticism fades away in its light.

Many people are not willing to accept or look at truth. I find it amusing when people we know well refuse to admit things that are blatantly apparent to everyone around them. Masks are worn by most of us at some time or another because we cannot stand to deal with the truth. I can personally recall times when I've refused to admit something about myself that I didn't like. I acted like the situation just didn't exist and expected others to believe that it didn't. All the while, the only one who was fooled was me. It isn't easy to face the ugliness we sometimes find within us. It is often easier to hide from something we don't like rather than face it and confront that which keeps us in bondage. Truth in oneself requires great maturity, which I believe is an equal amount of courage and consideration.

Open, honest communication allows us to uncover truth if we are dedicated to its end. Unfortunately, the process is like any honorable attempt—it often gets harder before it gets easier. We have to believe in the end result and be willing to subject our pride to a greater truth—understanding. We will never be able to walk in another's shoes, but we can certainly let others take us for a walk with them. And in the journey, we find an understanding of the challenges faced by others.

WRIGHT

Aside from personal role models, who are the people who have served as your role models for success?

RICE

My heroes are people who dare to be true to themselves despite the cost.

Jesus is an excellent role model for me. He served His Father, His self, and the world by pursuing God's purpose for His life. Gandhi's strength of character amazes me. He left a profound example of standing for one's values. He showed us what could be possible when we stand for our own truth.

Thomas Moore's commitment to truth and honor, and Ben Franklin's obsession with self-improvement have blessed me. Steven Covey's teaching on paradigms has allowed me to achieve quantum leaps in my endeavors. His systematic, commonsense approach to success provided me with a new understanding and helped me to implement a new level of structure in my life when I needed it most.

Scott Peck and Viktor Frankl both led me to new levels of discovery.

Last, but not least, is my beloved Arthur Burt, an evangelist from Wales, who nurtured me in the early years of my Christian walk and still speaks to me in everyday life lessons. He speaks in parables. His wonderful, real stories continue to open up truth to me. I saw him last year. He is in his nineties and still beams with truth and love. He called my partner, Marion, and me "the cemetery sisters." I can still hear his sweet cockney voice reminding me "our only struggle is not to struggle."

WRIGHT

Would you tell our readers a little bit about what drives you to be successful?

RICE

Judgment Day and those I'll leave behind. I want my Creator to say, "Well done, my faithful servant." I'm driven to live a full, courageous, compassionate life so that when I say goodbye to those I love, I will leave without regret. I want to live openly, freely, truthfully. I want to be able to laugh aloud at myself, and at life, at times. I want to work hard at those things that inspire me and to give of myself without concern for what I get back. I want to live in a way that my son and grandchildren and loved ones will know that they, too, can live in freedom and joy because they are incredibly rich based alone on what lives inside them.

I am driven to live without regret and to challenge myself daily to learn and understand more about myself, others, and nature.

WRIGHT

Cyndi, you have a different approach with many issues faced in becoming a success.

RICE

When I first became a Christian, I attended a Bill Gothard seminar called, "Basic Your Conflicts." The seminar taught the importance of accepting our parents and the other things about us that we cannot change.

I did some missionary work in Salvador during their Civil War in 1987. I had the opportunity to meet the man, Rene, who organized our mission. While attending college in Salvador, he was drawn into the propaganda that infiltrated the universities at that time. He took to the hills and joined the guerrillas to fight against the government.

One lonely night he had a visitation from God and realized that he needed to be teaching truth instead of fighting. He walked away and became involved in helping to promote understanding between the various parties at war. The Full Gospel Businessmen's Fellowship organization joined forces with him to minister to the soldiers who were often only fourteen- or fifteen-year-old boys. He gathered a handful of missionaries to offer hope to the soldiers as they went to war.

Rene's father was an abusive alcoholic who took all his money and treated him terribly. Rene once told me that he prayed and asked God why God gave him this man for a father. One day, God released him from all anger and resentment. Rene realized that God knew that this type of father was the tool necessary to turn him into the man he was meant to be and allow him to fulfill important roles in his life.

Our parents are our parents. There is purpose in what they were or were not and in what they are or are not. Even when we don't see that purpose with clarity, they were God-given and right. What we make of them and how we see them is up to us.

God reminds us with the famous serenity prayer to change the things we can and accept those we can't. When we do so, we can move forward without regret.

My parents are great blessings to me. I love and honor them with all my heart. I haven't always felt this way, but it became my choice to do so. Once I made the choice, I began to see all the wonderful roles they played in my life. Each has some excellent qualities that I like to think I inherited, at least in part.

My father taught me hard work, determination, and passion. My mom taught me unconditional love, hospitality, and the ability to dream big. What great gifts to embrace. All this from a very unconventional childhood!

No matter who you are, you, too can find reasons to honor and embrace your parents. When you don't—when you reject them—you reject yourself. You don't have to feel like accepting them. Just commit to it and the commitment will open your eyes to more.

WRIGHT

You have written a book titled *Don't Conform, Connect.* What did you hope to accomplish with the book?

RICE

My goal for the book was to encourage others to do the work of discovering what lies within them.

As I've said, most people work to live up to the expectations of others while ignoring their expectations for their own life. Often we become the people our parents see us as, or the employees our employers want us to be. We often work so hard to meet the expectations of those around us that we fail to realize that our real self is dying day by day as we fail to honor the Creator's creation! Ironically, once we stop trying to please everyone around us, we actually become more than enough for all of them! We become happy, satisfied people of value. We become leaders by example. Others want to be like us. Buried within us lies a true sense of who we are and that true self is dying to be let out!

We've all known people who are just happy with who they are. They are confident, alive, and energetically moving toward their dreams.

Throughout high school, I intentionally made friends with those who had what I wanted. I wanted to learn to be like them.

One of my friends came from a very affluent family. One day I called her on the phone, and I was startled by the voice on the other end. "Hello! How are you?" This could not have been my friend. We were in eighth grade and did not answer the phone with such confidence. The way she greeted me struck a deep cord within me.

I loved hearing the smiling concern and confidence in my friend's voice. It was inviting, polite, and so mature! I made up my mind that I would begin paying attention to the way I greeted my friends. This might sound like a minor thing, but it wasn't minor to me—it's as clear to me as if it happened yesterday. As you might imagine, our graduating class voted this beautiful girl the most likely to succeed. She married a popular guy. They both became doctors and humanitarians.

> *Bewildered, bewildered,*
> *You have no complaints,*
> *You are who you are and you*
> *ain't what you ain't.*
> *So listen up buster*
> *and listen up good,*
> *Stop wishin' on bad luck and*
> *knocking on wood.*
> *Signed . . . Dear Abby*
>
> —John Prine, Dear Abby lyrics

When we know who we are and where we are going, we affect people positively in even the smallest of ways. We forget trying to please everyone because we are too busy honoring the truth that lives within us.

Have you ever tried to be someone you weren't? Have you ever tried to conform to the expectations of someone else without success? What if you had used that same energy and time adhering to the vision you have for your own life?

How many classrooms are filled with people trying to learn to be someone they are not, and probably will never be? Many of us give years of our lives to learn things we don't care to know for purposes we don't care to serve. Obviously, a basic education is important and allows us to get a taste of different areas of life in order to find our niche. Extended education, when we have no idea about where we are going and why, is wasteful and usually fruitless.

I've always been told that I am a good communicator and an easy person to talk to. We do well by listening closely to the compliments paid to us by others. Here we find some good clues as to what is inside us. In high school, we passed around what we called "slam books." These were books with each page dedicated to a student. Everyone passed it around and wrote what they thought of each person. Everyone always put "understanding" under my name. I wanted the description of "best looking" or "most popular," but no, I got "understanding"—how drab. That was in high school. Forty years later, I'm a coach, counselor, and speaker on human relations! Duh! The difference is that now I am avid about my strengths and can't wait to learn more and get better. In high school I just wanted to be someone else with different parents and a different "specialty."

"Our only struggle is not to struggle." Once we accept who we were created to be and embrace it with passion, we begin to see clearly. That clarity fuels us with an energy, confidence, and passion that produce fruit, prosperity, and abundance.

The next step is connection. By connecting with like-minded people who also realize their purpose, we find the synergy that makes work fun.

WRIGHT

You're very proud of your accomplishments in speaking and radio and your title as Distinguished Toastmaster. Why are these so important to you?

RICE

Communication is such a key element in every area of success and happiness. We can live with disagreement if we understand the source of the disagreement. Disagreement is most difficult when we fail to understand the other party and, most importantly, when we fail to feel understood. People say that I'm a good communicator, yet I realize every day how much more I have to learn, especially when communicating with family, which is the real test!

WRIGHT

So how did you begin speaking and why did you choose communication and relationships as your topic?

RICE

I didn't choose it, it chose me. That's where I realized my purpose.

I was born to a fourteen-year-old mother and a seventeen-year-old father. I was the oldest of seven. As you might imagine, I learned to communicate right out of the womb. Who else was going to boss my siblings around?

I learned to communicate because I felt as though I had to be in charge. My siblings didn't necessarily agree, but I didn't mind. As I grew up, I needed to tell someone how things should be. My mom was easy to please, and my dad was always working and difficult to communicate with. I found respite though letters. I wrote long letters from my heart with my questions, thoughts, hurts, and hopes and left them at night for my parents. As I wrote, I gained some insight and understanding and felt comforted. My dad later told me that my letters made him cry.

It all made perfect sense to me! This may have been my introduction to counseling and coaching. It worked for me. I'm still bossy, and my sisters still remind me of how rough I was on them. Hopefully I've adapted those early skills into tools that help me to work with others in effective ways.

WRIGHT

I'm bossy too; I choose to call it forcefully helpful.

RICE

That's a good way to express it!

WRIGHT

So in addition to helping many people during your life, you've been successful at turning businesses around. What is your fundamental business strategy and how does it differ from coaching individuals?

RICE

Companies are like people. A company has an identity and strengths, weaknesses, and a personality. It has gifts to share with the world, and those gifts should be its focus. To empower a company, clean out the closet! Uncover the real goods and then entrust the very best people available to deliver them to the public. Uncover, accentuate, and capitalize the assets, minimize the liabilities, and focus on the core—the people who are the life blood of the company. Find their energy, find out what turns them on and you'll turn the company on. See that their needs are met in fulfilling the needs of the company. Find passionate, unbalanced people who are driven to succeed!

I'm a huge proponent of assessments. I use assessments that provide dependable information as to whether employees can do their jobs, how they will do their jobs, and if they will like doing their jobs. When you find someone who finds joy in doing the job well, assess him or her to find out if the person is a fit for the team culture. If the relationship between owner, company, and team member are all mutually beneficial, you're well on your way to success. Everything else is easy. Systems are tangible and marketing is basic. People are crucial. Now let the team clarify the vision, then clarify the vision, and then clarify the vision again!

I'm currently working on a project in Pittsburgh. The Pittsburgh Steelers just won a seat in the playoffs, so football is on my mind. What good would a talented, well-rounded, passionate team of football players be if they didn't know who the halfback was and where the goal was located?

Be a great coach to your team by listening and implementing what you hear from the players. Know them, help them, and find and identify their goals. Show them how to connect with the rest of the team and Go for it!

WRIGHT

One of your favorite speeches is called "I Hope You LAF." Would you tell our readers about that?

RICE

I hope you LAF!

L = Listen—Learn to listen with your whole heart. Listen to your Creator, your heart, your conscience, your intuition, and your still, small voice within. Listen to others. Although this takes a lot of energy, the rewards will empower you and move you to excellence. Listen with your eyes, your ears, your heart, and your spirit. Really feel the person speaking to you. The real issues will begin to appear and so will the solutions. Healing will take place in your presence. Soon you will find a wealth of solutions available to you. Answers to your questions will become apparent and others will heal before your eyes. In this way we give, we learn, and we find understanding.

A = Acceptance—Accept the things you can't change. Accept who you are, who you aren't, how you look, your parents, your age, your past. The real issues will begin to appear and so will the solutions. Healing will take place in your presence.

Accept others—just as they are. Accept that others also need space to find their own truth. We prevent them from finding their own truth when we judge them and reject them. Accept that we are all only human in this journey toward success. We make mistakes, we learn from them, and we move on together in grace. We need acceptance as we search for our true identity.

Accept that this life is a journey—move ahead with faith and determination to uncover your own treasure. Accept what you hear from within as part of the process. Don't stop at the junk on the top. Keep digging—you'll find the good stuff.

F = *Forgive*—Forgive your past, forgive yourself, and forgive others. Turn past mistakes into fertilizer for your future dreams. Forgive people who have hurt or harmed you. When you forgive, you are not giving someone a license to hurt you, and you are not saying that it was okay; you are simply letting go of some very heavy baggage—baggage that you do not need and that will hold you back. When you forgive and ask forgiveness, you set yourself free from the ugliness of anger and bitterness. You have more energy to fuel your own journey. You are choosing to look forward instead of backward.

WRIGHT

Well, what a good conversation. This has been great, Cyndi. I have really enjoyed talking with you. I've learned a lot and I've taken a lot of notes. I think our readers are really going to get a lot out of this chapter. I appreciate all the time you've taken to answer these questions.

RICE

You have blessed me, David. Thank you so much for taking time to speak with me. I hope that we can have a conversation in the future where *I* can ask *you* the questions!

WRIGHT

Today I have been talking with Cyndi Savage Rice, speaker, trainer, coach, consultant, and author of the book *Don't Conform, Connect.* Cyndi has enjoyed more than thirty-eight years as a consultant, speaker, and business leader.

Cyndi, thank you so much for being with us today on *ROADMAP to Success*.

RICE

Thank you, David.

About the Author

Cyndi is married to a handsome firefighter, David, who works in Jacksonville Beach, Florida. Cyndi loves gardening and walking on the beach where she practices "listening" to God. She enjoys spending time with her creative son, Hank, and her two granddaughters, Tori and Ashley. Snow skiing, mountain climbing, dancing, and yoga help her to stay in shape while having fun. She is committed to good health, open and honest relationships, her Christian faith, and standing up for the values that made America great.

Cyndi Savage Rice

Transformations
10 Marlin Ave
Ponte Vedra Beach, FL 32082
904-361-8302
cyndisrice@gmail.com
www.transformationconsulting.net

Chapter Twelve

AN INTERVIEW WITH

DR. KENNETH BLANCHARD

DAVID WRIGHT (WRIGHT)

Few people have created a positive impact on the day-to-day management of people and companies more than Dr. Kenneth Blanchard, who is known around the world simply as Ken, a prominent, gregarious, sought-after author, speaker, and business consultant. Ken is universally characterized by friends, colleagues, and clients as one of the most insightful, powerful, and compassionate men in business today. Ken's impact as a writer is far-reaching. His phenomenal best-selling book, *The One Minute Manager*®, coauthored with Spencer Johnson, has sold more than thirteen million copies worldwide and has been translated into more than twenty-five languages. Ken is Chairman and "Chief Spiritual Officer" of the Ken Blanchard Companies. The organization's focus is to energize organizations around the world with customized training in bottom line business strategies based on the simple yet powerful principles inspired by Ken's best-selling books.

Dr. Blanchard, welcome to *ROADMAP to Success*.

DR. KEN BLANCHARD (BLANCHARD)

Well, it's nice to talk with you, David. It's good to be here.

WRIGHT

I must tell you that preparing for your interview took quite a bit more time than usual. The scope of your life's work and your business, the Ken Blanchard Companies, would make for a dozen fascinating interviews.

Before we dive into the specifics of some of your projects and strategies, will you give our readers a brief synopsis of your life—how you came to be the Ken Blanchard we all know and respect?

BLANCHARD

Well, I'll tell you, David, I think life is what you do when you are planning on doing something else. I think that was John Lennon's line. I never intended to do what I have been doing. In fact, all my professors in college told me that I couldn't write. I wanted to do college work, which I did, and they said, "You had better be an administrator." So I decided I was going to be a Dean of Students. I was provisionally accepted into my master's degree program and then provisionally accepted at Cornell because I never could take any of those standardized tests.

I took the college boards four times and finally got 502 in English. I don't have a test-taking mind. I ended up in a university in Athens, Ohio, in 1966 as an Administrative Assistant to the Dean of the Business School. When I got there, he said, "Ken, I want you to teach a course. I want all my deans to teach." I had never thought about teaching because they said I couldn't write, and teachers had to publish.

He put me in the manager's department. I've taken enough bad courses in my day and I wasn't going to teach one. I really prepared and had a wonderful time with the students. I was chosen as one of the top ten teachers on the campus coming out of the chute. I just had a marvelous time.

A colleague by the name of Paul Hersey was chairman of the Management Department. He wasn't real friendly to me initially because the Dean had led me into his department, but I heard he was a great teacher. He taught organizational behavior and leadership. So I said, "Can I sit in on your course next semester?"

"Nobody audits my courses," he replied. "If you want to take it for credit, you're welcome."

I couldn't believe it. I had a doctoral degree and he wanted me to take his course for credit, so I signed up. The registrar didn't know what to do with me because I already had a doctorate, but I wrote the papers and took the course, and it was great.

In June 1967, Hersey came into my office and said, "Ken, I've been teaching in this field for ten years. I think I'm better than anybody, but I can't write. I'm a nervous wreck, and I'd love to write a textbook with somebody. Would you write one with me?"

I said, "We ought to be a great team. You can't write and I'm not supposed to be able to, so let's do it!"

Thus began this great career of writing and teaching. We wrote a textbook called *Management of Organizational Behavior: Utilizing Human Resources*. It just came out in its eighth edition last year and has sold more than any other textbook in that area over the years. It's been nearly thirty-five years since that book came out. I quit my administrative job, became a professor, and ended up working my way up the ranks.

I obtained a sabbatical leave and went to California for one year twenty-five years ago. I ended up meeting Spencer Johnson at a cocktail party. He wrote children's books—a wonderful series called *Value Tales for Kids* including, *The Value of Courage: The Story of Jackie Robinson*, and *The Value of Believing In Yourself: The Story Louis Pasteur*. My wife, Margie, met him first and said, "You guys ought to write a children's book for managers because they won't read anything else."

That was my introduction to Spencer. So, *The One Minute Manager* was really a kid's book for big people. That is a long way from saying that my career was well planned.

WRIGHT

Ken, what and/or who were your early influences in the areas of business, leadership, and success? In other words, who shaped you in your early years?

BLANCHARD

My father had a great effect on me. He was retired as an admiral in the Navy and had a wonderful philosophy. I remember when I was elected to president of the seventh grade, and I came home all pumped up. My father said, "Son, it's great that you're the president of the seventh grade, but now that you have that leadership position, don't ever use it. Great leaders are followed because people respect them and like them, not because they have power." That was a wonderful lesson for me early on. He was just a great model for me. I got a lot from him.

Then I had this wonderful opportunity in the mid 1980s to write a book with Norman Vincent Peale. He wrote *The Power of Positive Thinking*. I met him when he was eighty-six years old when we were asked to write a book on ethics together, *The Power of Ethical Management: Integrity Pays, You Don't Have to Cheat to Win*. It didn't matter what we were writing together,

I learned so much from him, and he just built the positive stuff I learned from my mother.

When I was born, my mother said that I laughed before I cried, I danced before I walked, and I smiled before I frowned. So that, on top of Norman Vincent Peale's influence, really affected me as I focused on what I could do to train leaders. How do you make them positive? How do you make them realize that it's not about them, it's about whom they are serving? It's not about their position—it's about what they can do to help other people win.

So, I'd say my mother and father, then Norman Vincent Peale, had a tremendous effect on me.

WRIGHT

I can imagine. I read a summary of your undergraduate and graduate degrees. I had assumed you studied Business Administration, Marketing Management, and related courses. Instead, at Cornell you studied Government and Philosophy. You received your master's from Colgate in Sociology and Counseling and your PhD from Cornell in Educational Administration and Leadership. Why did you choose this course of study? How has it affected your writing and consulting?

BLANCHARD

Well, again, it wasn't really well planned out. I originally went to Colgate to get a master's degree in Education because I was going to be a Dean of Students over men. I had been a government major because it was the best department at Cornell in the Liberal Arts School. It was exciting. We would study what the people were doing at the league governments. And then, the Philosophy Department was great. I just loved the philosophical arguments. I wasn't a great student in terms of getting grades, but I'm a total learner. I would sit there and listen, and I would really soak it in.

When I went over to Colgate and took some education courses; they were awful. They were boring. The second week, I was sitting at the bar at the Colgate Inn saying, "I can't believe I've been here two years for this." This is just the way the Lord works—sitting next to me in the bar was a young sociology professor who had just gotten his PhD at Illinois. He was staying at the Inn. I was moaning and groaning about what I was doing, and he said, "Why don't you come and major with me in Sociology? It's really exciting."

"I can do that?" I asked.

He said, "Yes."

I knew they would probably let me do whatever I wanted the first week. Suddenly, I switched out of Education and went with Warren Ramshaw. He had a tremendous affect on me. He retired a few years ago as the leading professor at Colgate in the Arts and Sciences, and got me interested in leadership and organizations. That's why I got a master's in Sociology.

The reason I went into Educational Administration and Leadership? It was a doctoral program I could get into because I knew the guy heading up the program. He said, "The greatest thing about Cornell is that you will be in a School of Education. It's not very big, so you don't have to take many Education courses, and you can take stuff all over the place."

There was a marvelous man by the name of Don McCarty who ended up going on to be the Dean of the School of Education, Wisconsin. He had an effect on my life, but I was always just searching around. My mission statement is: to be a loving teacher and example of simple truths that help myself and others to awaken the presence of God in our lives. The reason I mention "God" is that I believe the biggest addiction in the world is the human ego, but I'm really into simple truth. I used to tell people I was trying to get the B.S. out of the Behavioral Sciences.

WRIGHT

I can't help but think when you mentioned your father, and how he just bottomed-lined it for you about leadership.

BLANCHARD

Yes.

WRIGHT

Years and years ago when I went to a conference in Texas, a man I met, Paul Myers, told me, "David, if you think you're a leader, and you look around and no one is following you, you're just out for a walk."

BLANCHARD

Well, you'd get a kick—I'm just reaching over to pick up a picture of Paul Myers on my desk. He's a good friend, and he's a part of our Center for FaithWalk Leadership, where we're trying to challenge and equip people to lead like Jesus. It's non-profit. I tell people I'm not an evangelist because we've got enough trouble with the Christians we have, we don't need any more new ones. But, this is a picture of Paul on top of a mountain, and there's another picture below of him under the sea with stingrays. It says, "Attitude is Everything." Whether you're on the top of the mountain or the bottom of the sea, true happiness is achieved by accepting God's promises, and by having a biblically positive frame of mind. Your attitude is everything." Isn't that something?

WRIGHT

He's a fine, fine man. He helped me tremendously.

I want to get a sense from you about your success journey. Many people know you best from *The One Minute Manager* books you coauthored with Spencer Johnson. Would you consider these books as a high water mark for you, or have you defined success for yourself in different terms?

BLANCHARD

Well, *The One Minute Manager* was an absurdly successful book, so quickly that I found I couldn't take credit for it. It was published around the time when I really got on my own spiritual journey and started to try to find out what the real meaning of life and success was. That's been a wonderful journey for me.

The problem with most people is they think their self-worth is a function of their performance plus the opinion of others. The minute you think that is what your self-worth is, your self-worth is up for grabs every day because your performance is going to fluctuate on a day-to-day basis. People are fickle. Their opinions are going to go up and down. You need to ground your self-worth in the unconditional love that God has ready for us, and that really grew out of the unbelievable success of *The One Minute Manager*. When I started to realize where all that came from, that's how I got involved in the ministry I mentioned. Paul Myers is a part of it. As I started to read the Bible, I realized that everything I've ever written about or taught, Jesus did. You know, He did it with twelve incompetent guys that he hired. The only guy with much education was Judas, and he was His only turnover problem.

WRIGHT

Right.

BLANCHARD

It was a really interesting thing. What I see in people is not only do they think their self-worth is a function of their performance plus the opinion of others, but they measure their success on the amount of accumulation of wealth, on recognition, power, and status. I think those are nice success items. There's nothing wrong with those, as long as you don't define your life by that. What I think you need to focus on rather than success is what Bob Buford, in his book *Halftime,* calls significance—you know, moving from success to significance.

I think the opposite of accumulation of wealth is generosity. I wrote a book called *The Generosity Factor* with Truett Cathy, who is the founder of Chick-fil-A, one of the most generous men I've ever met in my life. I thought we needed to have a model of generosity. It's not only your treasure, but it's time and talent. Truett and I added *touch* as a fourth one.

The opposite of recognition is service. I think you become an adult when you realize you're here to serve rather than to be served. Finally, the opposite of power and status are loving relationships. Take Mother Teresa, as an example. She couldn't have cared less about recognition, power, and status because she was focused on generosity, service, and loving relationships, but she got all of that earthly stuff. If you focus on the earthly, such as money, recognition, and power, you're never going to get to significance. But if you focus on significance, you'll be amazed at how much success can come your way.

WRIGHT

I spoke with Truett Cathy recently and was impressed by what a down-to-earth good man he seems to be. When my friends found out that I had talked to him they said, "Boy, he must be a great Christian man, but he's rich." I said, "Well, to put his faith into perspective, by closing on Sunday it cost him $500 million a year." He lives his faith, doesn't he?

BLANCHARD

Absolutely, but he still outsells everybody else.

WRIGHT

That's right.

BLANCHARD

Chick-fil-A was chosen as the number one quick service restaurant in Los Angeles. They only have five restaurants here and they've only been here for a year.

WRIGHT

The simplest market scheme, I told him, tripped me up. I walked by the first Chick-fil-A I had ever seen, and some girl came out with chicken stuck on toothpicks and handed me one; I just grabbed it and ate it, it's history from there on.

BLANCHARD

Yes, I think so. It's really special. It is so important that people understand generosity, service, and loving relationships because too many people are running around like a bunch of peacocks. You even see pastors who say, how many in your congregation? Authors, how many books have you sold? Business, what's your profit margin? What's your sales? The reality is that's all well and good, but I think what you need to focus on is relationships. I think if business did that more and we got Wall Street off our backs with all the short-term evaluation, we'd be a lot better off.

WRIGHT

Absolutely. There seems to be a clear theme that winds through many of your books that have to do with success in business and organizations. It is how people are treated by management and how they feel about their value to a company. Is this an accurate observation? If so, can you elaborate on it?

BLANCHARD

Yes, it's a very accurate observation. See, I think the profit is the applause you get for taking care of your customers and creating a motivating environment for your people. Very often people think that business is only about your bottom line. But no, that happens to be the result of creating raving fan customers, which I've described with Sheldon Bowles in our book, *Raving Fans*. Customers want to brag about you, if you create an environment where people can be gung-ho and committed. You've got to take care of your customers and your people, and then your cash register is going to go ka-ching! and you can make some big bucks.

WRIGHT

I noticed that your professional title with the Ken Blanchard Companies is somewhat unique—Chairman and Chief Spiritual Officer. What does your title mean to you personally and to your company? How does it affect the books you choose to write?

BLANCHARD

I remember having lunch with Max DuPree one time. He is the legendary Chairman of Herman Miller. Max wrote a wonderful book called *Leadership Is An Art*. I asked him, "What's your job?"

"I basically work in the vision area," he replied.

"Well, what do you do?" I asked.

He said, "I'm like a third grade teacher. I say our vision and values over, and over, and over again until people get it right, right, right."

I decided from that, I was going to become the Chief Spiritual Officer, which means I would be working in the vision, values, and energy part of our business.

I ended up leaving a morning message every day for everybody in our company. We have about 275 to 300 around the country, in Canada, and the U.K. Then we have partners in about thirty nations.

I leave a voice mail every morning, and I do three things on that as Chief Spiritual Officer. One, people tell me who we need to pray for. Two, people tell me who we need to praise—our unsung heroes and people like that. And then three, I leave an inspirational morning message. I really am the cheerleader—the energy bunny—in our company, and the reminder of why we're here and what we're trying to do.

We think that our business in the Ken Blanchard Companies is to help people to lead at a higher level, and help individuals and organizations. Our mission statement is to unleash the power and potential of people and organizations for the common good. So if we are going to do that, we've really got to believe in that. I'm working on getting more Chief Spiritual

Officers around the country. I think it's a great title and we should get more of them.

WRIGHT

So those people for whom you pray, where do you get the names?

BLANCHARD

The people in the company tell me who needs help—whether it's a spouse who is sick, or kids who are sick, or they are worried about something. We have over five years of data about the power of prayer, which is pretty important.

This morning, my inspirational message was about an event my wife and five members of my company participated in. They walked sixty miles last weekend—twenty miles a day for three days—to raise money for breast cancer research. It was amazing. I went down and waved them all in as they came. There was a ceremony, and 7.6 million dollars was raised. There were over three thousand people walking, and many of the walkers were dressed in pink. They were cancer victors—people who had overcome cancer. There were even men walking with pictures of their wives who had died from breast cancer. I thought it was incredible.

There wasn't one mention in the major San Diego papers on Monday. I said, "Isn't that just something." We have to be an island of positive influence because all you see in the paper today is about Michael Jackson and Scott Peterson and Kobe Bryant and this kind of thing, and here you get all these thousands of people out there walking and trying to make a difference, and nobody thinks it's news. So every morning I pump people up about what life's about, about what's going on. That's what my Chief Spiritual Officer is about.

WRIGHT

I had the pleasure of reading one of your current releases, *The Leadership Pill.*

BLANCHARD

Yes.

WRIGHT

I must admit that my first thought was how short the book was. I wondered if I was going to get my money's worth, which by the way, I most certainly did. Many of your books are brief and based on a fictitious story. Most business books in the market today are hundreds of pages in length and are read almost like a textbook. Will you talk a little bit about why you write these short books and about the premise of *The Leadership Pill*?

BLANCHARD

I developed my relationship with Spencer Johnson when we wrote *The One Minute Manager*. As you know, he wrote *Who Moved My Cheese*, which was a phenomenal success. He wrote children's books, and I was a storyteller.

My favorite books were, *Jonathan Livingston Seagull* and *The Little Prince*. They are all great parables. I started writing parables because people can get into the story and learn the contents of the story. They don't bring their judgmental hats into reading. You write a regular book and they'll say, "Well, where did you get the research?" They get into that judgmental side. Our books get them emotionally involved and they learn.

The Leadership Pill is a fun story about a pharmaceutical company that thinks they have discovered the secret to leadership, and they can put the ingredients in a pill. When they announce it, the country goes crazy because everybody knows we need more effective leaders. When they release it, it outsells Viagra. The founders of the company start selling off stock and they call them Pillionaires. But along comes this guy who calls himself "the effective manager," and he challenges them to a no-pill challenge. If they identify two non-performing groups, he'll take on one and let somebody on the pill take another one, and he guarantees he will out-perform by the end of the year. They agree, but of course, they give him a drug test every week to make sure he's not sneaking pills on the side.

I wrote the book with Marc Muchnick, who is a young guy in his early thirties. We did a major study of what this interesting "Y" generation—the young people of today—want from leaders, and this is a secret blend that this effective manager in the *Leadership Pill* book uses.

When you think about it, David, it is really powerful on terms of what people want from a leader. Number one, they want integrity. A lot of people have talked about that in the past, but these young people will walk if they see people say one thing and do another. A lot of us walk to the bathroom and out into the halls to talk about it. But these people will quit. They don't want somebody to say something and not do it.

The second thing they want is a partnership relationship. They hate superior/subordinate. I mean, what awful terms those are. You know, the "head" of the department and the hired "hands"—you don't even give them a head. "What do you do? I'm in supervision. I see things a lot clearer than these stupid idiots." They want to be treated as partners. If they can get a financial partnership, great. If they can't, they really want a minimum of psychological partnership where they can bring their brains to work and make decisions.

Then finally, they want affirmation. They not only want to be caught doing things right, but they want to be affirmed for who they are. They want to be known as a person, not as a number. So those are the three ingredients that this effective manager uses. They are wonderful values if you think of them.

Rank-order values for any organization is number one, integrity. In our company, we call it ethics. It is our number one value.

The number two value is partnership. In our company, we call it relationships.

Number three is affirmation, which means being affirmed as a human being. I think that ties into relationships, too. They are wonderful values that can drive behavior in a great way.

WRIGHT

I believe most people in today's business culture would agree that success in business is everything to do with successful leadership. In *The Leadership Pill*, you present a simple but profound premise, that leadership is not something you do *to* people, it's something you do *with* them. At face value, that seems incredibly obvious, but you must have found in your research and observations that leaders in today's culture do not get this. Would you speak to that issue?

BLANCHARD

Yes, and I think what often happens in this is the human ego, you know. There are too many leaders out there who are self-serving. They're not serving leaders. They think the sheep are there for the benefit of the shepherd. All the power, money, fame, and recognition moves up the hierarchy, and they forget that the real action in business is not up the hierarchy—it's in the one-to-one, moment-to-moment interactions that your front line people have with your customers. It's how the phone is answered. It's how problems are dealt with and those kinds of things. If you don't think that you're doing leadership with them, rather you're doing it to them, after a while they won't take care of your customers.

I was at a store recently (not Nordstrom's, where I normally would go) and I thought of something I had to share with my wife, Margie. I asked the guy behind the counter in Men's Wear, "Can I use your phone?"

"No!" he replied.

"You're kidding me," I said, surprised. "I can always use the phone at Nordstrom's."

"Look, buddy," he said, "they won't let *me* use the phone here. Why should I let you use the phone?"

That is an example of leadership that's done to them not with them. People want a partnership. People want to be involved in a way that really makes a difference.

WRIGHT

Dr. Blanchard, the time has flown by and there are so many more questions I'd like to ask you. In closing, would you mind sharing with our readers some thoughts on success? If you were mentoring a small group of men and women, and one of their central goals was to become successful, what kind of advice would you give them?

BLANCHARD

Well, I would first of all say, "What are you focused on?" I think if you are focused on success as being, as I said earlier, accumulation of money, recognition, power, or status, I think you've got the wrong target. I think what you need to really be focused on is how can you be generous in the use of your time and your talent and your treasure and touch. How can you serve people rather than be served? How can you develop caring, loving relationships with people?

My sense is that if you will focus on those things, success in the traditional sense will come to you. I think you become an adult when you realize that you are here to give rather than to get. You're here to serve not to be served. I would just say to people, "Life is such a very special occasion. Don't miss it by aiming at a target that bypasses other people, because we're really here to serve each other." So that's what I would share with people.

WRIGHT

Well, what an enlightening conversation, Dr. Blanchard. I really want you to know how much I appreciate all this time you've taken with me for this interview. I know that our readers will learn from this, and I really appreciate your being with us today.

BLANCHARD

Well, thank you so much, David. I really enjoyed my time with you. You've asked some great questions that made me think, but I hope are helpful to other people because as I say, life is a special occasion.

WRIGHT

Today I have been talking with Dr. Ken Blanchard. He is the author of the phenomenal best-selling book, *The One Minute Manager*. Also, the fact that he's the Chief Spiritual Officer of his company should give us all cause to think about how we are leading our companies and leading our families and leading anything, whether it is in church or civic organizations. I know I will.

Thank you so much, Dr. Blanchard, for being with us today.

BLANCHARD

Good to be with you, David.

About the Author

Few people have created more of a positive impact on the day-to-day management of people and companies than Dr. Kenneth Blanchard, who is known around the world simply as "Ken."

When Ken speaks, he speaks from the heart with warmth and humor. His unique gift is to speak to an audience and communicate with each individual as if they were alone and talking one-on-one. He is a polished storyteller with a knack for making the seemingly complex easy to understand.

Ken has been a guest on a number of national television programs, including *Good Morning America and The Today Show*, and has been featured in *Time, People, U.S. News & World Report*, and a host of other popular publications.

He earned his bachelor's degree in Government and Philosophy from Cornell University, his master's degree in Sociology and Counseling from Colgate University, and his PhD in Educational Administration and Leadership from Cornell University.

Dr. Ken Blanchard

The Ken Blanchard Companies
125 State Place
Escondido, California 92029
800-728-6000
Fax: 760-489-8407
www.blanchardtraining.com

Chapter Thirteen

USE CONFLICT, CREATE SUCCESS!

DAVE GERBER

DAVID WRIGHT (WRIGHT)

Dave Gerber is a nationally known speaker, trainer, coach, author, and leadership coach. As an expert in conflict, he has helped more than fifteen thousand professionals use conflict to significantly influence their organization, build high performance teams, and develop relationships to increase performance, collaboration, and revenue! Dave works with C-suite executives, HR directors, leaders, and employees. He designs and delivers training/coaching/ADR to the corporate, non-profit, pharmaceutical, military, intelligence, space, manufacturing, and many other communities. Dave has written three books on conflict, has a BA and MEd, and is credentialed as an ACC coach, and he has ten certificates in conflict and leadership from Georgetown University, Notre Dame, George Mason University (NVMS), and others.

Dave, welcome to *ROADMAP to Success.*

What is your definition of conflict?

DAVE GERBER (GERBER)

Conflict occurs when anything or anyone gets in the way of something we truly need or want. Some might consider conflict between people about the end result of an issue or how they will get to the end result. More formal definitions include concepts like open clashes between groups or opposition between two simultaneous but incompatible feelings.

The reality is that conflict is both negative and positive—both a risk and an opportunity. We're all familiar with negative conflict. It can:

- Create more conflict
- Eliminate "response-ability"
- Create physiological responses that impede our ability to make sound, cognitive, logical decisions
- Sabotage decision-making
- Undermine creativity
- Re-emphasize our past poor decision-making
- Trigger our default behavior that creates more conflict
- Cause anxiety, mental and physical stress, and/or sickness
- Annihilate respect and trust
- Impede our ability to move forward internally or with others
- Create war

Positive conflict, however, may often be the only way to proactively deal with issues that people or groups need to address. Conflict can be the beginning of a great thing or the ending of something that needs closure. It can:

- Be the start of something new
- Initiate change
- Provide necessary closure
- Positively redirect something off track
- Leverage diversity
- Promote understanding
- Support dialogue
- Enlighten someone who is unaware of a problem
- Be the start of something unexpected
- Become a life-long learning opportunity
- Foster self-esteem
- Reinforce our current abilities, strengths, or contributions
- Help work to ensure life-long happiness

Even though it is positive, it may not be easy or painless to manage. Creating a mentality that promotes using conflict will help avoid the costly and difficult by-products of negative conflict.

WRIGHT

What is the difference between internal and external conflict?

GERBER

Internal conflict can mean feeling: torn about a situation, anger or fear in response to a situation or any disruptive thing we are dealing with in our lives that distracts us from feeling good and moving forward.

I would argue that much inner conflict can be traced to unmet needs or a belief system that is driven by symbols of success (e.g., home, car, affluence, family). In fact, we have twice as many material possessions but are reported by several experts to be nearly twice as unhappy as people were in the 1950s. We consistently compare ourselves to other people, other circumstances, other results, "the Joneses." This form of measurement creates suffering, which promotes internal conflict.

Measuring and understanding the type, amount, source, variables, and depth of internal conflict is necessary to make lasting changes. Our internal conflict may have roots in our childhood, adolescence, and young adult lives all wrapped into one. It could be anything from a situation we are dealing with now to an unmet childhood need, masking itself as a present pain.

Many people I have spoken with agree that the pain we will have to go through to grow may be more intense than the discomfort we currently feel; it's the Pain Portal. Nevertheless, it must be experienced to grow. If we are willing to take that step, then and only then will we see things the way they really are. "On the other side of every fear there is a freedom"— Marilyn Ferguson.

External Conflict

Conflict that is directed toward us may manifest as some more recognizable feeling such as irritation, envy, depression, or bitterness. Actually, these are all effects of a belief that presumes the outside world is the cause. The reality is we are responsible for generating our own response (e.g., anger), as we are both the cause and the effect. We are responsible for our own feelings. It may be easier to avoid a situation than turn anger into calm. But in any case, we must consciously and physically decide to make that change. The desires must come from inside as an effort to reduce inner conflict.

Take a moment to remember a time when you were upset. Didn't you see the world and those in it as the reason for being upset? Conversely, consider a moment when you felt great peace of mind. To whom did you give credit for that feeling, yourself or the external world? Most likely the answer is you. We must create positive peace of mind for ourselves.

Making peace of mind our natural default or response to any circumstance is no easy accomplishment. It requires a willingness and serious commitment to change. Those who seem to find themselves in conflict often will obviously get more practice. But practice without the proper techniques only reinforces bad habits. We can't afford to strike out in the game of life for long, relearn what we already know, or practice bad habits.

External conflict is a signal that we need to consider making new choices and understand the conflict we feel internally. We constantly struggle with what to think and how we will feel. External choice is really about internal struggle. We are the master of our minds. We can choose.

WRIGHT

What is the difference between conflict prevention, management, and resolution?

GERBER

Imagine someone trying to cover a gaping wound with a bandage. The bleeding may stop for a brief moment with direct pressure. Could it have been easier to prevent the accident in the first place? Could that individual have chosen to wear a long sleeve shirt or a jacket, maybe some gloves before hiking through the wilderness?

Our society does not want to think about or spend the resources to prevent conflict from happening before it starts. Consider crime. If we asked a group of parents if they would be interested in more police officers, emergency, and fire personnel, most would say yes. If we then told them how much their taxes would need to increase to support the approved initiative, most would rationalize a way to say, "Everything is truly okay and nothing happens around here, so, no, I won't support it."

Taking the time, energy, money, and other resources to prevent conflict before it starts is the only way to ensure that we are as prepared as we can be when conflict rears its head; and it will, daily. Human beings equal conflict. If we believe this, we can believe that preventing conflict is smart and rational and will affect our professional and personal lives. (Whoever said that business isn't personal wasn't looking beyond his or her experience.)

Conflict prevention incorporates a wide range of thoughts, planning, actions, and follow-up that creates informal and formal policies, procedures, and practice, all with a clear and established purpose, otherwise referred to as the "4-P State of Mind."

The 4-P State of Mind is used to describe the expectations courts of law will have on a company or organization. First, there must be policies. Secondly, we must examine the purpose of the policies in order to make sure that it is correctly stated and clear to all. Then the policies must have appropriate and clear procedures about how to follow those policies or what to do if a policy is broken. Finally, just like fire drills, procedures must be practiced. Everyone—both new hires and those who have been working for a while—need a refresher course.

Would it be acceptable for a school to have a fire policy but only practice it every other year? No. Policies and procedures must be put to the test and practiced. The end goal is to proactively address the problem or at least reduce the escalation and/or damage involved.

Conflict prevention includes:

1. Engaging in self-assessment, monitoring, and positive self-talk that will allow us to avert or manage potentially disruptive conflict. Self-talk is widely viewed as the little internal discussions that, during quiet times, we have with ourselves about our lives

2. Understanding the Agents of Socialization and other root causes directly related to the conflict at hand

3. Understanding our own buttons or default behaviors enough to warn ourselves of an impending conflict and/or a potentially harmful reaction

4. Developing a prevention-oriented mindset that understands, anticipates, and proactively considers the affect of conflict in each area of personal and professional life

5. Ensuring ourselves and those around us that we are dedicated to strengthening our skills and preventing conflict in every aspect of life

Conflict prevention addresses a desire to gain the appropriate tools and skills. But this new learning is only made useful when it is applied fairly and consistently with great reflection.

Conflict management is about using a conflict prevention mentality and working toward resolution, self-awareness, and a system or procedure for immediately dealing with conflict. Our goal is to prevent the initiation of conflict, quickly facilitate a method for containment when it happens, and enable ourselves to transform the experience into solutions, calmness, growth, and life-long learning.

Conflict resolution is a method or process of extinguishing or handling a conflict, preferably quickly, by:

- Identifying the main, secondary, tertiary, and related issues
- Addressing each side's or our own internal competing needs
- Adequately addressing personal and professional interests
- Investigating unmet professional expectations
- Understanding and anticipating the possible consequences of any decision (cause and effect)
- Allowing for the customized design of solutions between the parties involved in conflict
- Including all appropriate individuals and stakeholders
- Staying solution-oriented
- Creating a plan, making choices, and confirming the outcomes.
- Developing a plan for honest, effective feedback
- Actively listening to all parties involved, without interruption.
- Resolving issues through arbitration, mediation, negotiation, alternative dispute resolution, or a court of law.

The more we focus on conflict prevention, the less conflict we will have to manage and resolve. Each of these stages is a part of the process of transforming conflict into an agent for positive change. For instance, the identification and elimination of the conditions that fuel conflict support prevention. Management is appropriate when conflict, as positive change, is critical for achieving the desired results. Resolution encompasses prevention and management, resulting in a paradigm shift and win-win solutions for all parties involved.

WRIGHT

Who gets emotionally hijacked?

GERBER

Throughout our lives almost everyone gets hijacked. When we get upset, we can get *emotionally hijacked*—a changing physiological state where blood pressure increases and chemicals are released in the brain in such a way that they feel different and their ability to think creatively and logically is limited.

When you have a panic attack or become very anxious, your emotional response can actually bypass your "thinking brain." The amygdale, a small but powerful part of the brain, is involved with creating a "faster than thought" panic attack (i.e., it triggers the attack). It is very difficult—or even impossible—to think clearly when highly emotional because the part of the brain you think with is inhibited. This response has been termed an "emotional hijacking" by Daniel Goleman.[1]

One can think of this phenomenon as the *inverse* of "being in the zone." We have heard of blinding rage or have been so frustrated that we couldn't really make rational decisions or "see straight." Goleman and most other researchers in the field agree that when this phenomenon happens, the feeling can last a minimum of ten minutes. We all have experienced the disconnect between heightened negative emotions and an inability to be creative or to problem-solve.

Consider all of the things our brain helps us do—use logic and reason, it helps us breathe, make decisions, be creative, communicate, etc. When we are really angry and get hijacked, we lose many of those functions. When this happens, we have lost our ability to work with other people to find solutions that satisfy everyone. We have essentially, for the time being, lost our minds!

We are responsible for our behavior, whether we are hijacked or not. When reactions do not pass acceptable standards, consequences generally follow. Even if responses from others are not vocalized, witnessing someone who is emotionally hijacked is difficult to forget or even overcome.

---

[1]Panic-attacks.co.uk, "Part 5: The Brain and Panic Attacks: Emotional Hijacking," *The Panic Attack Prevention Program,* 2001-2006, <http://www.panic-attacks.co.uk/panic_attacks_5.htm /> July 26, 2006 (accessed November 26, 2010).

Emotional hijacking can escalate the negativity in a relationship or situation. While we are not responsible for other people's feelings, we do contribute to them and often make it easier for people to get frustrated. Language is powerful. People under stressful situations can be sensitive. A single word may be a bridge to more conflict if we are not careful.

WRIGHT

What is the role of telling the truth and lying in conflict?

GERBER

Presenting false impressions can be a source of conflict. For some, it can become an endless river of gas feeding flames of conflict, draining the parties involved for years or even decades. It takes new lies to keep the old lies fresh.

Why do we lie? We often fear being judged or being put in a position where we have to justify our decisions, behaviors, and comments. Remember a time when you created an impression based on information that was incomplete, reorganized, or removed to change the paradigm in the head of the person with whom you were speaking with at the time?

What is a lie? We define a lie as presenting any other paradigm, regardless of how minimal the difference, than the one we believe to be true. How is information deleted, removed, or reorganized to change the paradigm? How are elements of time manipulated? While these are only a few ways to manipulate the truth, it is important to investigate what our parents and extended family socialized us to believe is the truth.

Does truth mean the entire story? If details, insignificant or not, are left out, has a lie been told? Examine the definition of a lie, above, and determine whether the closets people in our lives view it the same way. If not, why? How does each person's understanding of truth affect the amount of conflict he or she creates, internalize from the outside world, and regurgitate back into the playing field from which the person works, lives, and spend his or her free time?

So, why do we lie? We often lie because we don't want conflict, we don't want to be judged or have our desires evaluated. We don't want to feel that we have to convince others that our choices are appropriate. We do not want to spend the time, effort, or work to make communication effective, often because we were never taught the skills. We don't want guilt, more confrontation, frustration, and disagreement. We don't want conflict.

Both truth-telling and lying are always about choice. One chooses to own the consequences and ripple effect that result from a false word, thought, or behavior. Even if we do not want to be judged or have to justify our legitimate feelings to each other, we still make a choice when asked to tell the truth or when we are expected to fill in the details. Each conscious thought, spoken word, and behavior is ultimately our own to choose and live.

WRIGHT

Why should we understand the difference between positions and interests?

GERBER

Stop focusing on where we are and focus on where we need and want to be when the conflict is over. Believe that a solution is possible, even if one is not clear at the moment.

As noted by Ury and Fisher in their book, *Getting to Yes*, positions are predetermined solutions or outcomes to a situation, conflict, or problem. They represent feelings and thoughts about where we are grounded, usually only solved with a single answer, most often a discussion-stopper. Interests are the underlying needs behind the positions that must be met to feel satisfaction, not necessarily victory. These represent feelings and thoughts about where we want to be and open the box for customized solutions and new conversations.[2]

Understanding and using interest-based conflict management styles in our lives will allow us to gain closure, build trust and relationships, and move beyond difficult situations with others. This is a beneficial and healthy transition from our old, social learning or a legalistic (to versus with) approach to conflict management. People often stick to their positions because they are angry, hurt, or feeling unheard. Yet these emotions get in the way of win-win solutions.

When two people enter into conflict focused on a resolution that satisfies their needs, they tend to resort to protecting their positions, feelings, and thoughts. But if they can focus on criteria that meet both parties' interests, the solution will be more acceptable to both.

---

[2] Robert Fischer, William Ury, and Patton, Bruce, *Getting to Yes: Negotiating Agreement without Giving In*, Penguin Group, New York, NY, 1981, pp. 40–41.

Consider the question, "What do you need?" This is a much more forward thinking approach. Focusing on interests allows us to concentrate on why a particular solution is preferred. It generates explanations, not justification, and promotes progress toward a customized, designed, and clarified win-win solution. Every exchange with someone sets a precedent in the person's mind for the next set of interactions.

WRIGHT

Why should we understand interest-based problem-solving?

GERBER

Good things happen when we stop focusing on where we are and focus on where we need and want to be when the conflict is over. When we believe that a solution is possible, even if one is not clear at the moment, we are more likely to create successful outcomes.

As noted by Ury and Fisher in their book, *Getting to Yes,* positions are predetermined solutions or outcomes to a situation, conflict, or problem. They represent feelings and thoughts about where we are grounded (stuck) and are usually only solved with a single answer, most often a discussion stopper.

For example, if a couple is planning a vacation, the discussion might sound like this:

"I want to go to Bermuda."
"I want to go to Orlando."
"I want to go to Bermuda."
"I want to go to Orlando."

How long can these two have a discussion like this without creating more conflict? Both have taken a position—a pre-determined outcome—before actually speaking with one another.

Interests are the underlying needs—not necessarily victory—behind the positions that must be met to feel satisfied. These represent feelings and thoughts about where we want to be and they open the box for customized solutions and new conversations.[3]

---

[3]Robert Fischer, William Ury, and Patton, Bruce, *Getting to Yes: Negotiating Agreement without Giving In,* Penguin Group, New York, NY, 1981, pp. 40–41.

Following the example above, if we were to ask the partners their reasons for choosing that particular destination, we might learn something fascinating. He wants to go to Bermuda for good golf and restaurants and to be near the beach. She wants to go to Orlando for good restaurants, to be near the beach, and to have Disney World for the kids. During conflict, when we look further into interests, we often find that both individuals actually have many similar, overlapping needs.

Understanding and using interest-based conflict management styles in our lives allow us to move beyond difficult situations with others. This is a beneficial and healthy transition from our old, social learning. Most K-12 school systems, colleges, universities, and graduate schools do not teach this type of thinking or problem-solving. It has been taken by the negotiation world. But we should all practice this thinking to even have a chance at a winning life.

This is one of the most important elements for individuals to capture as they move through these pages. People often stick to their positions because they are angry, hurt, or feeling unheard. Yet these emotions get in the way of win-win solutions—solutions that create desired outcomes for both parties based upon underlying, spoken, or unspoken needs.

When we enter into conflict focused on resolution that satisfies only our own needs, we tend to resort to protecting our positions, feelings, and thoughts. But if we can focus on criteria that meet both parties' interests, the solution will be more acceptable to both and often not as confrontational.

Asking the question, "What do you need?" focuses us on interests and needs and allows us to concentrate on why a particular solution is preferred. It generates explanations, not justification. Negative energy is similar to feeling backed into a corner. So we think about ways to let people explain themselves rather than justify their behavior or decision-making. Working with a forward-thinking, customized, flexible approach allows for a greater success rate.

Modeled after Ury and Fischer's work, the following diagram demonstrates one way to create a pre-planning guide for difficult conversations. Best practices demonstrate that the most effective communicators can shift the dynamic, remove some of the situational tension, and demonstrate genuine interest in the other party's needs.

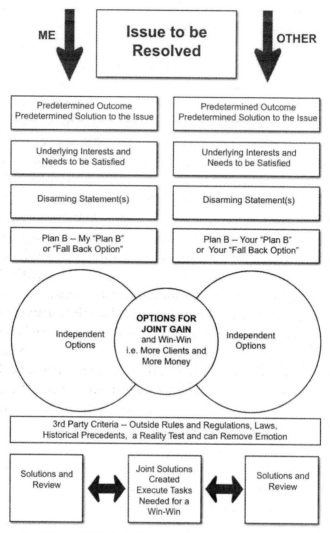

ME ↓ **Issue to be Resolved** ↓ OTHER

| Predetermined Outcome Predetermined Solution to the Issue | Predetermined Outcome Predetermined Solution to the Issue |

| Underlying Interests and Needs to be Satisfied | Underlying Interests and Needs to be Satisfied |

| Disarming Statement(s) | Disarming Statement(s) |

| Plan B -- My "Plan B" or "Fall Back Option" | Plan B -- Your "Plan B" or Your "Fall Back Option" |

Independent Options — **OPTIONS FOR JOINT GAIN** and Win-Win i.e. More Clients and More Money — Independent Options

3rd Party Criteria -- Outside Rules and Regulations, Laws, Historical Precedents, a Reality Test and can Remove Emotion

| Solutions and Review | Joint Solutions Created Execute Tasks Needed for a Win-Win | Solutions and Review |

Synergy Development & Training, LLC © 2006 & Modified from Ury and Fischer's Principles in Getting to Yes

After mutually acceptable outcomes have been generated, both parties should individually reflect on the content, outcome, and process of the conversation in order to improve the next one.

The benefits of the time taken to prepare and complete this form are numerous. When dealing with long-term solutions, conflict, or communication issues, it is best to be prepared. The following guide will help individuals feel more comfortable with the ambiguity of conflict and isolated situations. The steps to the model include:

Pre-determined Outcomes

Description: Happy or sad, right or wrong, good or bad—this is the outcome someone has in his or her head prior to the discussion taking place. Consider someone putting a stake in the ground. It is specific and definite—most often it is not a discussion-starter.

To use an earlier example, if a couple was going to discuss vacation plans, each individual might come into the discussion somewhat hard-headed, only wanting to go to the destination he or she has chosen. Imagine two people only discussing (probably forcibly) the merits of their predetermined vacation outcome.

Underlying Needs

Description: Everyone has underlying needs that drive predetermined outcomes. Examples:

- Respect
- Validation
- Recognition
- Organizational loyalty
- Build morale and high performance teams
- Money
- Family or time off
- Promotion/advancement

Disarming Technique

Description: The ability to diffuse conflict before it starts is a critical element when giving feedback. Demonstrating empathy right at the beginning of a conversation, for example, might disarm someone's anger, disappointment, or frustration level. If the underlying interests of the other party can be considered, it is possible to diffuse at the beginning of a discussion. Individuals brace for conflict. This technique will help encourage the person to relax and want to hear more because he or she now does not have to fight the original conflict.

Consider these common underlying needs to use as part of the framework for your first substantive words when having difficult conversations:

- Respect (i.e., "Before we continue, I want you to know that the company respects the quality of your work.")
- Recognition
- Validation
- Promotion/Advancement
- Accountability
- Meet the "Mission" or complete the objectives
- Money
- Family
- Loyalty
- Increased Communication and Feedback

It is vitally and fundamentally important to understand that this statement must be transparent, genuine, and appropriate for the discussion, relationship, context of the situation and more. Any opening, disarming statement that is misinterpreted as not being truthful, honest, respectful, or is misinterpreted as condescending will ultimately end up igniting more conflict.

Example:

- Apologies
- Statements of accountability
- Inquiries about family members (extremely sensitive one to use)
- Statements of respect
- Statements of appreciation
- Statements about increased feedback or communication
- Statements about loyalty or desire to support
- There are many more

Plan B

Description: A real, concrete, backup plan that is the "best/worst alternative to an agreement." It is something that can be actualized if the other party is unwilling to collaborate. It must be real and it must be able to be followed up with immediately. The ability to generate a backup plan prior to engaging in difficult conversations gives us choices. While we must be careful not to live a self-fulfilling prophecy or become negative, we do need to have options. Also, not everything is negotiable.

Examples:

- Quit
- File a Grievance
- File an EEO Complaint
- Go outside of the chain of command
- Leave (when buying a car)

Potential Outcomes

Description: Potential outcomes are created with the other party in joint brainstorming and discussions. It is recommended to brainstorm individually prior to the discussion in order to demonstrate preparation, empathy, and that we are solution-oriented.

Example: The greatest part about potential outcomes and engaging in this process is that individuals can come together to do more than they could on their own. Parties can create possibilities and solutions that are customized, within the boundaries of law, rules, regulations, and precedence, yet produce possibilities and solutions crafted to meet the needs of both parties.

Third Party Criteria

Description: Essentially, third-party criteria are those rules or guidelines that are placed upon us by someone or an organization that is greater than ourselves that dictate how creative we can be with our solutions. They help us to reality-test our results and remove the emotion from the equation (sometimes).

Examples:

- Kelley Blue Book
- Comparables on a house sale
- Rules, regulations, or laws
- Historical precedents

Solutions and Review

Description: The research shows us on many fronts, in many industries, with multiple studies that the most successful individuals are the ones who not only come to win-win solutions and meet the needs of both parties, they engage in the reflection process once the decisions are made.

Example: After decisions are made, the most successful negotiators reflect on personal verbal and non-verbal behavior, strategy, questioning techniques, the quality of listening, and if there was anything to change for the future.

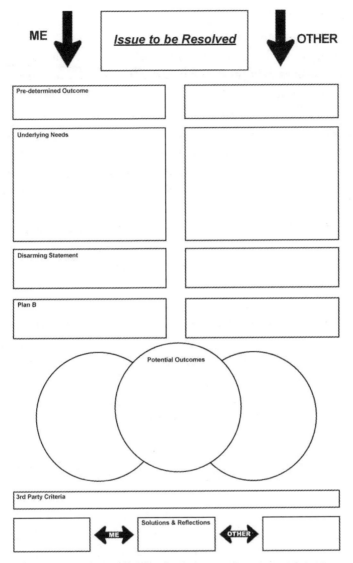

Synergy Development & Training, LLC © 2008-2011 & Modified from Ury and Fischer's Principles in Getting to Yes

By using this form to prepare for a negotiation, difficult conversation, or conflict, we can be more prepared to disarm the conflict and move to individual and mutual needs . . . and, win-win solutions.

WRIGHT

What is the difference between reacting and responding?

GERBER

Reacting versus Responding

We live in a society that is very reactive and fearful. People often feel defensive. No one likes to be judged or forced to explain why he or she did or did not do something.

The important distinction between reacting and responding is critical. Most of us react because we have not trained our brains to slow down. When we slow down in conflict, our brains have time to become flooded with options. This means we are actively choosing a response rather than allowing an internal, emotional, or physical change to dictate how we will speak or behave (i.e., react).

Reacting is a sudden, immediate internal or external action or feeling that contains lots of emotion and, quite often, no consideration of how it will affect others, including ourselves. *Responding* means to slow down and select a path, decision or behavior while considering the action itself, the people affected and the possible consequences.

The Reptilian Reaction describes how humans respond automatically to positive or negative events without consciously thinking about the consequences. It is grounded in emotion, not logic. Derived from the theory of the reptilian brain, this teaching principle describes the sequence of events in a cause-and-effect relationship. It claims that the primitive (reptilian) part of the brain controls lust, fear, hate, and love. When we *react*, we are actually operating with this primitive part, using emotion rather than logic and reason.

Reptiles and other animals do this instinctively. So do people who have not been taught to slow down and consider their immediate and long-term actions and consequences. Usually, the choice of reactive behavior is not a conscious choice at all, rather, it is a reaction that perpetuates negativity and often creates a cycle of conflict that spirals out of control.

People often resort to this behavior when their coping skills are limited or they cannot see other options. They stick with the approaches they are most comfortable with and experienced in using. But once they are consciously aware of how they feel, they can make a better choice.

While it is easy to believe that we are responding to the events in our lives, our feelings in the moment are related to our immediate, internalized interpretations and preconceived notions about the event. Therefore, the way we interpret events will often dictate our response or reptilian *react*-ion.

There are several ways to avoid reacting and to control decision-making:

1. Understand our own emotions.

   a. Understand the causes of our feelings.
   b. Become aware of our hot buttons.
   c. Develop frustration tolerance.
   d. Strengthen our sense of self-worth and reduce our dependence on external validation.

2. Recognize the isolated action.
3. Stop—do not *react*—and breathe.
   a. Avoid thinking in terms of extremes.
   b. Avoid believing that our perspective is the only one that exists.
   c. Do not over-generalize or blow things out of proportion.
   d. Do not personalize the entire conflict.
   e. Do not allow this experience to overshadow our successes.

4. Ask ourselves if it is possible that we misinterpreted what the other person said or if we were misinterpreted.
5. Step into the space of "now."
6. Acknowledge options, effect, and consequences. (What are my options for expressing my feelings?)
7. Select a response using logic rather than emotion.
8. Stated another way:

   a. Identify the action or behavior.
   b. Step willingly and knowingly into the space.
   c. Identify potential responses.
   d. Identify the consequences and effect of each option.
   e. Knowingly choose a response based upon a conscious decision.

WRIGHT

How do we honor our personal values when managing or resolving conflict?

GERBER

Values are said to be the elements in our lives that get us out of bed each day. They are the beliefs that make life worth living, whether times are good or bad. Perhaps we embrace some of the following:

- Honesty
- Accountability
- Teamwork
- Trust
- Personal growth
- Unconditional love
- Life-long learning
- Respect
- Freedom
- Recognition and validation
- Diversity

Whatever values we currently have, do we honor them in our thoughts, words, and deeds? When we are in conflict with someone, do we still honor these values that we hold true? The real question we must ask ourselves is how we actively choose to honor the most important values in our lives, even when things are not good.

WRIGHT

Why should we investigate the conflict in our lives now?

GERBER

- To improve the state of our lives and increase internal satisfaction
- To immediately improve our personal and professional relationships
- To improve our understanding of why conflict exists and how to prevent it from happening
- To develop a stronger "conflict fluency" that will help us dissect conflict in the moment
- To help create the best solutions while in conflict as our physiology changes
- To help others in our lives reduce their conflict

- To develop more tools to deal with the quickly-changing world around us
- To look at our lives from a different perspective

WRIGHT

David Gerber, I have truly enjoyed our talk today. Thank you for taking time to speak with us.

About the Author

David Gerber, President of Synergy Development and Training, is a passionate expert focused on helping organizations and individuals use conflict. He has worked with thousands of diverse participants from more than a dozen industries, including Fortune 500 businesses, intelligence community, U.S. Military, NASA, PMI WDC, state governments, and more. Dave brings fourteen years of varied conflict management, training, and coaching experiences as well. His motivating style is contagious and he is the author of three books on the subject of conflict management. In addition to having an MEd, Dave holds nearly a dozen certificates in leadership, coaching, negotiations, conflict management, and mediation.

Dave Gerber, President
Synergy Development and Training, LLC
Innovative Organizational Solutions
703-752-7588
Gerber@Synergydt.com
www.synergydt.com
www.davegerber.info
Twitter @KingofConflict
"Moving Forward Together"

Chapter Fourteen

IT CAN BE MORE THAN A DREAM

DR. IRENE PENDLETON

DAVID WRIGHT (WRIGHT)

Today I am talking with Dr. Irene Pendleton, a veteran leader, trainer, and motivational speaker. With more than twenty-seven years of federal government leadership, more than twenty years of teaching both undergraduate and graduate school at notable universities, and nearly thirty years as a board leader at national and international levels, Irene has yet to run into any industry where common language might be a problem. She is able to tie personal examples to topics at hand and demonstrate proven solutions that make sense to the listener and almost any audience. Quality is her passion and she believes that we must always strive to do our best.

Irene, welcome to *ROADMAP to Success*.

IRENE PENDLETON (PENDLETON)

Thank you, I'm very glad to be here.

WRIGHT

So what are some of the major reasons people never achieve their dreams for life?

PENDLETON

Primarily it's *lack of self confidence.* They don't believe in themselves. Perhaps they have been told they "can't do it" too many times. More often than not, the real problem is that they don't believe in themselves. They lack self-confidence and they don't believe they have choices, so they don't try. They don't get out of their comfort zone. With choices comes sacrifice, but many people are not willing to make the choices necessary to help their dreams come true. They allow others to make choices for them, to make decisions for them, and then they *blame* others because they've lost control of their own life.

Secondly it's *loss of hope.* Perhaps they have already seen failure or placed their trust and belief with the wrong person and got hurt once too often so they are not willing to try again.

Third, there may be *little or no support or encouragement from those they love.* Combine that with lack of self confidence and there is little incentive to take a risk to strike out into unknown territory.

Then lastly, it could be *fear of leaving their comfort zone.* This is sometimes reinforced by tyrannical bosses, teachers, or family. It takes a lot of perseverance and willingness to take risks to overcome this fear but it really is a matter of choices. Sometimes the underlying problem is real. Sometimes it's because the advisor failed at something and thinks it's not possible to succeed. Often it's a matter of planning or a matter of timing and setting milestones to achieve the dream.

WRIGHT

So realizing all these major reasons they never achieve their dream, why do people work in a career that is not their dream?

PENDLETON

Because they believe their own dream is impossible, they react to life rather than "live" it. They have no plan for success but they are passive and suddenly years have passed by with no action taken.

A better life begins with acknowledging your dream, creating a verbal or visual description of that dream, and taking action leading toward fulfillment.

You should love your life. So many people do not. People are locked into jobs they don't like. They don't know why they are there, but they are. The number of people who are in professions that are not their *first* choice is astonishing. Downsizing and massive layoffs have created a lot of fear and a lot of reluctance to change jobs, so people stay in jobs they don't like. With our current economic environment spiraling downward, it's even more difficult to make change. Unemployment keeps spiraling upward. Employers are more often requiring academic degrees, so it's even more important to continue your education. Too often, people believe they don't have a choice so they settle for less than their dream.

My experience with interviewing hundreds of people who are looking for a total life style change supports that idea. Many of them want to go back to school and improve their life, but they don't thoroughly research possibilities. They react to others without question or they accept marginally accurate descriptions of training or occupational opportunities and get locked into the first thing that offers a chance at survival. If they are lucky, following this route leads to a higher paying job that provides adequately for self and family. If not, the alternative may be a minimum wage job with no benefits, no security; but it fills today's most urgent need, so their dream goes out the window until "tomorrow" but then "tomorrow" never comes.

WRIGHT

Throughout my life, I've chosen to go into several businesses and various industries. My acquaintances and especially my friends have said negative things about it. I felt that they doubted I could do it or wanted me not to take the risk. Why do you think others try to talk people into not following their own dreams?

PENDLETON

They believe their own dream is impossible, so they live vicariously through others such as their child or spouse. They have their own personal agenda. Professional jealousy may be the reason. They don't want someone else to get ahead of them or get more recognition. Others may also believe life is "good enough" for them and therefore "good enough" for others, so they offer no encouragement for something different. They may believe it's a frivolous occupation or not in their realm of possibility and don't want their child or friend to get hurt. Parents always feel they know what is best for their children. Sometimes it's financial and they don't see the big picture or value in planning for the future. They see too much risk and pain in the short-term and don't see the potential for a better future for the long-term.

The whole idea of accepting this kind of advice is nonsense. We don't let others control our money. We don't let others tell us what to eat. Yet, we allow others to tell us how to live our lives and decide what our future should be. Then we are the unhappy ones who hate to get up in the morning!

WRIGHT

It's scary.

So would you tell our readers what people can do to get started on changing their life?

PENDLETON

Don't assume that all advice you receive is best for you without weighing all your options from a logical approach. Identify the pros and cons and determine how each will help you move forward or hold you back from achieving your dream.

Set goals/milestones/action plans. The choice is yours as to the direction you want to take. During your school years, you had the freedom to enjoy much of your time and with the right career that can continue. With the wrong career, you may "survive" but every day of your life you will wish you had made a different choice. Find your passion and go for it! As Confucius is credited with saying, "Find a job you love and you'll never work a day in your life."

Sometimes it takes a red flag or a critical emotional event to keep you on the path. One of my early dreams was to have a college education. I thought I wanted to be an architect but many things got in the way—family beliefs (girls didn't go to college), money, marriage, children, volunteer activities, time. For thirteen years I was in and out of courses pursuing my first degree. Then one day a favorite professor of mine said "If you keep going at this rate, it will be another *five* years before you finish—*if* you finish at all."

That was my Red Flag. When he said "if you finish at all" that said to me, get with it. Make a plan, prepare a road map, then take the first step to move forward on that plan. One year later I finished a Bachelor of Arts degree, immediately started a Master of Science degree, finished that, and went on to become the first person of my generation in my family to earn a doctorate. By the way, I didn't become an architect because by then I was sure I wanted to become a professor/teacher/speaker so that I could influence others in pursuing their dream. Once I had a clearly defined plan, I was able to relentlessly pursue it.

So to get started, create your own road map to success. Then, live every day to the fullest as if it might be your last, and make achieving your dream a top priority in your life. Keep an unwavering focus on where you are going. Make the hard choices. Don't feel like you are stuck. If you make mistakes, learn from them and move on. You can't change yesterday; that becomes history. But tomorrow is still a mystery so make your course corrections and continue with your choices.

WRIGHT

So what obstacles do people need to watch out for along the road?

PENDLETON

I see four major obstacles to achieving your dream. First, there are detours, distractions, and anything that takes you off course. As a newlywed, decades ago, I talked my husband into staying in the Navy so we could see the world. He stayed in the Navy and he did see the world, but I didn't! He deployed and saw a lot of it while I stayed at home port! So as soon as I had my degree, I started applying for jobs where I could travel and then I did see the world.

I also worked hard to get my civil service grade to the level I thought I would need to retire comfortably and be free to do what I wanted with my life. It worked! I transferred to Washington, D.C., continued to travel to some exciting places, and then took early retirement to pursue my dream.

Secondly, poor reading and writing skills will hold you back. Many of my former students, even at the graduate level, were poor readers and even worse writers so it was difficult for them to express their thoughts in words others would understand. Take whatever steps are necessary to improve those critical skills. Read a book a week—any kind and any topic is okay. Just keep reading to improve your skill in understanding and comprehension. Work on writing skills, too. Keep a journal or write in a diary. The key is to practice at every opportunity. Remember, both skills are needed for completing even basic tasks such as resumes, reports, and other workplace documents,

Third, beware of hungry recruiters for both jobs and education. Recruiters are frequently poorly educated salespeople who are driven by corporate profit motives and personal greed. Unrealistic production numbers are set to achieve "average" performance so your dream takes a back seat to the recruiter's need to perform. Don't fall into that trap. Follow your own dream, not theirs!

And fourth, your own attitude and beliefs may need to be examined. I hear so often "I have a family" or "my parents don't want me to leave home" or "I really want to learn electronics but my uncle wants me to go to business school."

Listen and evaluate but make your own choices. You can overcome each of these obstacles by sticking to your own choices and following a methodical, systematic, forward-moving direction along your personal road map. It's your dream, your choice, your plan, your life and you can do it!

WRIGHT

So how do I get started on my road map?

PENDLETON

Establish your goals for achievement using the same concepts and processes that you already use in your daily life (or in strategic business development). Figure out where you want to go. Describe your vision. What does your future look like? What do you have to know, and what do you have to do to get there? Then lastly, and most importantly, remember to clearly define your measure so you will know when you get there. You have to put your plan on paper. That's crucial. That makes it real. It becomes a tangible, almost magical, thing that you can see, speak, touch, and feel. It is *your personal* plan, your personal road map.

You've probably heard the saying "plan your work, then work your plan." The more difficult of the two is planning. The more difficult part of planning is putting the vision down on paper and laying out the goals to support that vision. As you are writing, express your vision in realistic, doable terms. Listen to your heart. Determine what your values are, what makes you tick. Make a list and prioritize it.

For example, if your list includes joy, love, friendship, security, freedom, or pleasure, determine why each of these values is more or less important to you. Ask "why." Ask "so what." Critically examine all of your assumptions. Don't just accept them. Ask why, and why, and why, and why again; then, come to an understanding with yourself that you will do what it takes to get the job done. Know where you want to be to fulfill your dream. Set goals along the way that are also achievable and realistic. Develop an attitude that allows you to think, act, and talk as you see yourself in the future. Pretend you are already living your dream. This will help keep your motivation in high gear. In simple terms, look at your dream as though it is a large pizza—you can never eat the whole thing, but you can eat a slice, then later another, and then another, and all of a sudden that huge pizza is almost gone!

Of course, you also need to plan for the necessary resources. You may not have them on day one, but your plan covers what is optimal and will serve as a guide for collecting those resources.

Lastly, the tactical portion of your plan addresses the details for the near-term. Remember, one usually must crawl before walking. Don't try to go multi-national before you have tested and succeeded at each step along the way. Be specific and include who, what, where, and when. Be realistic. Be confident. Be happy knowing it's your plan, not someone else's.

WRIGHT

Given the many successes you have achieved in your life, what major factors contribute to success?

PENDLETON

My version of "4P's" is persistence, passion, people, and plans. Make steady, forward, continuous movement by taking one step at a time toward the ultimate goal. We all have dreams and many are left in the dream stage. Don't let that happen to you. Follow your dream.

You may feel you have few choices. That is so not true. I am a living example. I know that feeling. I know what it's like to feel that you can't follow your dreams but instead have to accept an alternative because it seems to be impossible or because it pleases someone else. One branch of the military has a slogan, "Be all you can be," and I fully support those words. Anytime we achieve less than our full potential in life or in a career we can also have fun with, we are not being all we can be.

Don't put that choice in someone else's hands. It's up to you and no one else. It's your responsibility. It's your future. *You* are in charge of your own future. Surround yourself with people of like mind. Stay away from negativity. Most successful people have a mentor, so find a mentor or someone willing to share his or her ideas for success with you. Ideally, this would be someone you respect and trust who can also provide positive feedback when you are going off course. Tackle everything with a passion and have fun along the way

WRIGHT

So how does passion impact success?

PENDLETON

Passion and happiness shines through and helps sell others, whether it's you or a product. I met a young man who was an inbound call center sales employee who always had a big smile on his face. His smile transferred to his voice when he was on the phone. He was one of the most successful salespeople in the office. Real success requires that you love what you do, have a zest for it, and he did.

One of the most important things I learned during my school years was to ask the questions: so what, what are the choices, and what are the consequences of any decision? Life has dealt you a hand, what are you going to do with it now? Is your passion strong enough to fight for it? Are you going to let others run your life or are you going to make your own choices? Do you know where you are going or why you are where you are? Is it because it is your choice or someone else's? Is it because your parent is in that field and you wanted to follow in his or her footsteps? Is it because it's what your mother wants for you? If the answer is not what you dreamed of, I encourage you to get out your plan, look at it, and see what the next action should be. If you can't do that, start writing now.

If you have put the plan together properly, you will know where you are going and when you are there. You will be able to achieve your dream and you will know what you want to be. Don't be afraid; if you love doing something, you will be good at it and success and wealth will follow. Passion, therefore, becomes the motivating focus—I am who I am because I chose to be me; you, too, can be whatever you want to be and you can develop a plan to achieve your dream with passion.

WRIGHT

Many years ago I heard a man say that if I were walking down a road and saw a turtle sitting up on top of a fence post, I could believe he didn't get up there by himself. So who are the people who have been your personal role models and made you who you are today?

PENDLETON

Actually there are four people who come to mind. My grandmother taught me to read and write at a very early age; she is always first in my list. By the time I was in school, my reading habits were set for life. She also had me do memory work on long poems such as Longfellow's *Evangeline* and *Paul Revere's Ride*, which helped me understand better what I read.

A friend and coworker who was a corporate secretary for the manufacturing company where I worked at the beginning of my career is another one. Mabel belonged to an organization that sounded like an impossible dream for one from a humble working class background but I decided right then and there that one day I would be qualified to join that organization. I never lost sight of that dream and became eligible to join in my mid thirties after completing my first college degree and moving up in the business world.

The third person was a retired philosopher and friend who helped me to see the possibilities with the right planning and choices. Over time he introduced me to the ideas of Napoleon Hill, W. Clement Stone, and other successful people. He showed me how to navigate the paper bureaucracy to get noticed. At the time, promotion seemed hopeless but it did happen. I was able to use what I learned from Hill's *Think and Grow Rich* and the Science of Success Institute to strengthen my own resolve for success.

One of the more recent people who influenced me strongly was W. Edwards Deming and his quality management theories. Sitting in his four-day seminars several times and then years of teaching his principles imprinted his fourteen points in my mind, especially his "Do It Right the First Time." To this day, I have no tolerance for rework on what should have been the final product.

WRIGHT

That is very interesting. So what is the message you want most people to hear?

PENDLETON

Never give up! When I was growing up, I realized that my daddy was one of those people who felt trapped in a life he didn't enjoy. Every time he got moody, he would ask me to sing for him, and the song he requested was always "Que Sera, Sera." One line in that song is "the future is not ours to see" and he believed that. My daddy also believed quite strongly that we can mold that future into whatever we want it to be. But as so often happens, knowing is not doing, and he was afraid of the choices, so did nothing for himself. He did, however, convince me that anything was possible. I could follow my dreams if I worked hard, stayed focused, and really believed the risks were worth the effort.

So, I encourage you to stick to your own personal road map and never give up. Keep an unwavering focus. Let nothing deter you. Once you have defined your vision and your values, develop your strategy. Figure out the direction and route you need to take to get there, then follow your map. It will provide direction for you to fulfill your dream and be all you can be. Actively seek opportunities leading toward that dream. Face threats head-on and resolve them so they don't take you away from your focus.

It won't always be easy. Lots of things will get in your way, including your own self-confidence at times. Persevere! Life may pull you off track but get back on somehow. Be true to yourself. Follow your dream. Follow your passion. Be happy! Love your life! Again, it won't be easy, but *just do it!* It is your choice, your dream, and your life.

WRIGHT

What an interesting conversation. I couldn't take notes fast enough so I'm going to have to go back and listen to this interview again and take notes this time. This is good information. I appreciate your sharing it with us today. I also appreciate all this time you've taken to answer these questions.

PENDLETON

My pleasure.

WRIGHT

Today I have been talking with Dr. Irene Pendleton. Irene is a leader, trainer, and motivational speaker. She says that she has yet to run into any industry where a common language might be a problem. She is able to tie personal examples to the topic at hand and then demonstrate proven solutions that might make sense to the listener in almost any audience. Listening to her today, I can see how that is possible.

Irene, thank you so much for being with us today on *ROADMAP to Success.*

PENDLETON

Thank you very much.

About the Author

Dr. Irene Pendleton is a veteran leader, trainer, and motivational speaker. With more than twenty-seven years of federal government leadership experience, more than twenty years teaching both undergraduate and graduate school classes at notable universities, and nearly thirty years as a non-profit board member at national and international levels, she has yet to run into any industry where common language might be a problem. She is able to tie personal examples to topics at hand and then demonstrate proven solutions that make sense to the listener in almost any audience.

She has postgraduate degrees with a focus on education, behavioral psychology, sociology, supervision, and designing organizations. She has demonstrated abilities in academic, not-for-profit, and civil service careers in conveying performance expectations and providing feedback on actual performance. Her participation in a variety of leadership roles has included technical and general instructor training and professional organization development as well as establishment and assessment of programs. Dr. Pendleton has headed many committees where her work helped lead the group to sharper focus on issues and positive outcomes. Quality is her passion and she believes that we must always strive to do our best.

Irene Pendleton

Advanced Executive Solutions, LLC
26019 Lookout Oaks
San Antonio TX 78260
210-867-8788
info@irenependleton.com
www.aes-sa.com
www.bqxi.com

Chapter Fifteen

SERVICE LEADS TO SUCCESS

VINNI MIRZAIANS

DAVID WRIGHT (WRIGHT)

Today I am talking with Ashot Mirzaians, known to his many friends and clients as Vinni. He was born in Armenia. His family immigrated to America in 1985 and settled in Rockville, Maryland. Vinni attended public schools and The University of Phoenix where he majored in computer science. After graduation, he was employed by a federal contractor and performed highly classified IT assignments throughout the world during a fifteen-year period. These assignments included equipment installation testing and systems testing and evaluation.

Vinni opened his own firm Real Computer Solutions Inc. in 2007 with a modest cash investment and operated from his home. Since that time he has grown his organization significantly, starting with just himself. He now has four additional staff members, he leases a space in a modern building, and has increased his clientele by nearly 200 percent. In addition to installing and repairing business and personal computer systems, RCS installs and maintains an assortment of computer-based systems.

Vinni, welcome to *ROADMAP to Success*.

VINNI MIRZAIANS (MIRZAIANS)

Thank you.

WRIGHT

So you provide great coaching tips to people; where do they come from?

MIRZAIANS

Personal experiences, friends, and family, lessons learned, and knowing the model of life: Do it right, do it once, and you'll be successful all the time.

WRIGHT

So what would you say would be the biggest contribution to your professional success?

MIRZAIANS

Service, service, paying close attention to detail, and listening closely to understand what is being said.

WRIGHT

What do you think are the biggest obstacles people face in trying to become successful?

MIRZAIANS

Money, friends, family, time, and fear.

WRIGHT

How do you know what you need to be successful?

MIRZAIANS

You don't. You need to try different methods to accomplish your goal and try to achieve that goal with the fewest obstacles in the way. For example, if your goal is to get two plus two equals four and you tried one plus three equals four and that didn't work for you, maybe the two plus two combination might work, or the one plus one plus one plus one would work better. If one strategy does not work, you have to change gears to ensure the new process can work. This advice was given to me by Bruce Mattare, founder of Tronix Country.

WRIGHT

So would you tell our readers a little bit about what drives you to be successful?

MIRZAIANS

The satisfaction of knowing that people like what I do, enjoy what I provide, and do not hesitate to contact my business and use my services. That's the satisfaction I get from everyday life—knowing that my customers and clients are happy. Then I can sleep easy at night knowing that no one is going to call me tomorrow and start yelling and screaming at me.

WRIGHT

So do you feel it's important to balance your success in your life, and if you do, how do you do it?

MIRZAIANS

It is very important to balance success and life. The reason is that you don't want to be married to the job. The job will take over your life and pretty soon you're alone, lonely and it's you and QuickBooks. Then your personal life suffers because your friends and family never see you. Your wife kicks you out of the house and then you're back to being married to the job.

It's a fine line to balance life and work and ensure that you can maintain the relevancy and importance of each in order to be a success. Not only that, you can always relate to your clients because they're people just like we are. They have lives, they may have children and family and you can relate to them. If you don't have a similar private life, it is difficult to be successful in your business life. We work with people we are similar with. If they don't like us, then how can we force them to like us?

WRIGHT

What is the message you want people to hear so they can learn from your success?

MIRZAIANS

The message I want people to hear is to set your goals, know how to achieve your goals, and ensure that there are reasons why you would achieve your goals. Be realistic, don't fool yourself; be a little apprehensive of what's coming down the road, but do not be hesitant to grab the bull by its horns and move forward.

WRIGHT

You told me about people who influenced your life such as your father, Bill Gates, and Bob Ash. How do you suggest that people help others to succeed?

MIRZAIANS

Throughout the years in my experience as a contractor and even selling vacuum cleaners for one day, I learned that in order to be successful, you need to surround yourself with successful people. One thing my father always taught me was to treat people with respect, ensure you treat them the way you want to be treated, and no matter who the person is, always respect him or her.

Bill Gates is the person I strive to emulate. I would like to become as successful if not more successful than he is. Gates took a simple, genius solution, licensed it out to let everybody use it, and now he's fortunately made billions from it.

Bob Ash was one of the first instructors I had who provided customer service training skills to me. With that, not knowing how to even function in a corporate world or even how to deal with people, he provided a blueprint for me to know how to deal with people, respect them, treat people the way they want to be treated, be courteous, and provide the best customer service possible, no matter what it takes.

WRIGHT

Would you say that when people follow their passion and excel at it, does the passion bring success or does success bring more passion?

MIRZAIANS

This is one of those double-edged sword questions. It could go either way. You could say the passion of building the fastest super rocket in the world made you successful, but were you happy at the end? That's the question you have to ask yourself. My passion would be that if I am smiling when I'm going to bed at night, then I've been successful all my life.

WRIGHT

Of course you've been successful in turning businesses around. What is your fundamental business strategy?

MIRZAIANS

My fundamental business strategy is doing what I would do as if I were the customer. Think about what customers would want to see from you. Don't just say, "Mr. Customer, your solution is A and B, please sign on the dotted line." No, you have to switch hats here. "Okay, Mr. Customer, if I were in your shoes, investing X amount of dollars in this service or product, what do you expect to gain out of this?" Once you have that understanding from customers, you understand them, you understand what their need is, and you are able to deliver what they are asking for. It's not just a cut-and-dry solution.

WRIGHT

Well, it sounds like a simple philosophy. What is the root cause of why organizations don't focus on the customer?

MIRZAIANS

One of the root causes they don't focus on the customer is they get so convoluted with the day-to-day tasks of what needs to be done that day that they don't focus on the client. The business itself is a job but you can't forget the most important aspect of business. Without the customer or client, your business is worthless. No matter how good or great you claim to be, who are you? You can have the alphabet behind your name, you can have certifications, accreditations, but if you don't have customers who are you? These are some of the major reasons why organizations forget to focus on the customer; just too much going on. You have to stop, listen, and breathe.

WRIGHT

I thought I'd like to make this clear to our readers. You are actually not on the fence on this subject. How does customer focus differ from customer service?

MIRZAIANS

Customer service is what you do and in the process is what you actually provide to the customer. A simple example is: A customer purchases product A, but instead he or she gets product B. Why did the customer get product B? Somebody somewhere dropped the ball on the order. So what do you need to do to make sure the customer receives product A? That's where customer service comes in.

Customer focus is knowing what the customer wants. For example: a customer would come and say, "Vinni, I need to have a computer to perform my PhotoShop capabilities because I'm a professional photographer."

"Okay, Mr. Customer, we can certainly do that." In essence, we should we need to put ourselves in the customer's shoes. This being said, we know what the customer experiences and what we can provide to them to ensure their complete satisfaction. We must understand that aspect of the field work of a photographer, then we come back into the lab and say, "Okay, now I'm the photographer. I need to deliver ten perfect pictures to CNN to be broadcast on television live." Once we figure out those methods we can say, "Okay, this is how we're providing a computer for you, Mr. Photographer. This computer with XYZ configuration is going to do the job correctly for you and this is the price." That's being customer-focused versus just providing customer service. And when you put the two together, you have a win-win solution.

WRIGHT

When you do seminars and workshops, do you suggest ways that companies can track these things?

MIRZAIANS

There are standard methods of keeping track of these devices and things coming down the road. However, every business is different. If you have Jane on the phone, Jane is not going to keep track of the same things Thomas would if he were on the phone. So each corporation has to set up their own standard operating procedures, establish their own guidelines on what they want to compile and keep, and then have times when they can actually review the process, the materials, and the data. Once they've reviewed, analyzed, and learned from it, expand on it, and implement it for future use and reference. If you don't implement any of the information or data gathered and if you don't have a customer, what is your business really worth? If you have these processes and you don't take advantage of them, what are you doing? You're either just in a fancy office with just a name or you have something in hand that you can use.

WRIGHT

In this economy with high unemployment and people who are not productive and who are being fired right and left, how does customer focus boost employee productivity?

MIRZAIANS

It keeps the employees honest. Once employees have established those relationships with customers, they feel more in a personal relationship with them instead of someone they don't know walking into a store and just buying a simple pen for two dollars and walking out. If the employee focuses on the customer and says, "Wow, this is a great pen. It's made by XYZ Pen Corporation, but let me tell you this, Mr. Customer, the ABC Corporation makes a pen with a firm rubber grip,"

Mr. Customer states, "Ah, I like this."

The pen might be ten times more expensive than the two-dollar pen but you just boosted your sales and service because you focused on the customer's needs.

WRIGHT

How can customer service help me in my business?

MIRZAIANS

It's the cliché in Real Estate—what we all know as "location, location, location." As many organizations grow, they tend to lose focus on why they wanted to be in business or what they did initially to gain customers. You can be the best at what you do, you can be the top guy in the world and, yes, you'll have clients and you will generate income and have good revenue. However, if you don't have the service aspect, how are people going to know about you? Your best business comes to you by word-of-mouth and referrals. Referrals are generated by service—making sure people are happy and making sure they get what they want. If it's as simple as a five-dollar, ten-dollar, or twenty-dollar gift you give to that client to make them happy, so be it. "Customer services is a way of life, not a promotional campaign" (Jim Temme).

WRIGHT

So what can I do that the customer doesn't expect?

MIRZAIANS

Most customers expect to come into a retail location (they call us service technicians at our house) and this is the XYZ they've got to get. I'll give you a prime example that was actually used in many of my cases when we dispatch technicians to our client locations.

Years ago, when I initially had a cable provider come out to my house to install high speed Internet, the technician was a very nice guy. One of the first things he did was introduce himself, shook my hand, and next thing you know he started putting shoe covers on his shoes. To me it was strange. When I thought about it, the man is working for a cable provider and cares about my house, and he's covering his shoes so he doesn't drag dirt into my house. Wow what a concept! To this day I've actually even sent him out on some service calls that require cable work at some residential homes. He's always punctual and customer service is top notch priority. It's the simple things like putting shoe covers on before you walk into someone's house that make a difference, and that's something the customer doesn't expect and will always remember.

WRIGHT

So what can I do that my competition isn't doing?

MIRZAIANS

It's difficult to learn what the competition isn't doing that you could do. The best way is to put yourself in the role of the customer and approach the competition to figure out what the competition *is* doing. I'm not suggesting that you become involved in corporate espionage, just do some creative research and make some phone calls. See what's going on and what are they are doing. It might be something as simple as phoning John Smith, a customer you haven't heard from in a long time. You might say something like, "Hello, Mr. Smith," and ask how he is doing and asking if there is anything within the scope of what you do that you can help him with. The competition may not be doing this. They may just send out cards.

Do you value your customers or do just count them as a revenue-generating "machine"? It is also important to treat all customers with the same deference—the customer whose purchases are small as well as the customer whose purchases are large.

WRIGHT

How do I find out what my customer wants?

MIRZAIANS

That's when listening skills come into play. Customers can want, feel, and need lots of things, but to really understand and focus on what customers want, you have to understand what they need. To do that, you ask them.

One of the things I learned in my customer service training course with Bob Ash was to not just listen to the customer saying, "Yes, I want an—" I learned to really understand what the customer said during that conversation. Maybe the customer really wanted six of the items he or she mentioned.

First you have to listen, comprehend, and repeat what you think you heard back to the customer. For example, say, "Mr. Customer, you wanted just one XYZ. Is that exactly what you want?" Once you've fully understood the customer, the solution is simple. You deliver what he or she wants. Your customers receive what they want, they are happy, you are happy, business keeps flowing. Always remember this: you have two ears and one mouth and you can do more listening than talking by keeping your mouth closed.

WRIGHT

So to check yourself and to check your company, should you ask your customers how you are doing regarding your service to them?

MIRZAIANS

Always. No matter what the situation is, no matter what the customers are asking, the best way for you to know how good you are serving them, is to ask. Customers are not going pick up the phone and say, "Vinni, you screwed up my system" or "Vinni, you walked in with dirty shoes on my white carpet" or "Vinni, you didn't answer the phone when I called you and you said you answer the phone in two rings." But if I were to take the initiative and I called the customer, or the next time at the customer's location I ask, "Mr. Customer, I've been providing service for you and I'm trying to improve on everything we can provide. Is what we're providing up to your expectations? Do we meet your requirements? Are we taking care of everything you're asking for? Are you happy with the service we're providing?"

If we get good responses, great, if we don't, then we'll know why things didn't work and we have to fix them. If you don't ask, you'll never know what you're doing wrong. If you don't know what you're doing wrong, your wrongs may turn into simple processes that become standard operating procedures. You're then headed down the wrong path and doing the wrong thing all the time. This eventually leads to failure, which is not an option.

WRIGHT

Is it better to do this on a survey after the job or face-to-face?

MIRZAIANS

I'm more of a face-to-face person even though with the technology we have these days, we can send out multiple surveys and multiple letters. But you have to value the customer's time. If I'm sending customers a survey I'm asking for five to ten minutes of their time. I'm essentially either costing them money, depending on what they do, or taking time away from their loved ones or friends. If I make it easy for them and they just provide the answers to the questions, that makes the process easier.

One of the things I provide to my technicians is a customer service form. After the job is completed I ask, "Mr. Customer, with a quick survey we'll provide a coupon for your next visit. Will you answer these three to five questions quickly?" Usually we have satisfactory answers 95 percent of the time.

WRIGHT

Well, what a great conversation, Vinni. I appreciate all the time you've taken to answer these questions. It's been enlightening; I've learned a lot. And I'm sure our readers will as well.

MIRZAIANS

I hope so. This is what I've been good at. Yes, I majored in computer science but I never went to school to learn business. As for the material we discussed, it's a simple solution.

WRIGHT

Today I have been talking with Vinni Mirzaians. Vinni opened his firm Real Computer Solutions in 2007 with just a small cash investment. He has grown his organization to four additional staff. He leases a modern building and has increased his clientele by nearly 200 percent. His company installs, repairs, and works on computer systems and maintains an assortment of computer-based systems.

Vinni thank you so much for being with us today on *ROADMAP to Success*.

MIRZAIANS

You are most welcome.

About the Author

Ashot "Vinni" Mirzaians opened his own firm, Real Computer Solutions, Inc., in October of 2007 with a modest cash investment and operated from his home. Since that time he has grown his organization significantly. Starting with just himself, he now has four additional staff, leases space in a modern building, and has increased his clientele by nearly 200 percent. In addition to installing and repairing business and personal computer systems, Real Computer Solutions installs and maintains an assortment of computer-based systems.

Vinnie is a Microsoft Certified IT systems solution professional with diverse technical experience on LAN/WAN and Wireless technologies, including DSL/CABLE/WIRELESS/Fios Frame Relay, T-1, and T-3. He is fluent in English, Persian, and Armenian.

Vinnie's goal is simple: "I want to provide the best computer services in the quickest timeframe and as inexpensively as possible with a smile."

RCS is focused on providing 100 percent customer satisfaction. Vinni possesses the necessary qualifications and experience to successfully meet the challenges brought about by the revolutionary changes in information technology.

His specific areas of expertise include: strategic and business planning, business development, market positioning and benchmarking, and decision and change management.

"We must not only go above and beyond 'the sale to a customer,' but ensure a customer experience that is unrivaled and built on trust."

Ashot "Vinni" Mirzaians

Real Computer Solutions Inc.
19634 Club House Rd., Suite 310
Gaithersburg, MD 20886
301-330-7325
Vinni@RealComputerSolutions.com
Http://www.RealComputerSolutions.com

Chapter Sixteen

BE SUCCESS-FULL NOW

FARRA ALLEN

DAVID WRIGHT (WRIGHT)

Today I am talking with Farra Allen. Mr. Allen has an extensive background; he holds a law degree from The University of Kentucky, a Liberal Arts Degree from Center College in Danville, Kentucky, and a master's degree in Psychology and Counseling from West Georgia University. Mr. Allen has more than thirty-five years of experience in alternative and complimentary healthcare.

In 1980 he co-founded The Atlanta School of Massage, recognized as one of the top massage schools in the country, and taught more than fourteen hundred students. Farra designed the original curriculum, guided its development, and co-led the school until 1994. He and his ex-wife developed a startup company into a 1.26 million-dollar business before moving on to his next project. In 1994, he founded the Body Mind Center of Atlanta Inc. Having worked personally with many people from all walks of life via phone and Internet coaching, Farra has more than sixteen years of experience coaching individuals and groups.

In 2006 he founded The LifeWorks School of Coaching, training and certifying Life Coaches and Entrepreneurs. The year 2011 marks the sixth anniversary of the school's "in person" training. Life Works begins its International launch in 2011 whereby this unique body of work will be taught throughout the world.

WRIGHT

Farra, welcome to *ROADMAP to Success*.

FARRA ALLEN (ALLEN)

Thank you very much.

WRIGHT

So would you tell us a little bit about yourself and why you are an expert on the subject of creating success?

ALLEN

Absolutely. When I founded The Atlanta School of Massage, I was just following my passion. That's a big part of what creates success—being able to listen to what one naturally wants to do. Even with a law degree, I really wasn't interested in being a lawyer, so I started looking at who I wanted to be. Once I got in touch with doing massage, I realized that I wanted to spread the word—I really wanted to educate people. In the seventies, it was still a new concept.

So my focus became the product itself. It is so important that you refine the product to make it into something you really feel great about. Then we got our entire staff aligned with our Mission and our Vision. We created an intentional community where everybody bought into "being" an integral part of the business. We then got in touch with determining what we are in the business of selling. We realized we were really in the business of selling personal transformation—"a shift in the being that one is." So we began to focus our marketing efforts around that, distinct from selling a vocational training.

Then when I did the Body Mind Center, I got in touch with how important it is for people to have all of the areas of their lives working—body, mind, spirit, etc. Most recently, in creating The LifeWorks School of Coaching, I began to realize how important it is to completely support your people, to connect, and to create an intentional community. Seeking to empower people is what has led to a big part of our success. Lastly, and most importantly, our focus is on "who you are being" inside of whatever it is you are doing. So when we taught people how to do massage, we didn't teach merely how to do it, but rather how "to be" a massage therapist and similarly how "to be" a coach rather than just doing coaching. Similarly, as one experiences oneself as being successful, one in turn creates success.

When you authentically feel successful fully inside first, you naturally attract it externally.

WRIGHT

Do you have a systematic technique you use to train your students and clients?

ALLEN

We do. We have "a tried and true process"—a technique that we use. It was developed throughout years of research and development. We call this "flipping the coin"—you get in touch with whatever "childhood wounds" you had growing up and begin to flip that and start contributing to others what you wanted most emotionally from Mom or Dad.

What we do is help people listen to what their gift is—their passion. They connect with it and then begin to identify themselves with their passion, moving out of whatever old stories are living in their subconscious mind. Our students then get in touch with their vision, their mission, and an entirely new "re-identification of the self." When this occurs, people move from a "need base" where they are looking to "get something from others" to a "give base" wherein they are genuinely looking to contribute to others.

This is a very unique way in which we train our students because we focus on strengthening the individual and getting them to "own" who they truly are. We then assist people to form their own unique niche—what they naturally provide others. This is very specific to each individual and certain others are looking for this very thing. The Law of Attraction is activated and this is so important for generating success.

When our students discover *exactly* their niche and design their marketing approach around that, they attract the exact client they want to work with and *experience* more success as well as create more success in both their personal and professional life.

WRIGHT

Interesting. Would you give our readers more specific information about how you see one's application of how the Law of Attraction may lead to one's success?

ALLEN

Sure. Many people, for instance, may have seen the film *The Secret* or read about it. Of course they talk a lot about desire and then how to create your Mercedes or whatever it is that you want for yourself, which is all good. However, what we do in addition to that is assist people to listen into their calling, as if they come from a blank chalkboard and they can just be open to coming upon—discovering—what they are here to do on the planet—what their purpose is. Once one gets in touch with this, we say it has "legs." That is to say, it's a deep connection inside one's essence and one's soul. So one has a considerable amount of natural energy around this, thus one creates more emotional attraction. Furthermore, the person tends to stay with that and not just keep moving from one thing to another. This in turn adds to the likelihood of creating success.

The other way we work with the Law of Attraction is to make sure that everybody "lines everything up" without a doubt before they move forward into action. I've been studying the Law for many, many years prior to *The Secret*. I studied people like Ernest Holmes who were foundational instructors of this work. So what we do is not only look at the intellectual side, we're like a laboratory—we focus on direct experience. We assist people to do the inner work, to get into a "feeling tone" of having no attachment. This is so important to truly activate the Law in your favor and really maximize it for yourself.

The other thing we do is help people develop and design an "action plan," what we call the SPA or the Strategic Plan of Action. Because it's not just about what you are attracting, but it's also about what action you are going to take. Then, once people go into action, many times they hit roadblocks and/or they feel all alone. We encourage people to have coaches because the coach can assist and support people. I know that's really led to a lot of my success. I've had some great coaches who have been like mentors for me to help me create my businesses, which is priceless!

Lastly, feeling good about yourself causes you to vibrate at a higher frequency, which is going to naturally attract more of what you want. This is an experiential/emotional approach, not merely intellectual, and in our culture so much emphasis is placed on the intellectual. It's so important to really feel it—to actually *feel* it in your body—that's what we do. We don't just talk about things, we assist people to actually "have the feeling" of being successful and in turn they naturally attract success to them. Herein you have "lined it up"—it has to come to you. It's Law.

WRIGHT

What about listening skills and effective communication skills? How does that, in turn, assist one to create more success?

ALLEN

This is important because one really needs to have empathy, be able to get into other people's worlds, and then stay in rapport with them. Once you have lost rapport with someone, you have lost everything. The person speaking needs to be able to develop trust in the listener, whoever he or she is speaking to. So much of our focus in our culture is on speaking, rather than listening. Our work centers on listening and how important that is. Actually, listening is a powerful thing. That's what we train the public, not just our coaches, to do. Having good eye contact and "active listening" is important. You are fully present and "mindful" with the person in front of you. What is amazing about that is people feel it and they will open up. Then, all of a sudden, it shifts the conversation and that relationship to a higher level, which is so important, allowing meaningful change to occur.

We also work with people to speak to the concerns that people have such as asking questions, finding out what the person wants and needs. In our culture, we are taught that if we're a speaker or we're selling something, we tend to be focused on what we are saying, what we're putting out, and our performance. What we often miss is listening to the person we are speaking with. We should be curious, wondering who the person is and what he or she wants and needs. Then we can know what the person needs.

Curiosity, questioning and deepening those questions, and watching body language are areas that people aren't normally trained in. That is a lot of what we do in our interactions with not only coaches, but the public, too, because we also educate the public in developing these.

WRIGHT

Tell us more about how one gets in touch with one's purpose and passion and how that relates to success.

ALLEN

That's a pretty detailed subject. We actually do that in the trainings and in our teleclasses with people in general. We look for what occurred in your childhood—what did you want emotionally from Mom or Dad that you perceive you did not get, or did not get enough of? What happens is that when we have a desire for whatever we wanted as a child, day after day, month after month, year after year, it builds a passion in us. This keeps building and building; there is a great potential in that energy. So when you start to "flip the coin" on that and provide the opposite of what you didn't receive, all of a sudden you start having a really strong passion about that. People do it naturally, but often it's like water to the fish—they're not really aware that they are doing it.

What we do is assist people to become aware of what they are doing naturally that is providing a lot to others. In fact, if you talk to their friends, they'll say, "Oh yes, this person provide tremendous safety for me. I feel safe and accepted." You'll notice that when you dig, you find that the person didn't feel safe in his or her childhood and thus the person naturally provides that to others.

It's very important to gain awareness and to get in touch with what we call one's unique gift. Once you are aware of it, you can utilize and maximize it. Then it can become a very unique gift and a strength that you have. You can then start to build on that and focus on "what is working" about you distinct from what is not working. Then you naturally go into what we call "the flow"—your flow—where you are in the zone. You might say you are in the flow when you are providing your gifts to other people and it's coming naturally and normally for you. It's a very powerful force, as one begins to focus on "who one is," one moves away from "comparing" and competition. One then experiences and it's very effective in producing success in one's life.

WRIGHT

What have you discovered about dis-ease and its corresponding connection to creating success?

ALLEN

Yes, we call it dis-ease because there is a dis-ease in the system that is always a precursor to disease. There are many people who are researching this and learning more. We are starting to see that this is caused by a conflict that occurs inside the psyche—a battle between the ego and the soul that wants to go in opposite directions. They need to mediate and come together in order to create "ease."

We have discovered that we can literally go in and reprogram the DNA and literally get people to alter their subconscious mind. When I earned my master's in psychology and counseling I discovered that the great majority of what we do and don't do is literally tied to what is in our subconscious mind. In our culture we tend to think, "Oh, that's unconscious so we don't even think about going in there and trying to work with that." We think that if it's in the subconscious mind, we "get a pass" on that. Yet that is *exactly* where we should be looking and paying attention.

The work that we do literally reprograms the "old tapes" and in the book I am writing I go into detail on how to do that. Of course, that is an important element of our program. This dictates what we are going to do out here in the world and thus what kind of success we're going to have. Our focus is on "who one is being" prior to going into action, prior to the "doing." We connect people with their purpose and their vision. When you are connected to that, you don't have time for disease.

I very rarely have any dis-ease but when I do, I have ways in which I work with it. We teach inner work processes that help people get beyond that so they can put themselves into a state of "ease." As a result, we do not get sick or quickly recover. I'm so connected to my purpose and my passion and vision that I don't really have time for—I can't even remember the last time I got sick. So optimum health, vitality, spirit, inspiration, enthusiasm, is catching and people want it—they want what you have. When you think about it, people are "buying you" in a way. There is something about you that they may want in themselves, they are attracted to who you are being, and thus they are attracted to what you are offering. This is an important key to your success.

WRIGHT

How do you get people to authentically love themselves and accept others?

ALLEN

In our childhood, we interpret and assess what happens to us and this becomes our story. This then gets filed away in our subconscious mind. When something happens that reminds us of that, it activates the old story. We need to reprogram those "tapes" and demystify that old story because it literally pulls us down and limits us.

Once you demystify that old story and create what we call the True Self or the Authentic Self, then you start to naturally appreciate yourself. When you create your true self—your authentic self—you get in touch with who you truly are. You find your purpose, your passion, your vision, your mission, and your true self. Once you get in touch with that, you can love yourself. It's one thing to say you love yourself and accept others, but it's another to actually do it. We train people to experience "who they truly are." In our culture, too, we tend to judge and scrutinize, which are excellent tools at times. However, if we are doing that with other people, on some level they are feeling it. Everything is being communicated all the time anyway, thus this is occurring in people's subconscious minds. They may not realize this cognitively—they may not realize consciously that you are judging them, however, they feel a certain way around you. Instead, when you start to look for people's greatness, you start to see them that way. It's like a "loving presence." You start to listen that way and all of a sudden you notice that something "magical" is happening in that relationship you are having with someone. It's not just a conversation, there is energy inside of that conversation. You are connecting, bonding, you're in deep rapport, and all of a sudden this creates an entirely different interaction.

The work we do puts you in touch with appreciating yourself and loving yourself in spite of how many times we go out into the world and get thrown off. Our work is designed around "practicality" because we realize that mishaps are going to happen. The key is getting back on track—how quickly can you expedite "your return to You"? That's why it's so important to have a coach.

Our coaches are trained to teach you how to coach yourself because you can't always call someone. When you learn the body of work around coaching, you realize that it's all about how you can support your client. Getting back on track is the key to activating the Law of Attraction in your favor. In order for you to attract what you want, it's very important for people to "authentically" love themselves and accept others. When they do, they naturally attract success.

WRIGHT

Tell us all about vision and mission and how these create personal and professional success.

ALLEN

Yes, vision and mission create clarity and direction. They are like a compass or like a boat's rudder. When you have vision and mission, you can shine "your lighthouse." [Vision is the world that you are in "behalf of," what you see, what you want to happen in the world. Not only is that something you get in touch with, you really begin to merge with it.

People like Gandhi and Martin Luther King are examples in our lifetime of people who have done that and really become "one with their passion." Of course, they are extreme examples, but all of us have an ability to connect with our vision at a very deep level. This is important because you can begin to make your decisions aligned with your vision. You can make decisions such as where you want to live, who you want to be with, and so on. When you have your vision, you get clarity as to how you are going to live your life. This is why we call what we do "LifeWorks"—you begin to live the life you have imagined and dreamed of. All of a sudden your life begins to work, you start to feel your self apart from your ego. You realize something bigger than you, something that you are "in behalf of"— something that you are making happen out here in the world.

This then gives you a different experience inside yourself. Many of us who are highly creative have some aspect of attention deficit disorder (ADD). Many of us are interested in a myriad of things, and in our culture this is seen as something that is not good. In fact, doctors tend to medicate people who regularly demonstrate this condition. Instead, we merely need to assist others to gain clarity as to what is most important to them and encourage them to focus on that. They've actually done research that coaching has been highly effective working with people who have attention deficit. I don't like terms that "pigeonhole" people because in the case of ADD, these people are highly creative, I'm one of them myself.

So once you get clear on your focus, along with coaching support, you can "stay focused," which is again so important to creating success in your life. For instance, being able to focus can guide you as to how you formulate your business plan and marketing. If you formulate it your way, you are formulating it around who you are—your vision, your mission, your purpose, and your passion. At LifeWorks, we have an acronym we use for doing it your way. It's Who Are You—WAY. This is distinct from doing it someone else's way. It is more about who you are and what your mission and vision are. Your mission is your "job" inside of whatever your vision is. So the question is what are you going to do to help manifest that vision, and then how are you going to construct that? How are you going to design it—how are you going to shape your business and customize it around who you are? That's the work that we do. At LifeWorks, we assist people to literally customize their business exactly around themselves, what they want, and what they want to make happen in the world. When people do this, they have the most excitement and therefore they attract success.

WRIGHT

As you stated, you are writing a book. Will you tell us about that and does your book address the issue of creating success?

ALLEN

Yes, absolutely it does. My book will assist you to deal with ever-increasing stress inherent in day-to-day living. I don't know if you've noticed it, but it seems like in our culture the stressors are increasing all the time. There is more to do and more opportunities for stress. Stress can also be opportunities for growth if you see it that way. We teach a concept that we call "looking through a different lens." As life is fired at us "point blank," we have a certain perception. That perception will then create our thoughts, which creates our emotions, which creates whatever actions or non-actions we take. This in turn creates whatever success we achieve.

All of this hinges upon what our initial perception is. If we can begin to look for another perception, this opens up another "possibility" that didn't previously exist for us. We do need to be able to "connect the dots"—it must make sense to us. This is not just an affirmation. For example, "Before, I wasn't successful, but now I have a coach, and now I'm going to be successful with his [or her] assistance." You're looking through a different lens and now you can imagine yourself being successful; you are, in essence, activating the law of attraction.

So we do a lot of inner work—we are like the laboratory. There are a lot of places out there where you can go to learn what to do; however, what we do is focus on "how" you are going to change your subconscious and how you are going to get back on track. We actually do that. There are not many places that provide an actual experience that begins to alter one's life. This is especially true in our classroom where people come in and experience our training "in person." We form groups of twelve to fourteen students. The group energy is just incredible. People literally transform—they are not the same person. It's not just a change, it's literally a "shift in the being that one is" and that's the work we do. When others observe this shift, they want of that, too, and they become interested.

WRIGHT

If our readers found your information helpful, how can they deepen their understanding?

ALLEN

They can go to either of our Web sites. As you mentioned earlier, we are going international because we've spent a lot of time and energy putting this body of work together. We're now going to take it out into the world. But the teleclasses that are geared to everyday concerns, the book to come, the workshops, the in-person trainings, and the training that will soon be available via the Internet are ways in which people can steep themselves in their "authentic self"—who they truly are.

The training we do is not just to educate students in all of our powerful "coaching skill sets" or training them to be coaches. Indeed, some of our graduates choose whatever might be appropriate for them. It is also an entrepreneurial training where we assist people to listen to what is naturally moving through them and formulate a business around that. For some people it's public speaking, for others it's coaching. Some people want to learn how to manage other people and they want to empower those people. We are "the lab" wherein students can learn how to discover their purpose.

Once you feel in your body that personal power and you expand it, you feel the "vitality" it brings. Then you really are ready to go out and do whatever you need to do to make it work and you will stick with it. Results follow energy, and you find that you have a lot of energy for what you want to make happen.

If readers find what we have to offer valuable, they can hire one of our coaches. They can do coaching on the phone or in person. LifeWorks coaches are a little bit different from the traditional life coach. Life coaching itself is generally geared toward getting you in touch with your goals, holding you accountable, and making sure that you follow through with your goals. All of this is extremely important and our coaches do this also. However, most life coaches aren't equipped to work with the psychology and emotions and work from a spiritual perspective, including using the law of attraction. We've expanded coaching into these areas. So we're really somewhat unique. Our work is designed around what it takes to have your life work "on all cylinders." As one "feels" this, one becomes a "magnet of attraction."

WRIGHT

Is there anything else you would like to add to make this conversation complete?

ALLEN

Do your preparation. Focus on being distinct from your doing. In our culture, we don't emphasize where you come from as distinct from what you do. It's more about information, knowledge, cognitive-linear skills. There is also another part of us—the intuitive part, the part that listens, the part that is mindful and fully present, in touch with oneself. It is so important to focus on that part because when you look at results and being successful, a lot of that comes from "who we are being," not necessarily what we do.

Then secondarily, I think it's so important that everybody has a spiritual practice. I personally do "scripting," which is writing out what I am accomplishing each day. This is very powerful and effective. I do meditation, I exercise every day. These elements incorporate the mind, body, and spirit approach, including a connection with your Higher Source. Trust and have faith that, as you put things out there, they will come back to you. If you are serving and contributing to others you can feel that you are deserving. If you look at the word "deserve" and break it down, "de" is the Latin derivative for "about," so deserving is "about serving." If you are about serving, then you deserve to have a lot coming back to you. Once you feel that inside your body, then you are a magnet—you are at your "optimum attraction level" and you are optimally activating the Law of Attraction.

Then there are the three C's. The first is Commitment. You have to be totally committed to the work you are bringing forth in the world. Hold yourself in high regard. Realize that you have a specific, unique gift to share and "delivering your goods."

The second C is taking Care of yourself. This is important because *you* are your greatest resource. This can vary in many ways. For instance, frequently the phone will ring and I won't answer it because I'm sending that message to my Higher Self that "I" am more important. "Who I am being" is important—I'm taking full care of myself.

The third C is to Celebrate." Having fun and doing what you love is important. Start doing what you love and completely have fun. I don't feel like I work a day in my life, I enjoy what I'm doing. So I celebrate and that is an important tool for balance.

Lastly, it's important to have support. So often we develop what I call the "John Wayne syndrome" or "I'll do it on my own." It's so important to have a coach—everyone deserves a coach. In our culture we tend to say, "I'm doing great. I don't need a coach right now." Well, are you interested in being "all you can be"? Do you want to reach your highest potential? This work is all about reaching your full potential. This actually is the perfect time to hire a coach to assist in reaching your maximum potential. These individuals who have attained the highest levels of success know and practice this approach consistently.

Continuing to learn and grow is the focus that our people and I have. If you want to learn and grow, then you deserve to have a coach and you want to go to classes, workshops, and trainings. Following your inner wisdom, listening for guidance, synchronicity, and going with your flow are all ways to achieve success. I have created the word "abundancy," which is "the state of being in the experience of abundance." When you are in that state, you expect to attract the positive things you want in your life. When you expect it, when you know it's coming, when you feel inside your body that you deserve it, then that goes a long way toward creating success. In fact, it has to happen! One will, in time, create success. It's Law! So again, it goes back to "who you are being" as you go about what you do to create success in your life. I wish everyone great success in their lives.

WRIGHT

Well, what a great conversation. I learned a lot here today. With all your experience, you know what you are talking about. I'm sure our readers are going to recognize that. I appreciate all the time you've taken with me to answer these questions. It's really been delightful.

ALLEN

Thank you very much. I've enjoyed our time as well. It's my passion to do it. It's always uplifting to share and I feel that I could go on sharing because it's coming from my heart. The LifeWorks approach is very different. It actually empowers you as you are doing it, so it's always giving back to you. This gives you immediate fulfillment "in the act of doing and being your passion," which is creating success.

WRIGHT

Today I have been talking with Farra Allen. Mr. Allen has more than thirty-five years of experience in alternative and complementary healthcare. He has been training, empowering, and certifying life coaches and entrepreneurs at LifeWorks School of Coaching since 2006; he is starting his sixth class in 2011. LifeWorks is going international and Mr. Allen's unique body of work will be taught throughout the world.

Mr. Allen, thank you so much for being with us today on *ROADMAP to Success*.

ALLEN

Again, my pleasure. Thank you.

About the Author

In 1980 Mr. Farra Allen co-founded The Atlanta School of Massage, recognized as one of the top massage schools in the country, and taught more than fourteen hundred students. Farra designed the original curriculum, guided its development, and co-led the school until 1994. He and his ex-wife developed a startup company into a 1.26 million-dollar business before moving on to his next project. In 1994, he founded the Body Mind Center of Atlanta Inc. Having worked personally with many people from all walks of life via phone and Internet coaching, Farra has more than sixteen years of experience coaching individuals and groups.

In 2006 he founded The LifeWorks School of Coaching, training and certifying Life Coaches and Entrepreneurs. The year 2011 marks the sixth anniversary of the school's "in-person" training. Life Works began its International launch in 2011 whereby this unique body of work will be taught throughout the world.

Farra Allen

farra@LifeWorksSchool.com
www.LifeWorksSchoolofCoaching.com

Chapter Seventeen

IT TAKES GUTS TO BE SUCCESSFUL!

DEB COTTLE

DAVID WRIGHT (WRIGHT)

Today I am talking with Deb Cottle. Deb is the Founder and President of World on a String, a company focused on enhancing people's lives through inspirational seminars, coaching, self-help products, and professional speaking. Deb is the creator of the proven "4Step GUTS FORMULA," an easy process that individuals can use on a daily basis to manage their success. Originally from Chicago, she established herself as one of the highest ranking female executives in the television production industry, working with national clients such as Anheuser-Busch, Coca-Cola, Ford, Humana, and Oprah. Deb currently lives on Amelia Island, Florida, with her husband, Stan, and teenage son, Connor.

Deb, welcome to *ROADMAP to Success*.

DEB COTTLE (COTTLE)

Hello, David! Thank you for asking me to be part of the *ROADMAP to Success* anthology series.

WRIGHT

So, do we need a road map for success?

COTTLE

That is a good question, and the answer is *yes!* I think we *all* need a road map to success. If we don't have a road map, then we don't know where we are going or where we're going to end up. Imagine sitting on a plane and the pilot comes over the intercom and says, "I'm not sure where we're going today, but sit back and enjoy the flight." Or try driving to a destination without using a GPS system or a map to go somewhere you've never been before. Also, think about building a house. Does a builder build a house without referring closely to a set of blueprints? Why should it be any different in our lives when we want to have success?

We've come to depend on a road map in these other situations, but when it comes to seeking our own success, sometimes we fall short in the planning stage. So, designing our own road map to success is necessary. We can choose to take detours along the way when we feel like it, but at least we'll start out with a plan and have an end result in mind.

WRIGHT

I know that every person defines success differently, but how do you define success?

COTTLE

In my perception, success can be defined as a state of mind or a state of being that is empowering. Success can mean different things to different people and at different stages of their lives. Defining success in this stage of my life is the achievement of sharing my motivational techniques to help inspire others. I believe that if we can share ourselves with others through whatever talent, knowledge, or expertise we possess, we become personally successful and serve as an inspiration to others.

Most people think of success as having lots of money. And the more money we have, the more successful we become. Money can help us "feel" successful, but it isn't everything—not even close! Being rich in the quality of your relationships with your family and friends can be extremely fulfilling. It's all about perception; what spells success for you can be totally different to someone else.

WRIGHT

So, what do you think the key to success is?

COTTLE

The best explanation of the key to success is found in a quote from Albert Schweitzer. He said, "Success is not the key to happiness; happiness is the key to success. If you love what you are doing you will be successful." I firmly believe that statement. And in my coaching experience, I have found that most people are so worried about being successful that they overlook the process of just getting there. Being grateful in your life, no matter what your life may look like, is incredibly important to achieving success.

Another key to success is being grateful for the little things in your life—the people you see and the good you give to others. Gratitude is definitely a huge key to success. Everyone can think of something to be grateful for, whether large or small.

Here are five tips on expressing gratitude:

1. Keep a gratitude journal or a list that you can use every day to keep track of what you're grateful for. Then, review this list at the end of the day. You'd be surprised at how many items will add up for you.
2. Tell someone that you are grateful for his or her friendship. How often have you told a friend or family member that you are grateful to have them in your life and why?
3. Send a handwritten thank you note to someone who would least expect it (e.g., the mechanic who fixed your car, your doctor, the UPS delivery person, etc.).
4. Perform random acts of kindness. Buy a stranger a cup of coffee or help someone figure out where they are going. One time I bought a blouse for a young girl in front of me at the store because she didn't have enough money, and really wanted the blouse to match her pants! It was so gratifying to do that for someone.
5. Be grateful for *you!* Make a list of your unique talents and gifts.

WRIGHT

So, what is this 4Step GUTS FORMULA?

COTTLE

David, the 4Step GUTS FORMULA is something I created to help people make their lives just work better! GUTS is an acronym featuring letters to highlight each of the four steps in the process.

G = *Gain knowledge.* I really believe it is important that we all do whatever possible to gain more knowledge in our work lives and our personal lives. In our work lives it can be attending relevant industry seminars, earning more credentials or designations in our occupations, or learning from others in our industry.

Also, having a role model or mentor is important in whatever we do. My eighty-six-year-old father, nature photographer Leonard Messineo, continues to learn from other accomplished photographers and keeps up with the ever-changing world of digital photography.

What gaining knowledge does for us is twofold: not only does it build our own confidence level, it also gives us a competitive edge compared to others in our field of work or in our personal endeavors.

U = *Use positive affirmations on a daily basis.* This is what psychologists call self-talk—statements we declare on a regular basis that can truly work to define our outcome in life, good or bad.

If we focus on stating more positive statements consistently, we can realize more positive results in our lives. This isn't rocket science; these are concepts most of us have either heard about or are already doing. The challenge is to become more conscious of the words we use and what we declare to ourselves and others. If we aren't saying positive statements or affirmations, then the opposite may be true. Repeating negative statements either about yourself or others will attract more negative experiences in your life. The subconscious mind doesn't know the difference between a statement that is true or false—it simply responds to statements that are said more often and are packed with emotion.

Case in point: remember the phrase "Sticks and stones will break my bones, but names will never hurt me"? This is so not true. Look at what is going on in our society today with the problem of bullying. Verbal abuse is hurtful on many levels. That's why watching what words we use and how we say them are crucial.

Dr. Shad Helmstetter, author of *What to Say When You Talk to Yourself,* claims that before we are eighteen years old we have been told that we can't do something or heard the word "no" more than 148,000 times. He also says that 75 percent of what we say to ourselves is either negative or counterproductive. Therefore, it's important for us to work at reprogramming our self-talk. For example, how many times have you heard someone say statements like, "I can never remember names"? What that simply tells your subconscious mind is don't remember names because you can never remember names, and you continue to believe that about yourself.

What if, instead, you programmed your mind to start remembering names and you tell yourself, "I remember names easily and effortlessly?" You'd be surprised at how many names you would start to remember just because you told yourself that you are going to remember names. Your subconscious mind will latch onto that statement and help you remember more names. You can do this with anything in your life that you want to improve or change, merely by controlling what you say on a regular basis.

T= *Train your thoughts.* The National Science Foundation claims that we think about sixty thousand thoughts per day. Even if we think we are positive half the time, that's about thirty thousand thoughts. We need to concentrate on converting some of those remaining thirty thousand thoughts to be more positive. It's unrealistic to expect yourself to be positive all the time, but I'm sure you will agree that we can use improvement!

For example, this story really hits home to me. My mother was diagnosed with breast cancer when she was in her mid-fifties. Despite successful radiation treatments and a clean bill of health from the doctor, she still didn't believe that she was cured of the disease. So, she asked the doctor if the cancer could resurface, and he responded by saying, "Well, five years is a good guide to go by, if the cancer would reappear, but it is only a guide."

Unfortunately, my mom focused on the fact that the doctor said the cancer could come back in five years. That's what she thought, that's what she believed, and that's what she focused on.

Five years and two months later, my mom passed away from a reoccurrence of the disease. Now, maybe this is a coincidence or maybe it's not. Due to that negative thought pattern, though, I'm on a mission to help others change their thought patterns to be more positive. Ralph Waldo Emerson stated, "We are what we think about all day long." What are you thinking and what are you becoming by your thoughts?

S = *Set realistic goals.* This is the most important step in the process. Most people don't spend enough time setting goals or they set goals that are so unrealistic that it's almost impossible to achieve them.

In fact, let me quote the findings from a goal-setting study sponsored by The Ford Foundation. The study claims that 23 percent of the population has no idea what they want from life and as a result they float around aimlessly. Sixty-seven percent of the population has a general idea of what they want, but they don't have any plans on how to get it.

Only 10 percent of the population has specific and well-defined goals, but even then only seven out of ten of those people reach their goals just half the time.

The top 3 percent of the people in the study achieved their goals 89 percent of the time. So based on the study, they found that the only difference between the top performers and the rest of the group was that the top 3 percent *wrote down their goals.*

Wow, goal-setting can't be made any simpler—write them down and you are already ahead of the game!

The second part of the equation is this: you have to see yourself accomplishing the goals you set for yourself. Visualize yourself in that new position in the company, or living in the house of your dreams. And make sure you see all of it in the present tense. Whatever it is you want, put yourself in the picture as already having achieved that goal. Remember, the subconscious mind doesn't know the difference between what is true or false—it just manifests what you see and believe in your mind most often.

Set your goals, write them down, and visualize yourself already achieving them. With enough repetition, you can start to attract experiences into your reality. That being said, it's also important to make your goals realistic and achievable. I'd like to be taller than five feet, but chances are that's not going to happen.

WRIGHT

How do you use the 4Step GUTS FORMULA in your daily life?

COTTLE

Since I'm super conscious of the 4Step GUTS FORMULA process, my words, thoughts, and actions are constantly being refocused and fine-tuned during the day. If I feel myself drifting into a negative line of thinking, I'll say the word "stop" or "cancel" to break the negative pattern. Then, I'll work on replacing those thoughts with ones that are more positive. It takes discipline and attention, but when I really take notice and consciously make adjustments, my life works so much easier.

WRIGHT

You place a tremendous emphasis on setting and measuring goals. Do you have more advice in that specific area for our readers?

COTTLE

David, there is more to goal-setting than just writing down goals. Not only should they be measurable and realistic, but also balanced. It is important to set goals in several areas of our lives. I just read an article about actor Matthew McConaughey in which he states, "Last year it was really cool to open up a diary from 1989 and see I'd written down ten goals. I'd completely forgotten what they were, and you know what? I had all ten of them done." That's a great testimonial on the power of writing down your goals.

We can achieve more balance if we focus on five different life segments when setting goals: Financial/Career, Spiritual, Relationships, Educational, and Dreams.

Sometimes we can have so many goals in one area, especially in the financial or career segment, that we become imbalanced in other areas.

First, let's start with the *Financial/Career* goals. It's important to set measurable, realistic, and attainable goals in this area. Write down the steps needed for you to move forward in your career. Once you have done that and you feel confident in the steps necessary, determine the amount of money you'd like to make. Write down exactly how much money you want to earn by the week, month, and year.

After writing down each amount, add a line that states, "this or better!" Sometimes we limit ourselves in our thinking as to what we are capable of earning.

Next, you want to evaluate and create your *Spiritual* goals. How do you measure your spiritual activity and growth? Is it achieved by attending church every week, participating in a mission trip, or reading inspirational materials? The path isn't as important as deciding what is most important to *you,* and then setting aside time on a regular basis to move towards that goal. We are responsible for our own enlightenment. Whatever works for us and gives us comfort and peace.

The third area is in *Relationships*. Look at all relationships with your family, spouse, boss or coworkers, relationships with your friends or relationships with your boss or coworkers. Plan ways you can enhance the quality of your relationships in all areas of your life. Where can you make improvements?

For example, I am very conscious and proactive in building better relationships. I would say that this quality is one of my strongest. Being very conscious of people's feelings and needs help me to serve others easily. It's something that I focus on every day.

The next goal segment is in the *Educational* area which we talked about earlier in the Gain Knowledge step of the GUTS FORMULA. What do you have to do to gain more knowledge in your profession? What kind of classes or seminars can you take? Who in your field can you learn from? Would he/she be willing to mentor you?

If you are in college or considering college, what classes do you need for the degree you want? How long is it going to take you to get there? What action can you take *today* that will get you to where you need to be six months from now, a year from now? Setting goals in the educational area is very important.

Then, the last segment is the *Dreams* segment. It's the "pie in the sky" area, throwing caution to the wind and dreaming about something totally different than what you have in your life today.

After living in Chicago most of my life, I thought it would be great to live by the ocean, maybe on an island. It finally happened. We moved to Amelia Island, Florida just blocks from the beach. That was one of my "pie in the sky" goals. It took years to materialize, but it certainly came true.

Make sure you add your dreams to the goal setting process because you never know what is possible! If you think it, and you believe it, then the law of attraction may just bring it your way.

WRIGHT

So why is it necessary to set goals in different areas of our lives when many of us just want to focus on one or perhaps two?

COTTLE

It's important to diversify your goals into at least these five areas because it helps you become more balanced.

Also, when you set goals in different areas, you don't know which goals may happen sooner than others. Let me give you an example: In 1992, during a goal setting exercise with my husband Stan, I set goals in every area of my life.

One aspect that was missing was starting a family, so I decided to add a new area, a new goal. At that point neither one of us were motivated to have a baby, but I was getting older and we felt we should at least put it out there. If it was meant to be, then it was meant to happen, all in its own timeframe. Would you believe out of all the goals I set that year, the pregnancy goal happened first! You can imagine our surprise and elation!

That's what I'm saying about the process; leave room for those surprises, don't plan every detail of your life within the time frame that *you* decide. God may have another plan for you. But we still have to initiate a road map to success, otherwise we'd be just flailing around like a ship without a rudder, and not knowing where we're heading, but do leave room for unexpected surprises in life!

WRIGHT

Do you have a role model that exemplifies the 4Step GUTS FORMULA in action?

COTTLE

My most treasured and favorite role model is a dear friend from Illinois, Pat Gulick. Pat is truly an example of a woman with GUTS! We grew up together two houses apart and despite Pat's disability, she *never* complained about her condition or limitations. Armed with a never ending positive attitude, Pat always pushed the envelope.

You see, Pat was born with cerebral palsy and has limited use of her body from the waist down. She gets around on crutches or by wheelchair. But that never stopped Pat from doing just about anything she made up her mind to do!

Last summer I spent time with Pat and attended one of her weekly horseback riding lessons at the Hanson Riding Center, a therapeutic riding center that specializes in working with adults and children with special needs. Pat has been taking lessons for thirty years, many of those years at this unique facility and enjoys working with the qualified staff who truly understands her needs and capabilities.

Each rider has several spotters who not only help the individuals mount the horses, but also walk beside them as guides and spotters. The most amazing part of this program is the way in which the participants are lifted onto the horses from their wheelchairs stationed from a raised ramp. A modified type of crane apparatus comes down from the ceiling and scoops up the rider from their wheelchair and carefully places them on the horse's saddle. It's a very time consuming procedure, especially for only a half-hour lesson, but totally worth it for the rider.

Oh, by the way did I mention that Pat drives herself to her lesson (and everywhere else) with the use of a customized car with the gas and the brake controls located on the steering column? After her lesson, Pat drives home where she lives alone in the same house she grew up in. Both parents are now deceased, but Pat was determined to take care of herself at home. Not to mention taking care of a dog, and several other pets.

Once home, and before getting out of her car, she has to assemble her wheelchair, place it outside the car, get in it, and wheel herself down the driveway, down the sidewalk, up a custom-made ramp to the front door to enter the house.

It's hard enough in good weather, and downright treacherous in the Chicago winter with the ice and snow.

I've got to tell you on those days when it's difficult for me to stay motivated to do something, my heart goes out to Pat and I'm reminded just how much more difficult it is for her to do the simplest of tasks. Why should I complain? She is a role model and one who I think has the GUTS to do just about anything. Her thought process is stellar, she doesn't ever think about anything negative, at least from what I can tell. She has terrific self-talk, every statement she makes is positive and she gains knowledge by reading, she is on the internet, she has been taking these horseback riding lessons for thirty years, she sets goals for herself that are realistic and obtainable based on her condition. Pat truly lives the GUTS formula.

WRIGHT

How do we effectively find and use our own role models or mentors?

COTTLE

Finding a role model is pretty easy if you just stop and think: Who am I already relying on for advice in my industry? Or it may be someone who you look up to that has more experience than you, or someone who just seems to have found a better way of managing what they do!

Next, ask your prospective role model if they would consider being a mentor to you. Chances are they will be honored to do so. Make sure that you both agree upon what is expected, and determine goals and timeframes that will be measured. It's much easier for someone to help you when your objectives are clear, otherwise you are wasting their time and yours.

Sandra Schrift, who lives in San Diego, has been my speaking coach for about twelve years. Through phone calls, and more recently Skype sessions on-line, I've been able to communicate with Sandra for advice, expertise, and friendship throughout the years. Sandra keeps me on track with my career and tells me what I need to hear, not always what I want to hear!

When I went back to college to finish my degree, my mentor was Carole Darr, a prominent advertising executive in Chicago. Carole guided me in taking the right classes to not only learn more about advertising and marketing, but also accounting and business. At the time, it seemed unnecessary, but after becoming General Manager of a television production/editing company I was so glad I had listened to Carole.

Most recently I've engaged another role model and mentor who truly inspires me. That person is Denise Brown, the older sister of Nicole Brown Simpson who was murdered in June of 1994.

Since early 1995, Denise has worked to help pass a variety of legislative solutions for domestic violence. One of her most important projects was to lobby on behalf of the Violence Against Women Act. Denise testified to the U.S. Senate Appropriations committee for increased funding for the Violence Against Women Act.

After her testimony, funding was increased from $18 million to $32 million. Back then, U.S. Senators Biden and Hatch cited Denise Brown as "having done more for the issue of domestic violence than any other individual."

Denise and I are currently working on producing an educational DVD program that will help women (and men) understand and create healthier relationships, and take steps to solve relationship problems before they become unhealthy or even dangerous.

Also, I've conducted and included a video interview with Denise as part of my anthology documentary called *Women With GUTS!*

Yes, she is quite a role model and mentor!

WRIGHT

What holds people back from being successful?

COTTLE

The most common trait that I've heard from clients that hold them back from being successful is a general lack of confidence. Anyone can learn the tricks of their trade, do all the right things, but if you don't have confidence in yourself and in your abilities, you may still fail, or at least not perform at your best. Somewhere along the way, a well-meaning teacher, parent, or friend may have said something negative that caused you to doubt yourself.

For example, when I was growing up a teacher once made this defeating exclamation, "If you plan on being a teacher you better think twice about that profession, because those kids are going to be taller than you and you are not going to be able to handle them!" That *one* comment actually discouraged me from becoming a teacher. The good news is that eventually I developed my talents in professional speaking, and now use my gift to inspire others. It didn't have to take place in a classroom.

It's a shame that we believe something negative about ourselves based on what someone may have told us in the past. Such comments can either shake our confidence or make us stronger. Either way, they have an impact.

The other reason that some people don't become successful is because they don't take the time to learn what they need to know in their careers. They take a shortcut or they think they can do it easier or better without taking the steps necessary to advance in their field. Some give up when the job gets too difficult or frustrating. But that's when you have to be more diligent and confident. It takes GUTS to move forward when it's difficult because it's easier when the path is smooth. The truly successful person will overcome obstacles and smooth out the bumps in the road.

WRIGHT

Well, what a great conversation! I always love talking to you - you are awfully positive. You make me feel better every time. This is some really good information, especially the goal setting in the areas of your life. Of course your 4Step GUTS FORMULA, I'm sure you have proven it over and over and over again. I really appreciate you taking time with me this morning to answer all these questions, I've learned a lot again and I'm sure that our readers will too.

COTTLE

Thanks, David. And I really appreciate the time you spent with me today. It was an honor to be interviewed for your successful anthology book series.

WRIGHT

Today, we have been talking to Deb Cottle. She is the Founder and President of World On a String, Inc., which is a company focused on enhancing people's lives through her inspirational seminars and coaching, self-help products and professional speaking. Deb is also the creator of the 4Step GUTS FORMULA, as we have talked about here today. I think I'm going to start using it! I don't know about our readers, but I think it's a good idea. Deb, thank you so much for being with us today on *ROADMAP to Success*.

COTTLE

Thank you, David. I'm pleased that you are going to start using the GUTS FORMULA and I wish you much success in your businesses and in your personal life.

ABOUT THE AUTHOR

Deb Cottle is founder and president of World On A String, a company focused on enhancing people's lives through inspirational seminars, workshops, coaching, products, and professional speaking. With her proven 4Step GUTS FORMULA, Deb has successfully motivated individuals and groups in major corporations, associations, and non-profit organizations to exceed personal and professional expectations.

She says, "It is up to us, as individuals, to create innovative ways to live more enriching lives. Having found my own direction, I am passionate about helping others find the GUTS to reach their fullest potential."

On her website, www.worldonastring.com, there is additional information on speaking and workshop topics. Motivational products are also available such as: *Success Simplified* (book), *Music & Motivation* (CD), and *Special Moments* (DVD). The documentary titled *Women With GUTS!* featuring Denise Brown, domestic violence prevention advocate, and other inspirational role models, is now available.

Deb Cottle

World On A String, Inc.
118 Sea Marsh Road
Amelia Island, FL 32034
904-261-2712
deb@worldonastring.com
www.worldonastring.com

Chapter Eighteen

CHARTING YOUR COURSE TOWARD WORK-LIFE BALANCE

DR. HEIDI SCOTT

DAVID WRIGHT (WRIGHT)

Today I am talking with Dr. Heidi Scott, President of Learning Pursuits Consulting, a company that designs, develops, and delivers business and life-changing learning experiences for teams and individuals. Dr. Scott's speaking, training, and coaching focus on guiding executives and leaders to improve their performance and reach full potential within their organizations and within their lives. A former teacher, principal, and professor, Dr. Scott is a master facilitator, public speaker, and an ICF Certified Coach who holds a PhD in leadership.

She enjoys life in the Pacific Northwest with her husband and two teenagers, where she is an avid soccer player and water-skier.

Dr. Scott, welcome to *ROADMAP to Success*.

DR. HEIDI SCOTT (DR. SCOTT)

Thank you, David; it's great to be here.

WRIGHT

You talk about your "Work-Life Balance Roadmap." I like that phrase. Tell us about that.

DR. SCOTT

The Work-Life Balance Roadmap is your personal path to achievable and sustainable balance between success at work and success at home. It works for every person, no matter your profession, goals, age, or family situation.

WRIGHT

Sounds like something everyone needs. How do you create one?

DR. SCOTT

In my consulting and training, I teach a four-step process of defining, describing, filtering, and reviewing. The first step is to define what success means to you by knowing your desired destinations.

Next, you describe your destinations in a clear, emotionally compelling, vivid vision of what true success, in these areas, means to you. This detailed awareness opens you to new levels of diligence and motivation that energize and reinforce the behavior that propels you to success. These first two steps also establish a profound sense of clarity that guides you on your journey.

WRIGHT

What if you don't know where you want to go?

DR. SCOTT

Think of it like this: Have you ever entered a partial destination in your car's or phone's navigation system? Well, enter a destination that's somewhat like what you might want, and you'll get someplace—but not necessarily the place you wanted to spend precious years of your life reaching!

Whether in life or in business, it's only when we have the correct destination identified that the optimal path is revealed. If you want the kind of success that is deeply fulfilling to you—the kind of success that allows you to feel a profound sense of achievement, serenity, well-being and confidence and the kind of success that achieves what you truly want for your family, your relationships, your faith, your career, and your personal development—that's not something you stumble across. It's something you identify and wisely and strategically aim for.

WRIGHT

What you're describing is very compelling and very personal. What makes work-life balance a business priority?

DR. SCOTT

In my experience, *individuals* most often hire a business and personal coach because they want more time for themselves and their relationships, or because they want more money so they can have more time for themselves and their relationships. *Business and organization leaders* most often hire a consultant to increase profits. They may ask the consultant to improve morale, energize sales, enhance communication, reduce turnover, or any number of similar issues, but their primary motivation is to realize their vision of a successful and profitable company.

Wise leaders understand that employee well-being directly affects company well-being and vice versa. In other words, work and life outside of work are inextricably combined.

A hunger for living a balanced life intentionally and purposefully is evident across our society today. Most of us don't realize it, but this is nothing new.

Consider this quote: "Time is what we want most, but what, alas! we use worst; and for which God will certainly most strictly reckon with us, when Time shall be no more." Guess when that was written? Ten years ago, fifty years ago? It was written by William Penn, born in 1644. The quest for more time and the yearning for balance in a busy life has been part of our culture for a long, long time.

A successful balance between work and life nourishes us at the office and at home. When we have balance, our satisfaction and sense of "rightness" spill over into our work like water over a dam.

WRIGHT

So how does the kind of balance you're talking about lead to business success?

DR. SCOTT

Surveys show that achieving balance between work and life trumps career progression and salary in job seekers' decisions. This is so revealing! If you're an executive, leader, or manager, you need to know how to promote work-life balance among your employees to help them reach their work goals as well as their life goals.

Providing strategies and emphasizing increased work-life balance will set you apart as a leader or as a company. You'll earn your employees' loyalty and increase your own sense of achievement. Your commitment will pay off in improved productivity, reduced turnover, and more focused and self-directed work. When employees feel they are achieving their most desired priorities in their lives, their satisfaction across all important areas of their lives (including work!) goes up.

The best way to get anywhere is to know where you want to go and how you plan to get there. Success is that simple.

If you don't know or care where you're headed, any road will take you there. So the first issue is to have clarity about your desired destination. The next step is to determine your route.

With a road map, you have a plan that takes into account your desire to reach your destination quickly, as well as your need to enjoy yourself when you arrive. To extend the metaphor, it considers your need for rest, meals, and breaks. It addresses the terrain you have to cross, the vehicles and support you'll need to make the trip, and it's flexible in case you hit a snag—new construction, unexpected detours, and the kinds of things life is full of.

On the other hand, having no road map means your journey will likely be long, winding, confusing, and heavily dependent on luck. Even worse, the destination you reach may not be one you'd have willingly sacrificed years of life to reach.

The Work-Life Balance Roadmap helps you define *and* reach your desired destination. It puts you in touch with your own inner wisdom and builds a plan based on your values. It's your most direct track to success in the areas of your life that matter to you.

WRIGHT

If people desire work-life balance; what keeps them from it?

DR. SCOTT

The main obstacle to work-life balance can be summed up in one word: busyness. Think about how many times you've greeted someone with, "How are you?" and gotten an answer like, "Oh, I'm so busy! I've got so much going on I don't know whether I'm coming or going. Life is just crazy busy!" You hear it all the time.

Our culture esteems busyness even as we crave balance. A little bit of busyness is healthy, but there's a fine line between being energized with a full schedule and being exhausted or feeling out of control due to a completely over-committed life. Busyness can cyclone out of control and when it does, we get completely swept up. Suddenly, we're not leading the lives we wanted to lead, and we're not making progress toward destinations that are deeply meaningful to us. We're just barely getting through our day, sometimes without even realizing it. The cycle of busyness has taken over our lives.

WRIGHT

What is a "cycle of busyness"?

DR. SCOTT

There are four parts of the cycle: Busyness, Isolation, Loneliness, and Priority struggles. When you want to control your busyness instead of letting your busyness control you, you want to break the Busyness Cycle.

Here's how it works: It begins with busyness. Somehow— suddenly or slowly—we become busier and busier. We're living life on the fastest network speed available and can't seem to get off. We realize something is amiss as we race with exhaustion to the next

Busyness Cycle

Busyness

Priorities
STRUGGLE

Isolation

Loneliness

311

thing we must do, but we can't take time for self-assessment because we don't have any time!

Then, in our semi-conscious state of busyness, we realize we've become so busy that we've actually disconnected from others at a meaningful level. That's when we experience the next phase of our cycle of busyness, which is isolation.

Rushing from commitment to responsibility to the next thing on our to-do list gradually robs us of depth. We look up from our many commitments and harried schedules, and we realize something essential is missing. We are relational creatures. Deep down inside we crave connection and relationships with meaning. But we are isolated.

At some point, we realize we're not authentically connected to others the way we want to be, and we have next to no time to remedy that. Eventually, disconnection and isolation usher in the next step of the cycle of busyness: loneliness.

When we are spinning on the cycle of busyness, we're not just busy, isolated, and then a little lonely—we're so unconnected we can't remedy our loneliness. Experiencing loneliness in our relationships at work or at home is a stunning awareness.

Busyness can disguise starving relationships, neglected friendships, and missed opportunities with our children and friends for only so long. Sometimes in our state of isolation we've alienated or neglected those we care about so much that we don't feel we can reach out to them. Yet we long for relationships that matter.

We ask ourselves things like, "Am I the only one living out of control? Am I the only one who gets up feeling loneliness like this every day? Why am I doing all these things? How did my life get so out of balance?" This loneliness and self-recrimination leads us to the final phase on the busyness cycle—an awareness that we've lost or mixed up our priorities.

Without clearly established priorities that are true to our goals and our values and without definite priorities we can use as a filter in all of our activities, we flounder around in this fourth quadrant of the cycle of busyness.

Intense busyness has spun us into a state of isolation, which intensifies our perceived sense of loneliness. Isolation and loneliness lead us to question our priorities, or to recognize that we don't really have any. And often it feels most normal to just consume ourselves with more busyness than to deal with or examine our priorities.

Busyness, isolation, loneliness, and priority struggles, that's the cycle of busyness. It's a challenging cycle to break from.

WRIGHT

If the struggle for work-life balance is such a rampant one, what strategies exist for people who identify with your description of the out-of-control life?

DR. SCOTT

To combat and break the cycle of busyness—to tame our busyness, reduce and eliminate isolation, break our loneliness, and nail down our priorities—we have to examine the key building blocks of our road map to successful work-life balance.

There are four main stages on the Work-Life Balance Roadmap used to break the busyness cycle.

1. **Write Your Desired Destinations**. What are the most important priorities of your life? People generally answer with a list of items that often includes God, their significant other, career, health, children, recreation, financial stability, self-development, friendships, a hobby, etc. Common top destinations may have the same name, but may look very different to different people.

Once you get clear enough on those desired destinations to write them down, enrich those priorities with powerful images. In my workshops, I take clients through a process of describing their envisioned endgame for each destination in living color. What exactly does success in that particular destination or priority look like to you? How will it feel? How will you feel when you achieve it?

Without that type of clarity, you may be similar to the frantic traveler who, when asked how he is progressing on his journey responds, "Well, I've got bad news and good news. The bad news is that I'm not sure where I'm going. The good news is that I'm making great time!"

Ambiguous desired destinations in the most important areas of your life promote out-of-control busyness. This is the source of your inability to say no, your difficulty in prioritizing, and your inability to design a schedule that feeds you instead of one that starves and diminishes you. Having a crystal clear description in living color of your envisioned endgame for each one of your desired destinations is essential. In fact, it's the most critical step in your strategic plan to move toward work-life balance.

Living-Color

When I was a kid, we used to take an annual trip by car to the Oregon Coast. Typically, throughout this eight-hour drive, I pestered my parents with, "Are we there yet?" I knew in intense detail what the destination was like and I couldn't wait to be in this wonderful place. I was beside myself I was so eager to get there.

In my mind I could feel the wet sand squish between my toes and dry upon my leg. I could sense the mist of the surf upon my face as I walked close to the water on the beach. I could smell the salt air and feel the sensation of the salt in my hair after a few hours of playing on the beach. In the little beach town, I could picture opening a wooden door to the candy shop and hearing it slam against the doorframe while the sweet taffy smell wafted through the air. I could picture sparks from the evening bonfires whispering in the dark.

It's that type of clarity you need to create about your desired destinations so you can have a powerful desire to experience your goals with all of your senses. It's a desire so profound that it pulls you to where you want to go in your life. A living color, graphically-envisioned endgame is compelling. It describes exactly where you want to go and it fills you with an eagerness to experience it soon!

When we possess a focused, authentic vision in living color for what we want our lives to look like in all areas important to us, we create a new personal culture—at home and at work. Almost without effort, our behaviors become aligned to our vision.

WRIGHT

So once people have written their list of desired destinations, how do you recommend they create this living color envisioned endgame for each destination?

DR. SCOTT

When it comes to crafting your Work-Life Balance Roadmap, begin by focusing on three of your specific destinations from the list you wrote of your desired destinations. In my trainings we take the process further, but everything starts with these three goals. You will want one of those destinations to center on your work and your career.

Will you make an appointment with yourself for an uninterrupted block of time where you can think, dream, ponder, and envision what you desire your work and career to look, feel, and be like? We're talking about crafting a passionate picture of what you want to see in your work in three years or five years, depending on your age, industry, and situation. This isn't restating a metric-related goal (generally we're pretty good at doing that). This is a commitment to bring your main business-related, long-term goal from your brain to your heart. Imagine what that living color envisioned endgame—that larger-than-life, yet realistic stretch goal—in your work looks like.

Next, select two of the most important desired destinations related to your life away from work. What is of utmost importance to you? Is it a particular relationship with an individual? Is it self-development, recreation, or a hobby? What two destinations, away from work, are at the top of your chart?

Again, block out a few hours for envisioning each of those personal desired destinations. Free up your heart and mind to dream, regardless of your current reality related to each of those important destinations. Resist the temptation to get bogged down by considering "how" you will get there. Remain focused on the "what"—what will it look like? Begin to capture what that part of your life will look like when you successfully arrive.

If you had to design a high-quality marketing brochure or an interactive Web site in living color for each of these important desired destinations, what would you be sure to include? What is so compelling about the destination that makes you long to be there?

Writing and crafting that type of vision for each of your desired destinations takes a great deal of focus and mental energy and a lack of interruption. You've got to set yourself up for success by first selecting one work-focused destination and two life-related destinations so you don't become overwhelmed. Then, calendar a block of time when you're out of your normal work and life location. If you don't get away, crises, interruptions, and busyness will distract you. Give yourself permission, or perhaps an assignment, to write each of these descriptions in living color detail.

WRIGHT

So writing your desired destinations and crafting your living color envisioned endgames are the first two steps in designing your Work-Life Balance Roadmap. Would you share with our readers, what are the other two steps?

DR. SCOTT

Sure. Step three of designing your Work-Life Balance Roadmap is using your behavior filter. By writing and naming your desired destinations for your life and work, and by crafting a vivid, living-color endgame for each of those destinations, you now have a behavior filter.

Every activity you choose to engage in can be run through your behavior filter in a moment, in your mind, to ensure that it's aligned to your envisioned endgame for each of your desired destinations in your life. With this behavior filter, you can discern which choices are aligned to your goals and desires, and which are not.

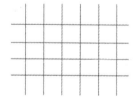

Behavior Filter

No matter what our culture tells us, no matter how driven we are, no matter what dreams we possess, we simply cannot do it all. Gaining awareness that every time I say "Yes" to something equates to saying "No" to something else can be life-altering. For example, when I decide to work late, that means I'm stealing time and attention from some other important priority or desired destination in my life. I may be stealing time and energy from my family or from my health or from friends and relationships. By choosing to work late, I may simply steal from myself the time to recharge, relax, or sleep.

When I choose to run late on one call or allow myself to lose track of time while I'm immersed in an activity, I am saying Yes to more focus in that area, but saying No to being on time for the people involved in my next meeting or No to planning time that would allow me to focus on the next activity or person in my day.

Learning how to consider that every Yes to one thing is a No to something else is a true challenge. Automatically reviewing our answer in light of our limited daily resources of time, energy, and focus, drives home the reality that we can't do it all. It creates a tangible awareness that each behavior and activity I say Yes to ought to be aligned to that living color envisioned endgame for my desired destination in order to stay on my Work-Life Balance Roadmap.

Living with an intentional awareness of each of our life destinations empowers us to say No to things, even good things, because they would distract us and pull us off course from the desired destinations to which our Work-Life Balance Roadmap leads us. With our desired destinations named and clearly in focus through our living color envisioned endgames, we have peace when we hit a roadblock or pull into a pit stop.

With the correct coordinates plugged in, we can easily get back on course.

Three R's

WRIGHT

And the fourth step?

DR. SCOTT

-*Reflect*
-*Review*
-*Revise*

The fourth step in sustaining momentum on your Work-Life Balance Roadmap is using the three R's: Reflect, Review, and Revise.

To reflect means looking at how we're working and living and considering whether we are balanced. It involves honest self-assessment, which leads to self-awareness.

To review involves revisiting our desired destinations and determining whether we're staying focused on moving toward them. As we review our journey and recognize our accomplishments, we gain energy and pick up momentum. Through regular reflection and review we can see specific changes that need to occur, and this may lead to revision.

To revise means fine-tuning, editing, or adding clarity to our envisioned endgames. Sometimes, due to external forces beyond our control, we may need to revise some of the recurring behaviors we allow through our behavior filter. Often, as we become more centered and balanced, we see our priorities change, shift, or expand. Revision means we are cognizant of the ever-evolving nature of life, and we are willing to grow.

The three R's bring us full circle back to our first step in this process, focusing on our desired destination. This isn't a one-stop shop. Creating and staying on our Work-Life Balance Roadmap is a continual process.

It becomes a way of life.

WORK - LIFE   BALANCE   ROADMAP

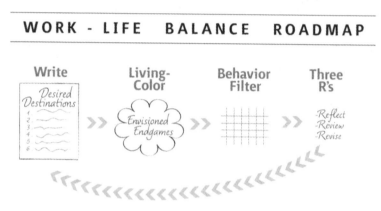

WRIGHT

You've given the four steps to designing a Work-Life Balance Roadmap. Are there other actions you recommend for those who desire a greater level of work-life balance?

DR. SCOTT

Yes. As you keep the mental description of each desired destination in mind, consider what I call "non-negotiables." When it comes to discovering and naming non-negotiables, the right question to ask is, "What are the things I would *never* willingly miss or not do related to my desired destination?" When you determine these activities, name them and calendar them.

For example, family birthdays go on my annual calendar. Nothing is going to switch those days and I want to be certain I don't schedule anything that would infringe on my availability to celebrate my family members' lives.

A few years ago, even though I'd calendared my son's thirteenth birthday, overachievement nearly got the best of me. I had a business event in New Jersey the entire day and evening the day before his

Saturday birthday. I dropped into my hotel bed late that Friday night and got up a few short hours later with my body still set on Pacific Time. I was bleary-eyed as my plane lifted off at 6 AM Eastern Time. Exhausted, I made it home at ten that morning to celebrate my boy's birthday with the party I'd planned the week before.

Yes, I was physically there. But in my heart I knew I'd cut it too close. What if one of my flights had been late?

Listing your non-negotiables helps you become truly aware of those golden, multi-million-dollar value events in your life. Is there an anniversary to remember? Are there family gatherings or celebrations you want or need to attend? Do you have your vacations calendared? Vacations are a critical event to calendar! Without time blocked for a true vacation, the odds are good you won't take one.

To get things started, consider the coming week or two. What business project, meeting, or event meets your criteria for a work-related non-negotiable? Remember, these non-negotiables *must* be aligned with your work-related destination.

After considering special non-negotiables, turn your attention to recurring behaviors you believe are necessary for you to have a shot at making your desired destination a reality. I encourage you to start with a small set of recurring behaviors aligned to one of your desired destinations. For example, in my desired destination for my health, I have a very clear picture of what I want to be able to do and how I will live life in ten and twenty years' time. With my health destination and living-color endgame clear, I know there are a number of recurring behaviors I need to be executing consistently. While I love the great outdoors, it can be very tempting to skip a run, a walk, or a workout. But when I keep my living-color envisioned endgame of my health destination in mind and I use it as a filter for my behaviors, my motivation level goes up. I know I'm confidently executing a daily dose of discipline as I journey toward my health destination.

If you schedule into your calendar the recurring behaviors that made it through your behavior filter, then the calendar reminder also serves as permission to do these things.

When we get into the habit of doing a quick mental check before we say Yes or No to a new project, commitment, or task, then we're in the process of living work-life balance!

Finally, don't overlook the three R's once you've started on your journey. Realize that living balance in your work and your life is a process.

Schedule time to regularly revisit and review your desired destinations as well as your living-color endgames for each.

Sometimes our seasons in life shift and our priorities will naturally shift with them. Change is a part of life whether we want it to be or not. Don't sit back and think that the strategic Work-Life Balance Roadmap you spent time on at one point is "good to go" for the rest of your life!

WRIGHT

What drives your personal interest in the topic of work-life balance?

DR. SCOTT

I am a successful recovering workaholic! Developing, testing, and implementing strategies to combat my own out-of-balance life ended up shifting my work and my career. When I began sharing what I'd learned, I saw men and women at all levels of organizations use these strategies to redraw their own road maps to success in every area of their lives. The busyness that leads to workaholism does not respect industry, status, or position. These strategies in the Work-Life Balance Roadmap can support anyone in improving his or her quality of life and chances for success in any area.

This past year, our daughter graduated from high school. As we left her at college a few states away, we hugged, shed some tears, and said goodbye. Over and above the intense emotion around this milestone, I also felt a very personal sense of relief. My relationship with her is exactly what I had envisioned back when she was in elementary school when I was forced to confront my workaholism. The relationship I have with my daughter today was one of my clear destinations back then.

What I teach and use in my speaking and consulting is not simply theory. It's not just book or research knowledge. It's how I live my life.

WRIGHT

What was your road into and out of being a workaholic like?

DR. SCOTT

I've always loved what I do, which is great, but over a decade ago I loved what I did in my career so much that I was constantly involved with work. I was physically, mentally, or emotionally distracted or absorbed in work most of the time. This left me unavailable to varying degrees at home. I didn't live as though I truly knew where I wanted to go in any area of my life—not even in my work! I was too busy solving work problems, facing work challenges, and leading my work team to know what it was I was striving and working so hard for.

One day I woke up and realized that I wasn't the wife, the mom, or the person I really wanted to be. I was successfully climbing that corporate ladder, but the rest of my life was not headed toward success. So I hit the brakes and immediately pulled into a pit stop for some major life repair.

Because I know, from personal experience, that work-life balance is a critical element in a healthy road map to success, I'm totally passionate about the topic. Help *does* exist for people who are overwhelmed by all they've taken on in work and in life.

WRIGHT

Do you think women lose balance between work and life more often than men?

DR. SCOTT

I don't believe the struggles involved in work-life balance place the noose more around the neck of either gender. When it comes to behavior, work ethic, family culture, and personality, each of us is wired uniquely. Each gender deals with different constraints, cultural norms, relationship roles, and child-bearing and child-rearing issues; but there are actually more similarities than differences.

Many men struggle with work-life balance as they strive to succeed in the workplace and lead personally rich and fulfilled lives. Throw kids into the mix, and many fathers find work success pulling them away from being the engaged fathers they desire to be. When it comes to women, I know all too well the work-life balance issues that women—especially professional women—struggle with, whether they are mothers or not.

Yet, in conversations with either sex, each seems to believe that the other gender simply does not understand the constraints and challenges he or she faces. Sadly, this is often true, but not because one gender has it much harder than the other! It's true because most people are so caught up in their priority struggles that they can't fully understand how issues of work-life balance include different pressures and demands for the opposite sex.

Today, record numbers of people struggle with work-life balance. This has much to do with our "always on" and "24/7 availability" culture. Living at breakneck speed keeps us from being aware of our desired destinations and priorities. But that doesn't mean we can't be extremely successful and extremely fulfilled. It just means we have to work at it, and we have to have a road map.

WRIGHT

What types of support do you recommend for people embarking on a fresh journey toward their desired destinations on their work-life balance road map?

DR. SCOTT

Sharing your goals and commitments and plans of action with someone you trust will increase the likelihood of your follow-through and success. A one-on-one business and personal life coach can be an effective route to go because it's tremendously helpful to have your own advocate who desires to see you succeed. Having a coach who knows how to ask the right questions often propels you forward in that journey toward work-life balance.

If that's not an option, there's another way to gain a guide and mentor. Lewis and Clark traversed the Pacific Northwest exploring the frontier, but without the Indian girl, Sacagawea, they would have perished on their journey. She knew about the paths they traveled toward their destination.

Find one or more mentors to serve as Sacajaweas for you on your work-life balance journey. This is something you want to approach carefully; it may be very challenging. Look for success in the person's history in areas related to your life's desired destinations. Look for an authentic level of care from him or her toward you. If you don't know the person at all or very well, look for evidence that he or she has an openness to authentically care for others with the desire to help. And definitely look for Sacajaweas you respect. Whom do you know with a successful track record in an area closely related to one of your desired destinations? Is it someone you respect and trust? List some names by each of your destinations.

Next, reach out to that person. As you prepare to connect with someone—either a one-on-one coach or an informal Sacajawea—review each of your desired destinations. What questions about each destination would you love to discuss with a mentor or subject matter expert?

With the names of the potential Sacajawea mentors in your life and your list of questions or topics, you're ready to calendar time to make contact and request the meeting. When? When will you make those inquiries and set up meetings? Get it scheduled.

Additionally, for whom can you be a Sacajawea? How can you pay forward to someone else the benefits you've experienced from being mentored? Can you name a few people you can offer to be a sounding board and mentor to? When will you seek out conversation of that nature with them? You may offer realistic support, and offer it sincerely, however, use caution so you don't offer more time than you can reasonably give or offer support you can't follow through on. In making this offer, remember that when you share wisely, you enrich yourself and the recipient. You build a new, value-based relationship and you deepen your connectedness to others.

WRIGHT

Thank you for providing us with strategies to create our personal work-life balance road map to success. Any send-off words for us?

DR. SCOTT

Begin now! Schedule an appointment with yourself to define and describe your top three desired destinations, then filter your behaviors and review your personal Work-Life Balance Roadmap. You *can* live a balanced life, and you can start living that way soon. Go for it!

WRIGHT

Today I have been talking with Dr. Heidi Scott, President of Learning Pursuits Consulting. She speaks to groups of all types about work-life balance and improving personal and team performance. She also designs, develops, and delivers business and life-changing learning experiences with teams and individuals. Listening to her today, I think she knows what she's talking about!

Heidi, thank you so much for being with us today on *ROADMAP to Success*.

DR. SCOTT

Thank you.

About the Author

Dr. Heidi Scott is President of Learning Pursuits Consulting. She is a speaker who engages audiences with authentic learning as they discover how to maximize the way they are naturally gifted and reach success while pursuing work-life balance. Leaders, teams, and organizations consult with her to help them improve their performance. From Blue Bunny Ice Cream to large hospital systems and financial planning companies, from training and education companies to college athletic teams—she helps clients reach their potential.

As an International Coaching Federation certified business coach, Dr. Scott helps people discern where they want to go, and helps them discover how to get there. For fun, she is an adjunct professor at Gonzaga University in Spokane, Washington, in both the Communications Department and the Masters of Leadership Program. She and her husband live in North Idaho and enjoy time with their high school and college teenagers.

Heidi Scott, PhD

Learning Pursuits Consulting
509-435-7470
www.LearningPursuits.com
DrH@LearningPursuits.com
Facebook.com/LearningPursuits
Twitter.com/DrHeidiScott

Chapter Nineteen

FIND YOUR OASIS

MILLIE GRENOUGH

DAVID WRIGHT (WRIGHT)

Today I am talking with Millie Grenough. Millie inspires people to do what they thought was impossible. She teaches non-singers to sing, shy speakers to present confidently in public, Type A personalities to work smarter, and frazzled folks to focus. A former nun turned nightclub singer, ex-shy Kentuckian turned international speaker, Millie walks her talk. After a near-death accident impacted her high-velocity lifestyle, she developed strategies to help herself live a saner and more balanced life. She incorporated her techniques in her book, *OASIS in the Overwhelm: 60 Second Strategies for Balance in a Busy World,* that has helped thousands. Coach, author of ten books, motivational speaker, and Clinical Instructor in Psychiatry at Yale University School of Medicine, she coaches people in all walks of life from CEOs to harried parents and imparts her strategies in workshops, lectures, and individual sessions internationally.

Millie, welcome to *ROADMAP to Success.*

MILLIE GRENOUGH (GRENOUGH)

Thank you, David. It's a pleasure to be here with you.

WRIGHT

Success is such a much-used word and has many connotations. How do you define it?

GRENOUGH

You're right. Success is used often, and it means different things to different people. It's a very personal thing. Someone may feel that creating something is success for them. Another person may define it by achieving financial success or having a strong family. Others might say it's being well thought of or pursuing higher education or even attaining a career goal. I like to think of success as my best self when I am living in meaningful, purposeful harmony with the world around me.

It's intriguing to me that when I ask friends and colleagues what success means to them I get widely varying responses. Each of their answers reflects who they are and where they are in their lives.

For instance, Brian, a sixty-five-year-old entrepreneur said, "Success means reaching a goal or an objective that you set for yourself."

Angelyn, a working mother and grandmother responded, "Somebody is successful who is happy, fulfilled, doing work that is satisfying, and is a productive member of the community." She added, "Somebody who is selling drugs may feel happy and fulfilled, but they're not doing much for the community."

Ben, age fifty, said, "I think success is feeling content within yourself." An engineer and CEO of his firm, Ben added "This contentment then leads to more material and practical things."

Diane, a thirty-year-old Manhattan attorney and mother of two, said, "Finding something you feel passionate about, whether it's your career or your family and following through to make it happen is my definition of success."

When I interviewed people, I was a bit surprised that the majority did not measure success primarily by financial means or even by material or intellectual trophies, a six-figure salary, how many books they'd written, or how many awards received. Almost all recognized that they wanted a connection between their inner selves and how they expressed that outwardly. This awareness of inner/outer connection may be a reflection of the people I interviewed, but at the same time they represent different ages, different gender, and different professions. I find that interesting and quite telling.

WRIGHT

You write about success meaning different things to different people. What questions can help us clarify what success is for each of us?

GRENOUGH

For my clients and for myself, I ask two simple but not always easy questions:

– Who am I?
– What am I here for?

I take each of those questions on two levels—the immediate and the "cosmic." If we begin at the immediate, right now, *"Who am I right this instant?"* my answer is: "I am Millie, coach, writer, being interviewed by you, David." And *"What am I here for right now?"* "To give the best, clearest, and most helpful interview possible."

Success in the immediate is to carry this out to the best of my ability. In this minute I am not cluttering myself with other goals I want to reach, other books I may want to write, other mountains I may want to climb, even though I greatly enjoy climbing mountains. Right now, this minute, success is knowing what I am here for exactly, now, in the present.

Now, here comes the more challenging part. On a "cosmic" level, the questions *Who am I?* and *What am I here on this Earth for?* invite us to pause and reflect on a deeper level: who am I, and what unique strengths, gifts, aspirations, and passions do I have? This is a really big question: how will the world be better because I am in it?

When I work with clients, I ask them to take time to feel, think, and write down their responses to these questions so that their answers become clearer. Then I ask them to dive deeper:

- What is your unique background?
- What did you receive from your family/friends/ neighborhood that shapes who you are now?
- What experiences have made an impression on you?
- What are your current circumstances—the good parts, the not so good parts?
- What are the challenges you are facing right now?
- What opportunities are in front of you?
- What barriers keep you from achieving your goals?

When my clients spend time with these questions, they shed light on the third important question:

– What do I want my legacy to be?

Again, the answer to this question varies widely. Andrea said, "I want to become a world famous architect and build something even more beautiful than the Chrysler Building." Curt, an engineer, commented: "If I can find a way to use water and energy that makes my state a leader in green beauty and functionality, that would be a wonderful legacy." Someone else may say he or she wants to raise a beautiful family or discover a breakthrough in the treatment of multiple sclerosis or start a nonprofit that helps children in the neighborhood.

What it really boils down to is what is important to you? Asking those three questions can help you to define what success is for you. It may not always come out the way you had initially dreamed. That's why it's important to ask yourself those questions on a regular basis—maybe even begin each day with them.

It's especially important to re-ask the questions after life throws you an unexpected curve such as illness for you or a family member, an economic shift, or a crisis in your community. Remember, you can *return to your core*. If you can define yourself and define your legacy, you can go from there.

WRIGHT

To accomplish these legacies we certainly will encounter barriers. What do you see as the chief barriers?

GRENOUGH

I believe there are four specific barriers:

1. Getting caught up in the fast lane
2. Lack of personal clarity
3. Competing pressures
4. The reality of everyday life

I'll begin with "getting caught up in the fast lane." I sometimes think about my dad who died a long time ago. He never heard that expression "24/7." If he had heard it, I believe he would have thought it was either something to get his old Chevy going in the morning or a laxative. It was not part of his life. My friend Jane, a mother, wife, and high school teacher, said, "Sure, we all live 24/7 lives. But the question is: what do we want those 24/7 lives to be?" She added, "If you get caught up in the rat race, even if you win, at the end you're still a rat."

The second barrier, about not being clear, is very real. Sometimes we just do not pay attention to the key questions: Who am I? and What am I here for?

I was speaking yesterday with a woman who is an extremely accomplished professional. She said, "I feel like a hamster in my cage. I'm just rolling all these balls around endlessly and don't know where I'm heading. I think I just need rest." I agreed, saying, "That's probably true." Along with scores of other professionals, she was not taking the time to care for herself and to get clear.

The third barrier, competing pressures, may include other people's ideas of what success should mean for you. Perhaps your parents wanted you to be an attorney or your college classmates are all making six-figure salaries or you feel as though you're doing everything you can, yet you're not achieving the American dream. Those might be somebody else's pressures that you are taking on yourself, when in reality that person doesn't have anything to do with who you are and why you are in this world.

The last barrier is about reality and refers to the fact that reality changes every minute. Maybe you were on the road to achieve your goals and then wham! the economy takes a tailspin that hits your profession and leaves you jobless. Or even worse, you find yourself seriously ill, or your twenty-year-old son is diagnosed with a life-threatening illness. All of these are reality factors that happen to all of us. I will address this barrier and how to deal with it later in this interview.

WRIGHT

So how can people get through these barriers and achieve success?

GRENOUGH

The key is to face yourself with clarity and to act with courage. When "reality" shifts, you need even more clarity and courage.

I'll give you an example. When Dave, a vice president in a large financial company, came to me for coaching, he was in his early thirties, married, and definitely on the upward track. He targeted two specific goals:

- I want to become the top salesman in my division.

- I want to lose weight and get active enough so that I can play basketball again.

Dave worked on his goals in very specific ways and was making progress. Then 9/11 happened.

Dave came in the following week and said, "Millie, is it okay if I change my goals?" I replied, "Sure. Let's talk about it." He went back to the key questions and it helped him refocus his intentions. Dave realized that he wanted to make some significant shifts, and he recognized that he would have to break through barriers and change some well-honed habits to achieve them. He wrote:

"I really want to spend more time with my wife. I have not been paying attention to her."

"I think I want to start going to church again."

"I realize I'd better take care of myself or else I won't be any good to anybody."

Within a few months, Dave reported that he was replacing his old habits with new "grooves" that were beginning to function more smoothly. He was feeling better personally (more content, bringing flowers to his wife, going to church, losing weight, playing in a weekly basketball game) and professionally (clearly focusing on desired clients and how to best serve them to achieve maximum results). He recognized more clearly how the personal/professional aspects of his life affected each other. He began bringing a healthy lunch to work three times a week instead of his usual time-consuming and calorie-filled cocktail lunches.

Six months after 9/11, Dave contacted me excitedly to say, "Great news! My wife and I are expecting and it's twins! I guess I will have to sharpen those questions again."

When I am working, either with an individual client or with a group for team-building, I ask them to begin by noticing what their strengths are, rather than focusing first on what is *not* working. You remember the old song, "You've got to accentuate the positive, eliminate the negative." Many times people try to be something different from what they are instead of recognizing their strengths and making them work in ways that are useful for them and for other people.

My *OASIS 60-Second Strategies* help people get in touch with their strengths.

The first strategy I would like to discuss I call *Changing the Channel*. Sometimes you realize you are in a funk or you are anxious about something, or you're sad or angry. If you let yourself *become aware* of the emotional channel you're on, that's the first step.

For example, let's say I'm on the angry channel. If I am aware of that, then I can ask myself what this anger is about and what is happening now that's triggering my anger. Once I am clear, then I ask: *is there anything I can do and want to do about this situation right at this moment?* If the answer is yes, and the action will not hurt me or anyone else, then I *do* it. But if it's simply anger about something past or future that is draining my energy now and making my brain clogged up, I can *change my channel*. I can switch to another channel that is more useful, more practical.

I am not a Pollyanna so I am not saying go to the *everything-is-wonderful* channel, because that's not realistic and it's not true. Simply find something right now that you can say, "Yes, that's okay." Right now I am looking out my window and I see that the sun is out. That's more useful, more pleasant, than being angry that there are two feet of snow on the ground and I can't get out to the office today. I change my emotional channel from, "*Ah, all my plans for today are messed up and I'll get even further behind*" frustration channel to, "*Ah, the sun is beautiful and I'm alive!*" positive channel. It can be as simple as that.

Changing your channel is not always easy when you are facing a major concern. However, it costs nothing financially, can be done in sixty seconds, and it has huge payoffs. When I stay on the anger channel, I actually impair my immune system and I impede the ability of my brain to think clearly, my blood pressure to work in my favor, and my heart to function optimally.

There are other simple ways such as writing in a journal. Sometimes I use an offbeat strategy—I invite my clients to sing their desires and their challenges.

Alicia talked about family pressure and her current frustration. She was from an Asian family of scientists and they clearly expected her to be a scientist. Alicia had climbed up the educational track and was involved in high-powered genetic research at a prestigious university. She woke up one morning and realized, "I love this work and I know it's very useful, but I really want to spend more time with my family. My daughter is growing up and that is more important to me." I asked her to sing her parents' dreams and she sang it out: "Be the best scientist you can be—" Then she sang her dream for herself: "I want to be a wonderful woman, a wonderful mother—" The simple act of shifting into singing helped her experience things in a radically different way. She aired out the parental messages and gave a stronger voice to a dream more closely attuned to her.

WRIGHT

Stress is so prevalent these days on all fronts. What are some of the ways that it affects us?

GRENOUGH

Hundreds of clinical studies affirm that stress is a factor in conditions such as:

> heightened anxiety
> fatigue
> depression
> inhibited memory function
> interrupted sleep
> less enjoyment of life
> elevated blood pressure
> disturbed relationships
> lowered sexual functioning
> poor work performance
> impaired immune systems
> lowered resilience regarding cancer
> increased incidence of strokes

Last week when I was conducting a workshop with a corporate group, I asked the participants not to tell me if they experienced the above stress factors, but just to put a checkmark by each one that might apply to them. As I read the list I could see lots of people checking.

Every day I hear complaints such as:

"I'd love to slow down but I can't. I'm afraid if I let up I'll lose my drive."

"I can never catch up. My life, my desk, my kids, my finances, the world [you fill in the blanks] is in such a mess now. I don't know where to start. And you know what? I think it's getting worse."

Medical experts say that we live now in a constant state of alertness, accompanied by an increased sense of helplessness. Simply stated, our lives are more complex and our world is less predictable and more dangerous than it used to be. In response to this state of affairs, our stress responses are going berserk.

Each of us feels this stress in tiny ways or big ways. Whether it's something as simple as "Where did I put my keys?" or something big like a spouse losing a job, stress hits all of us. In his book, *Why Zebras Don't Get Ulcers*, the neuroscientist Robert M. Sapolsky explains that animals make much better use of their stress responses than most of us do. Rather than turning our stress responses on and off as needed, we humans plug into them with extravagant frequency when we're sitting frustrated in traffic jams, worrying about expenses, mulling over intense interactions with colleagues, or even trying to find a quarter that we dropped on the floor of the car. Sapolsky says if we can't turn on the stress response when it's needed, as an animal does when it runs away from a hungry lion, we're in trouble. But even more, if we turn it on and cannot turn it off, that becomes nearly as damaging as the stressor itself. Sadly, most of corporate America today lives on 24/7 stress. Even more sadly, that 24/7 stress behavior is sometimes seen as a badge of success.

WRIGHT

You say you had a real wakeup moment that jolted you into a different view of success. Please tell our readers about that.

GRENOUGH

It happened at a time when I thought I was cruising along quite fine. I had just married, inherited three teenage stepsons, was initiating my own business, and I was developing another book. I was definitely in the fast lane.

On a beautiful sunny day in July, my work buddy Joe phoned to ask if I wanted to go for a bike ride. I had only five other things I needed to do that day, but I thought I could squeeze in a bike ride. I shoved my to-do's aside, hoisted my Raleigh bike onto my Camry, and drove to meet Joe. We were riding in a very hilly part of Connecticut and I'm a good biker, but suddenly I was thrown over the handlebars onto the pavement and knocked unconscious.

I don't remember much after that. Joe later told me that a LifeStar helicopter flew me forty-two miles to the Yale-New Haven Hospital's Emergency Room. I regained consciousness only once during that time and I remember hearing the whirr of the helicopter and feeling the hands of the EMT woman on my head. I thought, "She is good," and I let go into her hands. The next couple of days in the hospital were not at all pleasant. They told me I had three concussions and a ruptured kidney. I was unable to go back to work for six months.

During that time I had the chance, the opportunity, and the invitation, to reflect on my life in ways that I had never done before. Those key questions came up: *Who am I?* and *What am I here for?* I realized that unless I started taking better care of myself, I wouldn't be around much longer to do anything I wanted to do. That accident was my real wakeup call. I'm thankful I had a helmet on or else I wouldn't be here now. I still have a numb place on my upper lip. That's my little reminder to take a breath, take it easy, and hang out with those key questions.

WRIGHT

Life is so fast-paced now. How is it possible to balance life and work successfully?

GRENOUGH

That is the great and very present question for all of us in our fast-paced culture. Thankfully, corporate America is beginning to pay attention to this issue. Business leaders are beginning to be concerned about the effects of stress on their employees and recognizing that it is indeed a serious problem, not only regarding the health of their employees but also in terms of the bottom line. They're taking note of research that demonstrates that chronic stress is a serious interference to concentration, well-functioning memory, short-term and long-term judgment, wise decision-making, and overall productivity. They're bringing in experts to deal with practical strategies, not just to manage stress, but how to head it off personally and corporately.

Today, when I go into a corporate or nonprofit group, all of them have lived long enough to have experienced the unexpected in their personal and professional lives. They are very hungry for practical ways to get their lives in balance.

My *OASIS 60-Second Strategies* Training Program gives people easily-learned tools that produce immediate results. Practical knowledge about the best ways to take care of yourself can make a significant difference.

Sometimes it might take a personal accident or a corporate crisis for a person or a group to wake up. Nick, a CEO in his early fifties and the father of two teenagers, came around only after he had his second heart attack.

Prior to that, he was a victim of the corporate myth, the one that says, "The more pressure I feel, the better I work and the more work I produce." When we first met, Nick told me, "I love what I do. I don't have time for things like stress management. I'm a Type AA personality and proud of it." I listened to him and said, "I don't want you to *lose* your fire; I want you to learn how to *use* it so you'll be around to see your kids grow up and enjoy your grandkids."

Nick didn't want to hear that. But after a few weeks, he paused long enough to recognize that it might be useful for him to make a few tweaks in his lifestyle. He came in for one session, quickly learned the *OASIS in the Overwhelm 60-Second Strategies,* and began using them. Twelve years later, Nick reports that he continues to use the OASIS Strategies and they give him a true oasis in the "overwhelm" of his daily life. He especially likes the *1 Stone,* a ten-breath focusing meditation done with eyes open, looking at a stone held in the hand. Nick says, "I keep my stone in my pocket. It reminds me to chill with Mil."

When I studied with Jon Kabat-Zinn, a leader in stress research, I remember him saying:

You can't stop the waves,
but you can learn to surf.

True, we cannot control everything around us. But how we respond makes a huge difference. We can learn new ways to respond—to surf—in ways that will bring us improved health and happiness. It's almost like learning a new tennis serve. If I am used to serving a certain way, it will take a while for me to develop a new pattern. Similarly, if I am used to responding to stress or pressure in a certain way, it will take effort to develop a new response, a new habit. But the more often I am clear about what is going on, what channel I'm on, and what channel will be useful for me, I can strengthen that new pattern. Gradually, I will surf more easily.

WRIGHT

When you do your workshops and training, you often invite people to sing, *Enjoy Yourself! You're Younger Than You Think.* Why sing? And why those words?

GRENOUGH

Singing involves a different part of our brain than talking. When we were babies, we made all kinds of song-like sounds, and we did this without conscious thought.

When I go to senior centers, many people have lost the ability to speak or to remember things. When I start singing something from their past, like *"Oh, my darling, oh, my darling..."* their affect brightens. They come out immediately with, *"Oh, my darling Clementine!"* Songs register in a different part of our brains and they often bring out a different emotional feeling than simple words do.

I learned the song *Enjoy Yourself! It's Later than You Think* from my mother. But I changed the last line to "Enjoy yourself! You're *younger* than you think!" I do this to introduce the field of neuroscience research that has exploded in the last two decades. When I studied psychology in college in Kentucky, my professors told me that I was near my prime and I needed to take advantage of it because before long I'd start losing my brain cells. After all, I was twenty-one. They were wrong. The hot word in brain research today is neuroplasticity, a word that my professors back then had never heard of. So when I'm getting people to sing and to say "you're younger than you think," I give them some of the facts from this research. For instance there is this information from Dr. Richard Davidson from the University of Wisconsin:

> "Neuroscientists believed until very recently that we are born with a certain number of neurons and that is all we have for the rest of our life. Over the last two years we have discovered that to be false. It has now been demonstrated in humans that new neurons do grow throughout the entire lifespan."

Scientists can tangibly demonstrate this growth. Moreover, they say our brains are primed to continue learning new things as long as we live. Not only do new neurons appear, but *by what we choose to do and not do, we influence which neurons grow and how much they grow.*

This is true, not just on the physical level, but also on the emotional level. For instance, if I go to the gym and I lift weights with just my left arm, that left bicep will strengthen, but my right bicep won't grow; it may even diminish as I'm exercising the left arm. The same thing is true for what I do with my actions and my thinking. If I am constantly or pretty regularly on, say, the *worry channel* or the *anxiety channel*, that wiring keeps firing. If I shift it to another more positive channel, say the *walk-around-the-block* channel, that wiring will increase. I can rewire my brain, even into my nineties. That is very exciting for many people. Old dogs *can* learn new tricks. I even do a workshop called *Over The Hill? Now You Can Pick Up Speed.*

WRIGHT

You coach a broad range of people both in person and over the phone. What makes for a successful coaching engagement?

GRENOUGH

A successful coaching session is about clarity. Sometimes that involves getting people to pause and write down their responses to those key questions: who am I, what am I here for, what do I want to leave as my legacy, and more immediately what do I want from this coaching contract? The more clarity we have, the more we're able to deal with specific actions, and the more likely the coaching engagement will be successful. Merely thinking or dreaming does not put things into action. Building that clarity, building that trust, asking provocative and stimulating questions, celebrating movement, holding our mutual feet to the fire—my feet as well as theirs—all of those elements create a successful coaching engagement.

WRIGHT

We call this book *ROADMAP to Success*. You certainly have had an unusual life journey, from ex-shy Kentuckian to international presenter and Yale instructor, from ex-nun to nightclub singer, and from rat-race-speed woman to a more balanced successful life. Do you believe that each of us has a definite road map to success that we can follow?

GRENOUGH

I don't think there is such a thing as a definite road map. Sometimes I laugh when I reflect on my path. I had a life plan that I thought was complete. I went into it without reservation. I lived it with my whole heart, whole mind, whole body, and whole soul for eight years. Then it became apparent to me that the "plan" was for part of the journey, and was not meant for my entire life.

We make our plans to the best of our knowledge, choose our options to the best of our abilities, and we move forward. We never know exactly where the journey will take us. It sometimes reminds me of the GPS in my car saying "Recalculating... recalculating..." The importance of being aware of who I am and what's going on around me is almost like being able to judge what the weather is and how I will fare best in this weather, on this road. Where do I want to go? Am I helping that happen or not helping that happen?

In this instance I think of Tim, another of my clients who thought he had a definite road map for his life. His parents wanted him to be a successful businessman, but at the same time his father gave him the message, "You really won't ever amount to much of anything." So how was he supposed to achieve anything with that message in his head?

As a therapist, a coach, and a person who has lived through various chapters in my own life, I was able to help Tim realize, at age sixty, that it was okay for him to think about: Who am *I*? What are *my* dreams? What do I want to achieve now and leave behind as a legacy? He realized he did not want to waste any more years, so he made some abrupt turns to go for what was really important for him.

WRIGHT

Is there such a thing as normal?

GRENOUGH

I think normal is similar to success—there are so many different ways to define it. Sometimes I wish I lived in Spain where a normal work life might include three to six weeks of vacation a year. Another culture might think that normal is working eighty hours a week. I think "normal" is an overused word. I have never wanted to be normal. My friend Gene says, "You know, Millie, we're both eccentric."

At first I took his words as uncomplimentary but when I realized that the root meaning of *eccentric* is simply "off center," I realized that I like being off center. Each of us is truly one of a kind. Like the snowflakes, of which there are thousands outside my window right now, which ones are "normal"?

I think the real invitation to each of us humans is to be who we uniquely are with as much gusto, wisdom, enthusiasm, and sense of humor as we can.

WRIGHT

Do you have any final words for our readers?

GRENOUGH

Take some time each day to "not do." I try to spend twenty to thirty minutes each morning just being quiet. When I'm with corporate groups, I may not call this time meditation, I might call it focusing or filtering. Taking the time to get some space and some clarity for those big questions: who am I, what am I here for, what is really important to me right now and for the long run? If I skip several days and don't take that time, I really am much more easily rattled, get irritated more quickly, wander off course, and I become harder on myself and on others. When I find myself in that bad place, it's a reminder that taking the time to be there with those big questions is very helpful.

Last night in a teleconference with the current people in my Oasis Training Group, I said, "I'm having a challenging time this week. A very good friend of mine died suddenly from no apparent cause and she was only fifty. I'm still very rattled by that, plus the fact that for the last three days in usually fairly temperate Connecticut we've had almost two feet of snow. Things are all topsy turvy and I feel turned around." Thankfully, one of the people on the call reminded me: "Millie, time to change your channel." She continued, "Because of the snow, I couldn't get to my Manhattan office today. You know what I did right before this call? I went outside in two and a half feet of snow and I laid down and made a snow angel." I thought, "I haven't done that since I was a kid." I promised her and promised myself that after the phone call I would just go out in the front yard, lie down in the snow, and make a snow angel. I did.

So sometimes just having that ability to shift channels and give ourselves a little sense of humor helps us surf the waves. As my friend Rog says, "When you can't make love, make lunch."

I saw a quote this morning by Marian Wright Edelman, the founder of the Children's Defense Fund. It reminded me that life is much bigger than I am. It is bigger than my immediate goals, my immediate family, my clients, and my surroundings. Her words speak right to the heart of legacy. Edelman says:

"Be a good ancestor, stand for something bigger than yourself, add value to the Earth during your sojourn."

I think that is success.

WRIGHT

Well, what a great conversation. I really appreciate the time you've taken today to answer these questions. There is a lot of good information in this chapter that I can use. I'm sure that our readers have learned a lot from this as well.

GRENOUGH

Thank you, David. It was a pleasure talking with you and having you listen. We all love to be listened to, don't we?

WRIGHT

Yes, we certainly do.

Today I have been talking with Millie Grenough. Millie is author of *OASIS in the Overwhelm: 60 Second Strategies for Balance in a Busy World* and co-author of *OASIS in the Overwhelm 28 Day Guide: Rewire Your Brain from Chaos to Calm.*

Millie, thank you so much for being with us today on *ROADMAP to Success.*

GRENOUGH

Thank you, David.

About the Author

Coach, author, motivational speaker, and clinical instructor in Psychiatry at Yale University School of Medicine, Millie Grenough reaches people in all walks of life—from CEOs to harried parents, university deans to prison inmates. Her six years' work in Latin America and Europe gives her a rich appreciation of diverse cultures and distinct learning styles. She has developed curricula for groups as diverse as the Colegio de Médicos in Barcelona, the International Center at Yale University, and the CEO and Vice-Presidents at Foxwoods Resort and Casino. Her OASIS Training Program has graduates throughout the United States and in Panama, Puerto Rico, and New Zealand.

Millie was a key member of an international team in South America that provided organizational diagnosis, change management, team-building, and development of individual and group potential. In Europe, she designed practical learning strategies for multinational adult students at the Universidad de Salamanca. Her innovative approach to learning languages, *Sing it! Learn English through Song,* published as a six-book-six-cassette series by McGraw-Hill, won a national award and has sold more than seventy thousand copies internationally.

Certified in EMDR (Eye Movement Desensitization and Reprocessing), Level II, with a specialty in Performance Enhancement, Millie imparts her strategies in trainings, workshops, lectures, and individual sessions internationally. Her passion is to help individuals and groups reach their full potential while remaining sane and healthy.

Millie Grenough

Grenough LLC
200 Orchard Street, Suite 301
New Haven, CT 06511
203-789-2191
millie@milliegrenough.com
www.milliegrenough.com